THE KING'S WIFE

The King's Wife

George IV and Mrs Fitzherbert

Valerie Irvine

Hambledon and London

London and New York

Hambledon and London

102 Gloucester Avenue, London NW1 8HX

175 Fifth Avenue
New York, NY 10010
USA

First Published 2005

ISBN 1 85285 443 X

A description of this book is available from the
British Library and from the Library of Congress.

Typeset by Carnegie Publishing, Lancaster,
and printed in Great Britain by Cambridge University Press.

Distributed in the United States and Canada
exclusively by Palgrave Macmillan,
A division of St Martin's Press.

Contents

Illustrations

To my daughters
Marie-Claire and Antonia

Introduction

On moving to Brighton some years ago, I came across Maria Fitzherbert's burial place and memorial. Curious about her, I began to research her life. I discovered that it was a long and extraordinary one, of double widowhood and great grief but also of love and joy. It brought her to the centre of Society and to marriage to the heir to the throne, George, Prince of Wales. Their relationship shaped their lives and might easily have changed the history of Britain. As a story, it is both dramatic and touching; it is certainly one worth retelling.

I would like to thank the many friends who have listened to me talking about 'Mrs Fitz' and encouraged me to write this book. I am grateful to the National Portrait Gallery for permission to reproduce plates 1 and 3; and to the Ashmolean Museum for permission to reproduce plate 2.

Mary Anne

Mary Anne, the first child of the handsome Mr Walter Smythe and his bride of one year, Mary, née Errington, was born at Tong in Shropshire in the summer of 1756. Her family background appeared to set her apart from most girls of her age, both Smythes and Erringtons being Catholic, part of a network of landowning families who had kept the old religion, and their estates, through times of persecution. With their resident priests, living in hiding when times were dangerous and openly when things were easier, and with the respect they commanded as lords of the manor, these families had played a vital part in keeping a Catholic community alive when the official policy was to stamp it out. Now, in mid eighteenth century, with persecution over, they still lived quietly, marrying among themselves. They formed a Catholic 'cousinhood', connected, however distantly, by blood or marriage, who though spread unevenly across the country, stood as godparents to one another's children, and planned suitable marriages for their sons and daughters. Later in the century, when they re-entered fashionable society, and met at London's balls and assemblies, Lady Jerningham noted that 'all knew one another intimately'.[1]

The baby's father's family was originally from Nunstanton in County Durham, but in 1568 William Smythe had married Margaret, daughter and coheiress of Anthony Eshe of Eshe, also in Durham, and the manor house there had become the main Smythe home. Perhaps it was a good place for Catholics to lie low, pay their fines for not attending the new church of England services, and have the old Mass said secretly, defending their priests from the death penalty that discovery would bring, because no Smythes were martyred, and none of their estates were forfeited.

It was from Eshe that the Smythe men rode south to support the King in the Civil War, supplying him with a considerable sum of money.

With the war lost, and the King dead, they suffered for their generosity under Cromwell; but when Charles II returned to his father's kingdom in 1660 one of his first acts was to create Edward Smythe a baronet. The family fortunes were improved the following year when Edward married Mary, daughter and coheiress of Sir Richard Lee of Langley and Acton Burnell.[2] After that the Smythes, though retaining the estate at Eshe, lived at Acton Burnell Hall in the softer climate of Shropshire. Their coat of arms, left carved on the stone gatepost at Eshe, was three roses argent, and their motto, 'Regi Semper Fidelis', to the king ever faithful.

The troubled reigns of Charles II and his brother James brought Catholics no lasting relief and, after James II's departure, the arrival of William and Mary brought new penal laws. They looked severe. Men proved to be priests, though no longer put to death for treason as they had been under Elizabeth I, were subject to life imprisonment. Catholics could neither inherit nor purchase land, hold fire arms, own a horse worth more than five pounds, nor become barristers or officers in the armed forces. A hundred pounds reward was offered to anyone supplying information leading to the conviction of a 'Mass-saying priest'. And, after 1700, Catholic landowners had to pay double land tax. However, none of these laws were enforced, with the exception of the hundred pounds reward for informing and the payment of double land tax. No priest was imprisoned for life, those who were imprisoned being released after a short sentence, and Catholics continued to inherit and purchase land. The laws passed after 1688 were political rather than religious, Catholics being penalised, at this time, for being faithful to the Stuarts rather than to the Pope. The new laws were there as a threat, to show Catholics what could happen to them if they ever tried to bring a king of their religion back to England. The 'cousins' did well to remain quietly on their estates.

Later, with Queen Anne dead and Hanoverian George on the throne, the Smythes probably regarded the Old Pretender, James III, as the King to whom they were secretly 'ever faithful'. He was recognised as King by the Pope, and kept a sad little court in Rome's Piazza dei Santi Apostoli. But there is no record of a Smythe riding north to fight for him when he landed at Peterhead in 1715, nor in 1745, when his son, Charles Edward, Bonnie Prince Charlie, made his attempt to regain the throne for his father, leading his Highlanders into England, before retreating to defeat on Culloden Moor in 1746. It seems likely that the Smythes, along with most of their fellow Catholics, saw no reason to risk everything for a cause that was clearly doomed, especially as Richard Challoner, the most influential of their bishops, urged Catholic men to stay at home.[3]

Yet they must have had Jacobite sympathies, for when one of their kinsmen, a Mr Welles of Brambridge, Hampshire, went too far in publicly denouncing the Hanoverians and found it necessary to disappear, John Smythe gave him a hiding place at Acton Burnell until his outburst was forgiven, or just forgotten, and it was safe for him to return home.[4]

By the middle of the eighteenth century Catholic landowners could live comfortably; the penal laws, though still on the statute book as a threat, were no great hardship, agriculture was paying well, and such fines and taxes which were imposed were not crippling. Catholics of humbler origin, living on or near Catholic estates, could practise their religion without difficulty; but those living out of reach of such houses had by this time drifted away. There were few Catholics living in the towns, with the exception of London, where their numbers were surprisingly high. Poor Catholics, and the priests who served them, in London's East End, still lived a dangerous life, no-popery attitudes surviving in the poorer areas of London long after they had faded elsewhere.

John Smythe and his wife, Constantia, had a daughter, also named Constantia, and two sons, Edward, who would inherit title and estates, and Walter who, debarred by his religion from a political or military career in England, became an officer in the Austrian army. At one time a portrait of him hung in Acton Burnell, showing him to be remarkably handsome, splendid in green and scarlet uniform, with a dark-eyed, long-nosed but curiously sensitive face for a soldier.[5]

In 1754, or early 1755, Walter left the Austrian army and returned to England. A marriage was being talked of between him and Mary Anne, the daughter of John Errington, a younger son of a well-known Northumbrian family. Mary Anne was young and beautiful, with a fortune of her own and Walter was no doubt pleased with the match. At the same time, Henry Welles, the outspoken Jacobite, who, though the second of three brothers, now found himself the sole survivor of the family, and approaching old age with no children, made Walter Smythe the heir to Brambridge Hall. Walter and Mary Anne married in 1755.

The marriage took place at Acton Burnell in Shropshire, and the couple began their married life at Tong Castle, in the same county. Tong was owned by Lord Kingston, but, as he did not live there himself, he seems to have invited Walter Smythe to act as land agent and make his home in the castle. It was there, in the Red Room, according to tradition, that their first child was born, and named Mary Anne after her mother. Her parents may have sometimes called her Maria, but it is more likely that she adopted this version of her name later in life. A second child, Walter (known as Wat) was born a year later, followed by two more sons, John (known as Jack) and Charles. There is some mystery about another boy, Henry Smythe, born in 1760, the same year as Charles, and sent with him, in their teens, to the Jesuit college in Liège.[6] He was possibly an illegitimate relative brought up with the Smythe children, but there are few records of him beyond their shared school days.

The year 1762 was an eventful one for the Smythes. Lord Kingston sold Tong to the Durrant family, which necessitated a move to another house; a second daughter, Frances, was born; and Henry Welles made a final will confirming Walter Smythe as the heir to Brambridge Hall. Welles died in November 1763, but it is not known where the Smythes lived between the sale of Tong and the move to Brambridge. Henry Welles's widow moved out of the house very quickly, but the Smythes may have delayed their move to Hampshire until the spring of 1764. If this was so, Mary Anne would have been seven years old when Brambridge became her home. Travelling from Shropshire to Hampshire, must have been a long and exhausting journey, but to the older children, the overnight stops at inns, the changing of horses, the inevitable breakdowns, even the fear of highwaymen, would have made it a great adventure.

The approach to Brambridge Hall, in those days, was very beautiful. In the reign of Charles II, a double avenue of lime trees had been planted along the drive (some accounts say that the King himself planted them, while he stayed at Brambridge awaiting the completion of his palace at Winchester). Unusually, all the branches of the outer line of trees had been trained downwards to touch the ground, and those of the inner line trained upward and inward, to meet overhead. Up this driveway Mary Anne and her siblings, their long journey over, were finally swept to their new home. Their mother's brother, Henry Errington, married and became the owner of Red Rice, an estate near Andover some twenty miles from Brambridge, in 1769.[7] He became a kind and protective uncle to all the Smythe children as they grew up, but especially to Mary Anne.

Brambridge Hall was spacious and comfortable, the sort of home a country squire of moderate means might be expected to live in. It stood on the banks of the River Itchen five miles from Winchester, and had originally been known as Brambridge Mill House. At one time it had been the home of Swithin Welles, now St Swithin Welles, who was hanged outside his London house, during Elizabeth I's reign, for allowing a Mass to be said there. The Welles family lost Brambridge after that, but it was restored to Gilbert Welles by Charles I. The house had a long history of resident chaplains, many of them Jesuits. When Bishop Challoner visited Hampshire in 1742 he noted, in the careful records of his visitation, that over a hundred people regularly attended Mass at Brambridge.[8] Numbers were possibly much the same when the Smythes came. By that time Catholics no longer expected to die for their faith, but the story of Swithin Welles was still told in Hampshire, and Mary Anne may have thought about him sometimes while she waited in the chapel for the door to be locked before Mass began. The locking of the door was a precaution against would-be informers. However, in Hampshire, at that time, Catholics had little to fear. Catholic priests lived openly in Winchester, owning their own house not far from the cathedral, and no action was ever taken against them. Several Hampshire estates were Catholic-owned, and the large Catholic community in the region, happily accepted by their Protestant neighbours, enabled Mary Anne to grow up without that feeling of exclusion from the mainstream of society that afflicted less fortunate Catholics.

Walter Smythe had been educated by Benedictines, and a Benedictine priest arrived at Brambridge some time in 1765. This was William Walmsley, who remained near Brambridge until his death in 1815.[9] For some years after his arrival he lived at Brambridge Hall, as his predecessors had done, and seems to have been both respected and liked by all the family. It is thought that the Smythes added a chapel to the house soon after their arrival. In earlier times, Mass was probably said in an upstairs room which could be returned to domestic use afterwards, but, as anti-Catholic feeling faded, many Catholic families began to extend their houses to provide permanent chapels.[10]

The romantic park surrounding the house, with weir and mill stream, was the children's playground and Mary Anne's closest companions were the two older boys, Wat and Jack. A sixth child, Barbara, was born in 1769.[11] Mary Anne may not have been there to watch the baptismal water poured over her new sister's head, for by 1769, aged thirteen, she had embarked on the next adventure of her young life; school days in France.

The Smythe children grew up knowing they would go to school on the Continent, as their parents and aunts and uncles had done before them. A Catholic education was thought necessary for the handing down of their religion to the next generation. That education not being available in England, children had to be sent abroad to obtain it.

Sending children abroad to be educated was forbidden by one of the early penal laws, but it was a law consistently broken by Catholics. By the second half of the eighteenth century it was also a law unlikely to be enforced. Even so, once the children were in school on the Continent, it was thought advisable for them to stay there until their schooling was finished. This meant being away for several years, keeping in touch with home by letter and family visits. So when Mary Anne left the secure life of Brambridge for school, she was saying a long goodbye. She was probably the first of the family to go, and it must have felt like a journey into the unknown; exciting, but a little frightening, especially as she had no sister close enough in age to start school with her.

Her brothers, Wat and Jack, would leave home together, following their father's footsteps to one of the French Benedictine schools and possibly going on to a continental university for a few years, though they may have hoped, even as boys, to follow their father's footsteps even more closely, and become officers in the Austrian army as soon as they were old enough. The education thought suitable for girls like Mary Anne was shorter and less arduous than that for boys, but it is interesting that the Smythes, and parents like them, believed in, and were prepared to pay for, a formal schooling for daughters as well as sons.

France and Flanders had plenty of convents with small schools for the education of Catholic girls. Some of them were extremely small, no bigger than a large family. The Benedictines at Cambrai could only take eight girls, the Conceptionists in Paris had room for just fourteen, and the largest schools had a maximum of about thirty places. Because the girls lived in the convents, and paid for their board and lodging separately from their tuition fees, they were always known as 'pensioners'. It is not known for certain at which convent the young Miss Smythe became a pensioner. No letters from this period have survived, and most of the convents lost their records when the nuns fled during and after the French Revolution. Those who returned, years later, were a new generation of sisters with only scanty information about their pensioners in pre-Revolution days. Many, unable to claim back their original building, opened new schools elsewhere. It has been suggested that Mary Anne went to the Conceptionists, the Blue Nuns (named for the colour of their choir mantles), an English Order in the Faubourg St-Antoine. But the 'Blues', as they were affectionately known, kept a daily diary, which, surprisingly, has survived, but makes no mention of a Mary Anne Smythe in the meticulous record of every new pensioner's arrival and departure. Nor does her name appear in a list of the Blue Nuns' pensioners published with Lady Jerningham's letters.[12] Paris offered a wide choice of convents with schools, but the Blue Nuns, a very English establishment, were at one time the most popular with English families. When their popularity began to decline during the second half of the century, it was the French Ursulines in the Rue St-Jacques who rose in favour with the English as the 'Blues' faded. (Lady Jerningham had been with the Blue Nuns from the age of eight, but she sent her only daughter to the Ursulines.) The Ursulines, founded solely to educate girls, possibly offered a better organised curriculum than some of the other schools, and it has also been suggested that the Smythes followed the new trend and took their daughter to the Rue St-Jacques, but Lady Anne Lindsay's diary indicates that Mary Anne went, not to Paris, but to the Benedictines at Dunkirk for at least part of her education.[13]

The life of a young pensioner was, however, much the same in all the continental convents and, wherever she went, Mary Anne's days would have followed a similar pattern of lessons, prayers and recreation, with the same close friendships, partings, disappointments and small excitements that make up school life.

Great emphasis was placed on the French language in all the schools, but a variety of academic subjects were offered – ancient history, geography, literature and heraldry being the most popular. It was rare for Greek and Latin to be taught to girls, but other European languages were often an option, along with drawing, embroidery, singing and deportment. Music was considered important, the harp being the favourite instrument, and dancing lessons were taken at least once a week, not just to prepare the girls for a graceful performance in future ballrooms, but also for exercise (at a convent in Liège the girls had to dance the quadrille every night between supper and bedtime). Most of the teachers were lay people, so, though the pensioners lived with the nuns, they were not cut off from the outside world. The aim was to get the correct balance between acquiring useful knowledge, practising social graces, and gaining an understanding of, and love for, their religion, all in preparation for their future place in society. The major feasts of the church's year were the girls' holidays, marked by two or three days of recreation. Free from lessons, they celebrated with concerts and special dinners, their classrooms filled with flowers, and everything accompanied with much excitement and laughter.[14]

Mary Anne probably began her convent education at the age of twelve, but has left only one story of her life there, dating it with the single phrase 'while yet a child'. She thought the story interesting enough to include in the memoir of her life which she later dictated to her cousin, Lord Stourton.[15] Her parents took her on a visit to Paris, perhaps before taking her to start school, and they obtained places to watch the King, Louis XV, at dinner. The arrangements were stylish, with a lavish touch of theatre. When, amid all the elaborate ceremonial, the King began to tear a chicken apart with his hands, Mary Anne gave a burst of astonished laughter. Her parents, seeing the French King pause, and look straight across at their daughter, must have been deeply embarrassed. What Louis saw was a young girl with abundant gold hair, dark hazel eyes, a flawless complexion, and that special beauty belonging only to the early teens. Louis had a weakness for young girls. He had a harem of them in the Parc de Cerf, where they lived with every luxury. When they were old enough to marry, he gave them dowries and sent them home. No one thought the worse of them, and parents of pretty girls with no dowries would sometimes approach the right members of the court with a discreet offer. Could Louis have, momentarily, mistaken the Smythes' laughing daughter for a candidate for his Parc? He sent her a dish of sugar plums, not by a footman but by a duke. The Duc de Soubise must have been impressed by the young Miss Smythe because he not only found out who she was but always remembered her, often reminding her of this episode when they met again, years later. The Smythes probably knew nothing of the French King's tastes, but the nuns may have heard the gossip of Paris and have looked a little fearfully at the attractive child who drew unwanted attention so easily.

Mrs Fitzherbert told Lord Stourton that she looked back on this story as a portent of the part royalty was to play in the dramas of her life ('to prognosticate her future destinies' was how Lord Stourton put it). But she could hardly have seen it like that at the time. It would just have been a splendid story to tell her school friends, and not one the nuns would have encouraged her to keep repeating.

No doubt she achieved the desired balance between learning, correct behaviour and religion. She certainly perfected her French, which she spoke and wrote fluently all her life. But there is no reference, anywhere, of her playing the harp or the harpsichord or singing in any of the drawing rooms she later frequented, though there were plenty of ladies who did all three. Nor, so far as we know, did she draw or paint. She did do very fine embroidery,[16] which she may have learned from the nuns, and she always moved gracefully and was a beautiful dancer, owing this to years of deportment and dancing lessons.

Writing in her diary a lifetime later, Lady Jerningham's daughter, Charlotte, recalled that she had been so happy at school with the Ursulines that she had wished her time there would never end, and that it was only the thought of being with Mama and Papa again that made leaving the Rue St-Jacques bearable.[17] As Mary Anne kept no diary, and never mentioned her schooling in any of her later letters, we do not know how she felt about her school days. But, coming from a large family, the transition from home to the group life of a small school may have come easily to her; perhaps she found it pleasant to be among girls of her own age, instead of younger brothers. When she became responsible for the education of her niece, thought to be her brother Jack's child,[18] she sent her to a French convent, even though, by that time, there were a number of convent schools in England. This suggests that she had happy memories of her own school days in France, or at least that she valued what she had learned there.

Her school friend Catherine Dillon, younger sister to Lady Jerningham, who was greatly attracted to convent life, decided to join the Benedictines at Montargis when her school days were over. If Mary Anne ever thought of doing the same, she clearly changed her mind, and at the age of about sixteen she came home to Brambridge to prepare for her grown-up life in the world.

The world as Miss Smythe saw it, in 1774, her eighteenth year, must have looked very enticing. By this time the 'cousins' were taking their place in London Society again, and the glittering world of balls and theatres, carriage rides in the park, and admiring glances from beaux and dancing partners, was awaiting her.

In the same year, Mr Edward Weld, a young widower, wealthy and sought after, was in London buying a town house and enjoying the entertainments of the Season with his younger sister, Mary, known in the family as 'Molly'. Before long Molly was writing to her other brother, Thomas, dropping hints that Edward looked like marrying again. It has been said that Mr Weld, 'fell straightway in love',[19] when he met Miss Smythe for the first time, in her uncle's house at Red Rice; but, from the timing of their first meeting, it seems more likely that it took place in Henry Errington's London house, while his niece was having her first taste of a London Season. Neither of the pair kept a diary, and all that has been preserved of their courtship is an entry in Edward Weld's appointment book, 'To see M.S.' By the end of the year, however, a marriage was certainly being 'talked of' by Edward Weld and the Smythes. In the spring of 1775 Miss Smythe gave her consent, the marriage settlement was drawn up, and the forthcoming marriage announced.

Young girls were not expected to be 'in love' when marriages were arranged. Acceptance was usually based on practicalities; romance was a bonus, but not necessary. Edward Weld, though sixteen years older than Mary Anne, was one of the most eligible men of the day and a Catholic. Both his parents had died by the time he was twenty and, as the eldest of the three surviving children, he had inherited not only

Lulworth Castle in Dorset but several other estates as well. He had married early, but his wife, Julianna Petre, had died, young and childless, in 1771.

Well educated by the Jesuits at St-Omer and the university of Reims, he had spent time in Italy learning how to appreciate good paintings; he played the harpsichord beautifully, was an accomplished horseman, kept a good stable and a small pack of hounds, and owned a yacht ('my cutter'), of which he was proud. He had a London house, in Bond Street, and spent as much time travelling and visiting as he did at Lulworth. When at home he liked to entertain, and kept a French chef to make sure his table was among the best in the county.[20]

He was described as a 'man of gaiety and charm', and it seems likely that Miss Smythe accepted his offer without much hesitation, and that she and her parents were as charmed by him as was everyone else. Edward's brother and sister were delighted that he had found a second bride. Thomas and his wife, another Mary, were present at the marriage which took place in the chapel of Brambridge Hall, celebrated by William Walmsley amid general approval.[21]

Marriages at that time were quiet affairs, with only close family present as witnesses. Since 1753, when Lord Hardwicke's Marriage Act became law, everyone (apart from Jews and Quakers) had to be married by a Church of England clergyman, and a proper record kept. No other form of marriage would be regarded as legal. For Catholics this meant that two separate ceremonies were necessary, one before the incumbent of the parish church, regarded purely as a civil ceremony to make the marriage legal, and one, the 'real' wedding, before a Catholic priest.[22] This law was not intended to penalise Catholics, its sole aim was to reduce the high number of clandestine marriages.

It was fashionable for brides to wear gowns of white and silver made up in the style of the day and lace caps with flowers and ribbons, and no doubt Miss Smythe wore hers with grace and confidence, and was admired by all who saw her. The ceremony and festivities over, the young Mrs Weld, a few weeks short of her nineteenth birthday, left Brambridge for her new life at Lulworth.

Lulworth Castle was undoubtedly grand. Four square, with battlemented towers at each corner, it stood among lawns and woodlands with a view of the Purbeck hills, and a glimpse of the sea through the Arishell Gap. The house may have looked a little forbidding from the outside, but Edward Weld knew how to enjoy the good things of life, and Lulworth was never dull.

A history of friendship existed between the Welds and their Protestant neighbours, the Framptons of Moreton Manor. It was there that Edward Weld took his bride for dinner on her nineteenth birthday. At a later date, Mary Frampton described Mrs Weld as she had looked that day: 'She was then very beautiful. She dined at Moreton on the day she was nineteen, perfectly unaffected and unassuming in manner.'[23] It was this 'perfectly unaffected' manner, along with the striking beauty of her skin and hair and natural grace, that attracted both men and women to her, not just at this moment of youth and happiness but throughout her life.

There is a story told of her bouncing out of the room at Lulworth while her portrait was being painted. She had taken a peep at the early version and seen her hair, of which she was probably proud, temporarily filled in in grey. 'He's given me a grey wig!' she is said to have cried out in anger, vanishing from the room and vowing not to return. She must have been easily mollified, because the portrait was resumed. Her outrage is partly explained by a contemporary description of the 'marvellous aureole of hair which she persisted in wearing *au naturel* when all wore wigs and other hideous erections'. She obviously wanted the portrait to do her hair justice. A further description of Edward's young wife claims: 'She was *pétillante d'esprit*, and would convince the most incredulous of her early beauty and originality.'[24]

All the portraits of Mary Anne of this time show her early beauty with the rather long nose inherited from her father; a face still retaining the roundness of youth, and dark eyes looking out from the canvas with a calm, intelligent gaze. The 'grey wig' episode is more than just a story of an impetuous girl, not quite grown up. It reveals a characteristic that would remain part of her personality for life: a quickness to anger, and willingness to retract, gracefully, if proved wrong.

It is unlikely that the Welds spent any time in their London house at 158 Bond Street. Thomas Weld and his wife, three months pregnant with their third child, joined them at Lulworth in August staying until late September. Two weeks later Edward was taken ill, so ill that Thomas was recalled from his house at Britwell. Ten days later Thomas entered in his diary for 26 October, 'my poor brother dyed'.[25]

The cause of Edward Weld's death is not known. Doctors attended him, but, with few aids to diagnosis, may not have discovered what had made him so ill. Sudden deaths, even among the young and apparently healthy, were common, and detailed medical explanations were often neither given nor asked for.

The Framptons called to pay their respects. Finding the young widow in a shocked state, and no relative with her, they took her back to Moreton, away from the grief-stricken house, which had so recently been full of music and laughter, and plans for the future. She spent the sad days between the death and the funeral with them. 'This friendly conduct', wrote Mary Frampton, 'was on her side always repaid with great civility and attention.'[26]

Thomas Weld, as the nearest male heir, inherited Lulworth and the other Weld estates. He noted in his accounts, which he began to keep immediately, that two hundred pounds was given straight away to the widow, 'at my brother's request'. Presumably Edward had made the request verbally before he died, concerned that his wife should have enough for her immediate needs until her first annuity was paid from the estate. But the young Mrs Weld had understood that, should Edward die, she would be left more than the eight hundred pounds a year fixed in her marriage settlement. Thomas must have been asked about this. No will, however, other than the one leaving all the estates to Thomas, could be found. The story that Edward had prepared a new will leaving everything to his wife, but had neglected to sign it, seems to have no foundation. Thomas believed, however, that his brother had told his wife that he planned to leave her more, and his accounts book shows that he instructed the family lawyers to check if any other instructions had been left with them, and if the marriage contract could be interpreted more generously.[27] Edward Weld seems to have been happy go lucky about money, and probably thought he had plenty of time to find out what could, legally, be left to a wife; or perhaps he was waiting for the birth of a child before changing his will. Perhaps, when he realised he was dying, he decided that Thomas and his sons had more right to the income from the Weld estates than a very young wife who would certainly marry again. Thomas was anxious to handle the estate affairs correctly. He was a kind man, and would have taken time to explain to his young sister-in-law that, though Edward had been a rich man, his property and land had not been his to dispose of as he wished, but Mary Anne seems to have gone on thinking she was entitled to more.

Eight hundred pounds a year was a sum on which a single woman could live comfortably with several servants and a carriage, and few financial worries, and it would have been a very useful sum to bring to a second marriage. Second and third marriages were common in the eighteenth century, when so many died young, and no one would have doubted that Mary Anne would marry again.

In addition to the question of the will, there was something else. Years later, after Mary Annes's death, Charles Bodenham, husband of one of Thomas Weld's daughters, wrote to a Miss Dormer about various documents connected with her, ending with an intriguing reference to diamonds, 'Lord Holland's document says nothing of course as to the diamond squabble between Mrs Fitzherbert and the brother of her first husband (my wife's father) which seems to interest you so much so I have omitted in this instance all mention of that'.[28] Few clues exist to explain this 'squabble', and no reference to it appears elsewhere. There was a diamond necklace, a Weld family heirloom, referred to several times in the Weld papers, and this may have been what the disagreement was about. But whatever lay behind Charles Bodenham's remark, it leaves the impression that Mary Anne felt she had been unfairly treated, and had said so. This did not, however, create a rift between her and the Welds and several of Thomas's sons became her friends in later life.

After Edward's funeral, Mary Anne returned to her father's house. Black gowned and veiled in her 'weeds' she was driven home up the avenue of limes, down which she had passed as a bride so short a time before. There is a sad little sequel to the story of her brief marriage. Thomas and his wife delayed their move to Lulworth until after their third child was born, and the Britwell records show that they called him Edward, the family name they had promised to leave for Mary Anne's first son.[29]

2

Thomas Fitzherbert

Living at Brambridge again, Mary Anne observed the formalities of mourning: gowns of unrelieved black with cap and veil, and a quiet domestic life, with no invitations accepted or given. A severe regime for a girl of nineteen, whose friends were still enjoying the pleasures of the social round which she had known briefly and lost so soon. Older women assured her that time would pass, that life was not over; but before she could come to terms with her loss, she had a second tragedy to face. Soon after Edward Weld's death, Walter Smythe had a stroke that left him partially paralysed. She had lost her husband, her new home, all her dreams of the future, and now she saw her father turn into a helpless invalid. Life, once so full of joy and promise, now seemed too sad to be borne. She might have found support from her siblings, but few of them were at home.

It has been said that the Smythe boys ran wild without a father's firm control, but there seems to be little foundation for the story.[1] The records of the Jesuit college at Liège show that the younger boys, Charles and Henry, went there in 1775, with their fees paid in advance up to 1781.[2] If all the brothers had been given the same education, which seems likely, then Wat and Jack would also have studied on the Continent until they were about nineteen. They both served in the Austrian army for a time, so it is unlikely that any of the boys were at Brambridge for long during the years immediately following their father's stroke. Frances Smythe, aged thirteen, was probably away at school as well, leaving Barbara, aged six, the only child at home with Mary Anne and their mother at this unhappy time.

When widows reached the 'second mourning', a year after their husbands' death, they could add a touch of white or violet to their gowns and bonnets, and begin, in a small way, to take part in social life again. Even when in full mourning, black gowns and veils were not always as dowdy as they sound. Lady Jerningham wrote to her daughter in 1799, 'Yesterday I had Madame de Saisseval, looking uncommonly pretty in her weeds'.[3] Mary Anne possibly began to look 'uncommonly pretty' too, once the worst of her shock and grief were over. It was probably in her second year as a widow that she visited London and called on Lady Jerningham, who, writing to her daughter some years later, recalled this visit and asked, 'Do you remember her when she was the widow Weld?'[4]

She was not to remain the widow Weld for very much longer. In the early summer of 1778, she agreed to marry a Mr Thomas Fitzherbert. Thomas Fitzherbert, aged thirty-one, was the eldest son of an old Catholic family with estates at Swynnerton in Staffordshire and at Norbury, over the border in Derbyshire. His father, also Thomas, had built an imposing new mansion at Swynnerton, and Thomas junior had a house of his own in London's Mayfair, where he liked to entertain in the Season. Like Edward Weld, he was a gregarious and popular man, but he belonged to a new breed of young Catholic gentlemen who now saw the road to political freedom opening up in front of them. It wasn't enough for them to live comfortably in their mansions on incomes from their estates, to travel in Italy, to keep a good stable and sail their cutters. They wanted full citizenship and that role in public affairs which the anti-Catholic penal laws denied them. Suddenly, it looked as if they might get what they wanted. Mary Anne, soon to be a bride again, and probably in London buying her trousseau, found herself swept into the midst of a campaign for a Catholic Relief Bill, kept informed of events by Thomas and his Throckmorton first cousins, who were deeply involved.

Lord North's government, stuck at an indecisive stage in the American War of Independence and threatened by Spain and France, desperately needed recruits for the army. They had already wooed the Irish with a revised oath of allegiance, made acceptable to Catholics, and many Irishmen had enlisted; but more men were needed. The Scottish Highlanders were the men they wanted, but they, too, were largely Catholic and a new oath, and other concessions, would be needed before any of them would join an English army. The government was unsure what offers would prove effective and sent Sir William Dalrymple to consult Bishop Hay, Vicar Apostolic for the Scottish Region.

Bishop Hay was the friend, one might say the disciple, of the highly respected Bishop Challoner, who had for many years been in charge of the London region. Hay suggested that English Catholics should be included in both discussion and concessions, and a meeting between Challoner and Dalrymple was hastily arranged.

Richard Challoner worked among the very poor in the East End of London, a far cry from the *beau monde* of the Catholic gentlemen. Of humble origin himself, he possibly felt more sympathy with the poor than with the Catholic gentlemen's desire for a role in public affairs. He was a man of high intellect and great piety, but he was now an old man. Dalrymple said he found him, 'timid and using twenty difficulties'.[5] Challoner feared change. He thought a Catholic Relief Act might bring down the wrath of the anti-Catholic lobby on the heads of his flock. He did consult with Bishop Hay, however, and drew up a number of possible concessions, summing them up in a plea for 'general toleration'.

In the meantime, Dalrymple had been introduced to William Sheldon, a young lawyer of Grey's Inn, who told Dalrymple that, in his opinion, gaining relief from the penal laws was a matter for the Catholic gentry, not for the bishops. Dalrymple accepted his advice and invitations were sent out to over two hundred members of the leading Catholic families, including the Smythes, Erringtons and Fitzherberts, requesting them to attend a meeting at the Thatched House Tavern on 12 April 1778, their company being desired 'on some particular business'.

By this time, Mary Anne Weld's marriage arrangements were well under way, but, with her Smythe cousins, the Erringtons, the Fitzherberts and Throckmortons all planning to attend the Thatched House Tavern, family talk was all of a new oath, and Catholic Relief Bills. Before long, she heard how the meeting had agreed to send a loyal address to the King, to elect a committee from among themselves to draw up a new oath of allegiance, and to reach agreement with Parliament for as much relief from the old penal laws as was possible.

Events moved fast. Both sides hoped a Relief Bill would be passed before the summer recess. Mary Anne might also have hoped it would be satisfactorily settled before her wedding day at the end of June. Everyone's hopes were fulfilled. George III received the loyal address graciously, a first Catholic Relief Bill was prepared, introduced into the Commons by George Saville, and passed by both Houses without a division. George III found no fault with it, and royal assent was given on the 3 June.

The new Act removed from the statute book some of the old laws, hardly ever enforced, but which Catholics always feared might be brought into use again: Catholic priests were freed from the penalty of life imprisonment; Catholics could buy and inherit land; and, most importantly, for everyday purposes, the £100 reward for informing against a priest was abolished. Catholics could now take an oath of allegiance to the King, with the religious clauses, preventing them doing so in the past, omitted, but with a renunciation of Charles Stuart, and a denial that the Pope could claim temporal jurisdiction 'within this realm' included.

It was not a great deal but it was a beginning, and optimism ran high in the Catholic community. The lawyer Charles Butler, looking back in old age on the passing of this Bill, wrote: 'No Catholic who recollects the passing of the Bill will ever forget the general anxiety of the body, while it was in its progress through Parliament, or the smile and friendly greeting with which his Protestant neighbour met him the day after it had passed into law.'[6] Bishop Challoner rose to the occasion and instructed his priests that: 'all and every one of you should offer up your most ardent prayers to the Almighty for our most gracious sovereign, King George III and his Royal Consort Queen Charlotte, and all their royal family ... this being the duty which by the law of God all Christian people owe to their respective Sovereign'.[7] After this, no one could say Catholics were Jacobites, and the King to whom the Smythes' family motto bade them be Ever Faithful was, from now on, a Hanoverian.

Thomas Fitzherbert could therefore turn his mind entirely to thoughts of marriage, both he and Mary Anne seeing the Relief Act as a happy omen for the future of the sons and daughters they hoped they would have. On 24 June 1778, Mary Anne married Thomas Fitzherbert at Swynnerton Hall. Her black gowns had been replaced by colourful silks, her gold hair, freed from cap and 'weeds' and still unpowdered, was abundant as ever, and her admired white skin was still fresh and clear. Putting her sad past behind her, she had come to Swynnerton to begin a new life, and brought with her a maturity she did not have when she married Edward Weld. As an outward sign of a new beginning, she not only took her husband's name of Fitzherbert, but changed her first name as well. From that time on she signed herself 'Maria Fitzherbert', and was addressed as Maria by the few who were intimate enough to use her first name. Perhaps Thomas liked to call her Maria, and she adopted that form of her name to please him. But to the rest of the world she was, and would remain, 'Mrs Fitzherbert'.

Thomas Fitzherbert senior was still alive in 1778 and his family was a large one. Thomas junior had four younger brothers, Basil, John, William and Robert, and, in addition, there were two married girls, Theresa and Constantia, and a younger sister, Barbara, still at home. The youngest boy had just gone to study at Liège, where he joined Charles and Henry Smythe. Some of the other brothers were probably in residence at Swynnerton, or coming and going between travels abroad and country visits. But Maria was used to sharing a home with brothers and sisters, and the Fitzherbert siblings no doubt found her every bit as charming and sympathetic as the younger Welds had done in her brief time at Lulworth. Swynnerton Hall, built in the classical style, with its surrounding park by Capability Brown, was an impressive house, large but well proportioned, and said to have so many rooms that no one had ever counted them.

Her entry into the family would have been celebrated with dinners and evening parties, and a ball, to introduce the bride to neighbours and family connections. All this, however, came to an end with the death, later in the year, of Thomas senior. Perhaps his death was expected, but it was a sadness to his children, and entertaining ceased for a time.

Like the Welds, the Fitzherberts got on well with their Protestant neighbours, and Maria frequently visited the Jervis family at Meaford. Edward Jervis, whose father became Lord St Vincent, after naval triumphs in the West Indies, became a great friend of hers. A Jervis daughter later wrote in her autograph book: 'The famous Mrs Fitzherbert then living at Swynnerton was a great friend of my father's and used to like to come to Meaford as it was more gay than Swynnerton'.[8] She went on to recall that her father gave Maria a miniature of Wat Smythe, who was also a friend of his and 'wonderfully handsome'. No doubt Swynnerton could be full of life and gaiety when the numberless rooms were full of guests, but when the younger members of the family were away, and there were no visitors, Maria may well have enjoyed driving herself in the phaeton to pay calls on nearby friends.

Thomas Fitzherbert is described as, 'A tall and powerful man with a tendency to corpulency which he endeavoured to counteract by great abstemiousness in diet and by the most astonishing efforts of bodily activity and exercise'.[9] This must have taken up much of his time, and was perhaps another reason why Maria, if left alone for long periods, may have found Swynnerton rather quiet. But it cannot be assumed, from Miss Jervis's single comment, that she was in any way discontented. She told Lord Stourton that she was 'sincerely attached' to Thomas Fitzherbert, and Swynnerton was not their only home. Visits to their house in Park Street were made in the Season, and London at that time was certainly 'gay'. Lady Mary Coke's journal describes the social round: 'calls and card parties, opera, assemblies, breakfasts and driving in the park ...' The Fitzherberts possibly preferred a less hectic Season than Lady Mary's, but a full and enjoyable life centred around their Park Street house, and the town, of which Maria had seen so little before her first marriage, offered much to divert and delight a young woman.

London society was nocturnal. Theatres began at 7 o'clock, but it was fashionable to arrive late. There were usually two plays, and the first could be missed. The theatre was followed by late suppers and balls, and no one would think of arriving at an assembly before eleven.

London was spreading westwards, with spacious new streets and squares providing tall, narrow town houses for the wealthy wishing to move from the City. Park Street, running along the side of Hyde Park, was fashionably situated. The town was now much too big for sedan chairs, and travel from one place of pleasure to another was by carriage. Huge country waggons arrived daily with loads of hay and fodder for London's large number of horses, causing traffic jams in the narrow streets.

The town was full of music. Concerts abounded during the Season, many held in the Hanover Square Rooms, where Johann Christian Bach (the 'London Bach') performed, and Haydn sometimes played his own compositions; or at Hickford's Rooms in Brewer Street, where the child Mozart had once played. There was much playing and singing in homes, taverns and churches, and musical street cries echoed round the new squares and terraces, charming visiting foreigners. Handel had first come to London in 1710, and although he had died in 1759, his oratorios and orchestral works still dominated the town's musical life. Thomas Arne's Shakespearian songs were still sung at Drury Lane where he had composed them, and his 'Rule Britannia!' sounded round the pleasure gardens at Vauxhall. But by far the most fashionable musical venue was the Royal Italian Opera at the King's Theatre in the Haymarket. Here all the fine world listened to operas and observed one another.

The chapels of the Catholic foreign embassies were full of music as well, with the Sardinian, Bavarian, Portuguese, Neapolitan and other embassies all opening their doors to London's Catholics; and Sunday High Mass was sung in them with bravura. The Portuguese Embassy, in South Street, was particularly famous for its fine music, and members of the Italian Opera Company sang free of charge in the Sardinian Embassy chapel in Lincoln's Inn Fields.[10]

With or without their music, the embassy chapels had always provided Catholics with a place to worship in safety.[11] Most of the chapels were large and well staffed with priests, many of whom were English. On Sunday mornings there were lines of carriages all round Golden Square as the fashionable and faithful, the Fitzherberts among them, were put down in time for Mass at the Bavarian Embassy. Years later, Maria recounted an episode from her London life at this time:

> Mrs Fitzherbert told us this evening, that the first time she ever saw the Prince, was when she was driving with her husband Mr Fitzherbert. They were in Park Lane, when he turned round and said: 'Look, there is the Prince!' The second time was a few days subsequently when she was going with her husband to a breakfast given by Mrs Townley at Corney House Chiswick ... As they were turning down the Lane she perceived that the Prince had followed her and had stopped to look at her.[12]

George, Prince of Wales, would have been seventeen, at the most, not yet of age, but he already had the habit of staring at, and following, any pretty woman who caught his eye. Regarding him as a boy, not yet used to the manners of polite society, the Fitzherberts were probably amused by the episode. The young Prince was strikingly handsome in his late teens, which is perhaps why Thomas Fitzherbert instantly recognised him, even though he was not yet the well-known figure about town he would later become.

Happy though Maria was in these early years of her second marriage, she knew that her first duty as a wife was to provide an heir to the Fitzherbert name and estates, and, as their second wedding anniversary approached, the lack of a longed-for child was a source of private disappointment.[13] But Maria was young, and it was far too early to worry. Any anxiety or sadness was well hidden as she carried out her duties as châtelaine at Swynnerton and hostess in Park Street.

The debates and dramas at Westminster during the Season provided fashionable society with gossip, and a chance to take sides. Although Catholics usually remained aloof from party politics, in 1779 the Fitzherberts became deeply interested in a political drama involving their neighbour, Sir John Jervis. With a French invasion feared, and both French and Spanish fleets sighted in the Channel, the court martial of Commander Augustus Keppel for neglect of duty in a sea battle with the French was dividing London Society. Sir John Jervis was the key witness at his trial. The Whigs supported Keppel, and the Whig ladies went to the opera wearing 'Keppel caps' to show their allegiance. Lord North's Tory government was heavily criticised for allowing the court martial to take place, based, as it was, on the accusation of a junior officer.

Keppel had commanded a fleet of thirty-two ships in squalls and thick fog in a battle off Brest. When the French got away, Keppel was accused of making serious mistakes. Jervis had been commanding the ship immediately astern of Keppel's in the line of battle, and his evidence was crucial to Keppel's defence. Keppel was acquitted, amid Whig rejoicing, but the celebrations got out of hand with the Whig MP Charles James Fox, and his drinking companions, encouraging the crowds to break Lord North's windows in Downing Street and do similar damage to the homes of other Ministers, whose addresses Fox was said to have supplied. When Keppel received the Freedom of the City, a few days later, Fox's windows were broken and Whig houses attacked as the other side retaliated and the fickle crowd joined in. Bishop Challoner observed the violence in the streets and wondered, prophetically, how long it would be before the same crowd turned against the Catholics.

In the hot summer of 1780 a petition was presented to Parliament which riveted the attention of all Catholics, including the Fitzherberts, in Park Street for the Season. The presentation of petitions to Parliament was a regular feature of business in the House of Commons, but this was to prove a petition which Londoners would not forget for many years. The government had delayed the Catholic Relief Bill for Scotland until 1779, but it was withdrawn almost immediately after causing rioting in Scottish cities. This led some Protestants south of the border to believe they could get the English Relief Act withdrawn also.

Lord George Gordon, a man whom many regarded as deranged, and even his friends thought extreme, had become president of the recently formed Protestant Association the previous year. As a Member of Parliament, Gordon had observed the presentation of petitions, and heard them debated straight away, and decided to get the English Catholic Relief Act withdrawn by the Petitionist method. He invited the Protestant Association and its supporters to sign a petition for the abolition of the Act, and to meet him at St George's Fields, Southwark, on 5 June, to march over the river to Westminster. Handbills advertising the event were passed around all over London, and Catholics, well aware of what was happening, waited in apprehension.

Something like 60,000 supporters turned up in Southwark, all being given blue cockades, provided by Gordon at a cost of £25,000. Then, in the full heat of the midday sun, Gordon raised his blue banner, and led his supporters over the river to Westminster. It never looked like being a peaceful demonstration. As the vast crowd marched through the City it picked up the inevitable gangs of petty criminals, and those drifters in society who would join any march with a chance of violence.

When they all arrived at Westminster it was the peers, entering the House of Lords, who were the first to suffer. Many were kicked, seized by the throat, lost their watches and wigs, or had their carriage wheels removed, and generally thought themselves lucky to escape with their lives. Members of the Commons were let off more lightly, Lord North only losing his hat. The petition was presented and a debate followed. The crowd pressed into the lobbies, and it was only then that the guard was called to force them back into Palace Yard. The size and anger of the crowd caused noticeable fear among Members, and one was heard to tell Gordon that, if the mob entered the Chamber, he would kill him. In spite of their fear, only seven MPs voted in favour of abolishing the Catholic Relief Act, with 192 voting against. The news travelled fast; but, before the Catholics could express their gratitude, relief turned to dismay.

The furious and disappointed crowd left Westminster. Divided into two groups, one went to the Bavarian Embassy in Golden Square, damaging the building and torching the chapel; the other went to the Sardinian Embassy in Lincoln's Inn Fields, where the damage was more serious and the chapel destroyed. This began six days of terrifying and unchecked rioting, by far the worst violence London had seen for well over a century. But it was organised rioting in most places; only Catholic houses and those of Catholic sympathisers were burned, and fire engines followed the crowd to prevent the fires spreading to Protestant homes, or to houses of very poor Catholics. Priests, especially those who worked in the East End of the town, were greatly at risk from the mob, and many Catholic men, including Thomas Fitzherbert, hastened to rescue them from their vulnerable houses and get them out of London. Challoner was the one the rioters most wanted, shouting for him as they searched, and it was feared they would burn the old man alive if they found him. He was smuggled from his lodgings and taken, in Lady Stourton's chariot, to Finchley, where he was kept safe in John Mawhood's house.

It was important that Catholics did not retaliate, no matter how provoked, and some Catholic men, Thomas Fitzherbert among them, stayed in the streets trying to maintain calm. Everyone in authority seemed too frightened to act. The magistrates could have brought in the army to restore order, but hesitated to read the Riot Act in case the violence was turned against them and their homes. Lord North watched from the roof of Downing Street as London burned. There were plenty of troops standing by, in various parts of town, but no one gave them orders to act, so they remained spectators.

On the third day of rioting, Lord George Saville, who had introduced the Relief Bill into the Commons, saw his house in Leicester Square fired, and his books, paintings and furniture piled up in the centre of the square and burned. Dozens of houses were destroyed, and by the fourth day terror had become general. Those who had to go out wore a blue cockade, there being no safety for anyone without this 'badge of riot'. Newgate Prison was burned, and all the prisoners released. The mob then moved down Snow Hill to Langdale's distillery at Holborn. Langdale was a Catholic, and the crowd threatened to destroy his house if he did not supply them with spirits. He brought out tubs and pails for them to help themselves.

Maria's fear and dismay knew no bounds in the early stage of the rioting, when her husband was out and she had no idea where he was. Years later, when she was living in a house on the Thames when the river was about to flood, she wrote describing how she ran down the garden every five minutes to check how high the water had risen, working herself up into 'a state of anxiety scarcely to be borne'.[14] It is easy to imagine her, in a state of even greater anxiety, with houses two streets away burning, flying from front windows to back, from garden to stables, looking and praying for Thomas's return. He did return, overheated, face blackened, lungs full of smoke, and flung himself into a cold bath.[15]

By the fifth day, almost every house in London had hung out blue flags or 'No Popery' banners, and the Fitzherberts could only hope Thomas was not sufficiently well known for the rioters to have his address. It was not safe for them to try and leave, even though Thomas had begun to feel ill and weak, with some difficulty in breathing. News probably reached them that Sir John Fielding's house, not far away in Grosvenor Square, had been wrecked, and his priceless library of books burned. The mob had also rolled out casks of spirits from Langdale's which spilt into the gutters, where the firemen used it, mistaking it for water, causing the fires to spread in a terrifying way, and by night both fires and and the gin-drunk crowds were out of control.

On the sixth day the King, after attending a meeting of the Privy Council, gave orders himself for the troops to be sent in. Twenty-five thousand troops attacked the mobs in various parts of the town. By the end of the day, five hundred lay dead in the streets. Hundreds were arrested, and fifty-nine were condemned to death.[16]

The damaged embassies were assured of compensation, and so were those whose homes had been damaged or destroyed. The chapels were rapidly rebuilt, in many cases larger and finer than before. Lord George Gordon was put in the Tower awaiting trial for treason. The French did not invade, and the English army did a little better, for a while, in the American War. In September Lord North called a surprise election, which he won. By October John Mawhood was recording in his diary a series of visits to reopened chapels, 'All to the Bavarian', he wrote, 'To the Neapolitan for Vespers', 'To prayers at Moorfields', just as if the restored chapels had never been destroyed.[17] The Prince of Wales became eighteen that summer, and was given his own apartments in Buckingham House. The Season had ended abruptly, and the Fitzherberts had returned to Swynnerton, hoping that Thomas, who was now very unwell, would recover his health. The doctors described his condition as 'a chill', but John Kirk's opinion,[18] that he had picked up some pulmonary infection while mingling with the crowds, seems more likely. The quiet weeks at Swynnerton did not help Thomas, and in October the Fitzherberts left England, travelling slowly to Nice, hoping a warmer climate would improve Thomas's deteriorating health.

The year 1780 was a bad one for Maria. In March her sister, Barbara, had died at Brambridge, shortly before her eleventh birthday;[19] the summer of violence in London had shocked and terrified her; and now Nice's winter sunshine seemed to be her husband's last hope of regaining his health. Nice was still a small town in 1780. The Promenade des Anglais and the fashionable hotels were not yet built. Charles James Fox, when travelling as a young man, had described it as 'probably the dullest town in the world',[20] but the Fitzherberts were not there for entertainment; they rented a house and settled into a gentle daily routine.

Nice belonged to the House of Savoy, Kings of Sardinia, in 1780, and the society there was a floating one, a mixture of French, English and Italian, some pausing there en route to other places, and some staying to enjoy the warm climate. The young wife, caring solicitously for an ailing husband whose condition did not improve, attracted sympathy, and Maria made many friends. In spite of his wife's care, and the soft climate, Thomas's health deteriorated. At some stage they were joined by John, the second of Thomas's brothers, who came to Nice to represent the family and give what help he could. Thomas survived the winter and spring, but died in the early summer, on 7 May 1781, aged thirty-four.

Maria had watched a husband die for a second time. Edward Weld's death had been a shock and a loss, but she had been married to Thomas Fitzherbert for three years and this time her grief was much deeper. She must have been glad of her brother-in-law's support while making all the arrangements that follow a death.

They did not attempt to take the body home for burial in the family vaults at Norbury. Instead Maria purchased a chapel in the Dominican church, and had a tomb prepared for him there. 'Purchasing' a chapel may seem unusual, but that was the word she used herself, twenty-five years later:

> How very kind of you, dearest, to think of me and all my suffering at Nice. Your search after the tomb must have been fruitless. It is in one of the Chapels I purchased in a Church, and I conclude there could have been no one at Nice who could recollect me at such a distance of time.[21]

She and John Fitzherbert chose a brief Latin memorial for Thomas's tomb:

Nobili Viro
Thomae Fitzherberto Anglo
Maria Smythe Conjuge B.
Johannes Frati
Moerentes P.p.
III Id Maij MDCCLXXXI [22]

The Fitzherbert estates passed to Basil, the eldest surviving brother, but Mrs Fitzherbert was comfortably provided for. The house in Park Street became hers, with an annual income of nearly £2000,[23] and all the carriages and horses. Rather touchingly, Thomas had added that she should also have 'the ponies or Galloways she usually drives in the phaeton'.

Once more in 'weeds', Maria Fitzherbert remained some months in Nice. Possibly the tomb took a long time to complete, and she would naturally wish to see it finished before leaving. Even then, she may have wanted to stay on for a while in the place where her husband was buried, and where, in Nice's shifting population, there would soon be few to remember him. Deep in grief, aged just twenty-five, she must have found it hard to make a decision about where to go, and what to do with the rest of her life.

When she did leave, she went to Paris. While there, she heard of a number English Catholic women living in poor circumstances and befriended them, able to offer financial help from the Fitzherbert money now at her disposal.[24] Eventually, she made the decision to return to England – crossing to Brighton where she spent the summer of 1783. An artist, much attracted by her looks and manners, begged leave to dedicate four of his paintings to her.[25] She had lost none of her power to attract, in spite of her 'weeds' and obvious sadness, or perhaps because of them.

From Brighton she travelled on to Brambridge where her parents, for a second time, welcomed home a grieving daughter. The family hoped her grief would not last overlong, and efforts were made to persuade her to return to London when her mourning drew to an end. She was reluctant to do so, but did rent a villa near Twickenham, probably Ormeley Lodge on Ham Common, close enough to London to visit friends, but far enough into the country to provide the seclusion she felt a widow should maintain.

Before leaving Brambridge, she endowed William Walmsley's mission with a bond for a thousand pounds. Priests were beginning to move from the protection of the manor houses into houses of their own, and William Walmsley had recently left Brambridge Hall for a house-cum-chapel in the nearby hamlet of Highbridge.[26] From there he could minister to the Catholics of the region more effectively, while still remaining on close terms with the Smythes. Maria's endowment gave him a small income to add to whatever the local Catholics could provide. Here, as in Paris, she was making generous use of her Fitzherbert money.

After a time, her half-uncle Lord Sefton (connected to the Smythes through the second marriage of an Errington widow) persuaded her to open her Park Street house, and enter into society again, spending as much time as she liked with him and his wife. Lord and Lady Sefton moved in the most fashionable of circles, into which they introduced their niece.

Mrs Fitzherbert's return to London life, in 1784, was noted by the press. The *Morning Herald* announced, on 20 March, 'Mrs Fitzherbert is arrived in London for the Season'. Later in the year, on 27 July, the paper went further, becoming quite excited,

> A new Constellation has lately made an appearance in the fashionable hemisphere that engages the attention of those whose hearts are susceptible to the power of beauty. The widow of the late Mr Fitzherbert has in her train half our young nobility. As the Lady has not, as yet, discovered

a partiality for any of her admirers, they are all animated with hopes of success.

Even allowing for exaggeration, it is clear that Mrs Fitzherbert, at twenty-seven, an age when charms were supposed to fade, was still admired.

Lady Sefton, described by Georgiana, Duchess of Devonshire as 'a compound of vanity, nonsense, folly and good nature',[27] had her own box at the Italian Opera, and was determined that Maria should go with her and Lord Sefton to this most fashionable of entertainments. But Maria was reluctant. Although enjoying her return to Society, she felt the opera was too fashionable, and too public, an entertainment for a widow of just three years. She agreed to go, however, but wearing a widow's cap and veil.

3

'Who the Devil is that Pretty Girl?'

Maria was right in thinking the opera was the place to be seen by fashionable people; and, that night, the most fashionable young man of them all was there. George, Prince of Wales, lost no time in scanning the high tiers of boxes to see who else was there, and with whom. His eyes were drawn to the fair, pure-complexioned young woman, with widow's veil thrown back, seated in Lady Sefton's box. Years later, George Dawson Damer heard, and recorded, Maria's own account of what happened next:

> She left the opera leaning on Henry Artan's arm and when at the door with her veil down, waiting for her carriage the Prince came up to him and said: 'Who the devil is that pretty girl you have on your arm, Henry?' The latter told the Prince who she was and then introduced the Prince to Mrs Fitzherbert.[1]

The Prince, impressionable and passionately romantic, probably believed himself to be falling deeply in love as he stood looking at her. He had fallen in love many times before, and was familiar with the sensation. Maria, though used to men's admiring glances, was aware of the Prince's reputation with women and may have been a little flustered by such open royal admiration, just when she was trying to slip away unseen. But, whatever her feelings, she dropped the low curtsey due to royalty and was handed into her carriage, unaware that her life had been changed for ever by that brief meeting on the theatre steps.

The Prince of Wales was a disarming young man, tall and floridly handsome, with clear blue eyes and wavy brown hair. Although heavily built, he carried himself with grace and dignity. Witty and musical, he spoke French and German fluently, was already showing signs of the taste and style for which he would be famous, and had, when he chose, exquisite manners. Above all, he had charm. His extravagance, drinking and reckless adventures of the heart gave his father sleepless nights, but fashionable society excused his faults.

The eldest of fifteen children, his had been a joyless childhood. Born on 12 August 1762, he was declared to be a 'strong, large and pretty boy'. He was created Prince of Wales five days later, and on 16 September was baptised George Augustus Frederick by the Archbishop of Canterbury. Though made much of by both his parents as an infant, he was soon handed over to governess and teachers to begin his education. He was thought to be an intelligent and precocious child, and at the age of three he was made a Knight of the Garter. By the age of five he had made good progress in all his lessons and could write 'a clear hand'. From time to time he attended his mother's Thursday afternoon 'Drawing Rooms' where he was admired as a healthy and attractive boy. Apart from occasional appearances in public, he spent most of his childhood either in the Bower Lodge at Kew or in Buckingham House (not yet a palace) and was denied any companions other than his brothers and sisters. By the year 1773, when he was eleven, he had eight siblings: Frederick a year younger than himself, William, Charlotte, Edward, Augusta, Elizabeth and Ernest. The royal nursery was not only overcrowded, it was becoming increasingly unruly,[2] and it was decided that the two eldest boys should be moved to the Dutch House at Kew (later known as Kew Palace) to complete their education, separated both from their siblings and from outside distractions. They were also separated from any kind of family life, with governor, sub-governor and tutor to organise their days. Their regime was strict: lessons, based on the classics and modern languages, beginning immediately after breakfast at seven and continuing, with breaks for supervised exercise, fencing, riding and boxing, until eight at night. Light relief sometimes came in the form of music; George learnt to play the cello competently and developed a pleasant singing voice. The King and Queen took a great interest in the boys' development and health, but seemed unable to show them love and affection. On their father's orders they were beaten severely for inattention at lessons, and for dishonesty. The Prince was an habitual liar, his father often complaining that he had 'a bad habit of not speaking the truth'.[3] It was a habit that remained all his life. But by the age of sixteen he had become a handsome youth, was an amusing talker and a wonderful mimic, with a gift for making people like him.

Frederick, George's only companion and the King's favourite son, was sent to Hanover for military training at the age of seventeen. The King wept to see him go, but it was Prince George who was left lonely and envious. The younger brothers were also sent abroad in their turn: William, destined for the navy, became a midshipman at the age of fourteen, and the others, now including two younger sons, Adolphus and Augustus, all went, in their middle teens, to the university of Göttingen to study military history, and to train, later, with the Hanoverian army. The sisters, now including Mary, Sophia and Amelia, remained with their parents in chaperoned seclusion, their orderly days of lessons, sewing, reading and walks being supervised by the Queen.

George saw little of his siblings, but his uncle Cumberland, the King's brother, took a liking to him and, to his father's distress, introduced him to a licentious way of life. The King's disapproval of the Duke of Cumberland went back to 1772 when the Duke had openly contracted a marriage with Anne Horton, a young widow, undoubtedly beautiful, but said to be disreputable. Unable to prove the marriage either illegal or canonically invalid, the King, who believed that all royal dukes should marry Protestant princesses, decided to ensure no more 'shameful' marriages could take place in the family, and forced a Bill designed to prevent them through a reluctant Parliament.

The Royal Marriages Act, passed in 1772, forbade any Prince or Princess descended from George II, and under the age of twenty-five, to marry without the consent of the ruling monarch. Should one of them wish to marry without royal approval after the age of twenty-five, he or she could apply to the Privy Council, and could then marry a year later, provided neither the Lords nor the Commons had raised an objection. Unfortunately for George III, a second regrettable marriage had already taken place, in 1766. His brother the Duke of Gloucester, of whom he was very fond, came to him and confessed that he had secretly married Lady Waldegrave, widow of Lord Waldegrave and illegitimate daughter of Edward Walpole. Both Gloucester and Cumberland were banned from Court. The King was eventually reconciled to Gloucester, and his two children,[4] but he never forgave Cumberland.

He could not, however, forbid his son to see his uncle and the Prince continued to do so, though hardly needing lessons from him when it came to living for pleasure. He had seduced one of his mother's ladies in waiting when he was sixteen, and then embarked on a series of passionate attachments. His first public affair was with the actress, Mary Robinson, but she had been preceded in the Prince's affections by a secret attachment to Mary Hamilton, to whom he had written daily letters declaring no one had ever loved before as he loved her: 'I love you', he had vowed, 'more than ideas or words can express ...' Miss Hamilton wisely refused all gifts except friendship, and was easily dismissed with, 'Adieu, Adieu, Adieu, *toujours chère*'.

Mrs Robinson was very beautiful, and when she played Perdita in *The Winter's Tale* she became the toast of the town. The Prince went to the theatre especially to see her, and as soon as she stepped onto the stage she became the next object of his desire. He made her not only promises of undying love, but agreed, in writing, to give her a fortune of £20,000 as soon as he came of age.

As early as his son's eighteenth birthday, the King had written, 'your love of dissipation has for some months been ... trumpeted in the public papers', but a bond for £20,000, was something he could not have anticipated and he felt obliged to buy Mrs Robinson off. The Prince had tired of her anyway, and progressed recklessly on down a long line of other loves, including Liz Armistead (who later became the mistress, and eventually the wife, of Charles James Fox), and Lady Melbourne, whose fourth son was said to be his. He almost eloped with the 'divinely pretty' wife of Karl von Hardenburg, but the King put a stop to that affair by sending the von Hardenburgs home to Hanover.

When the Prince met Maria Fitzherbert on the steps of the opera, he had recently moved to Carlton House in Pall Mall, and his mind was consumed, not with current mistresses, but with ambitious plans for that mansion's glorious refurbishment.

George III was deeply uneasy about his eldest son. The Prince had taken up with Charles James Fox, the last man the King would have chosen as his son's companion. Apart from being the heaviest drinker and deepest gambler in Brooks' Club, Fox was the leader of a group of radicals within the Whig Party who believed kings should reign but not rule, and that Parliament should hold the real power. In the King's eyes, he was a threat to good government. But his son saw 'My dear Charles' as a magical companion whose company he would never give up.

The Prince's debts were another source of pain to the King. Something like £30,000 was currently owed to boot-makers, hat-makers, jewellers and wine merchants. The Cabinet suggested that his debts be written off, and that he should in future receive an income of £100,000 a year. The King was outraged. Public money should not be squandered to 'gratify the passions of an ill-advised young man' was his not unreasonable comment. A compromise was reached by which Parliament was to find money to pay the debts, the King to find £50,000 a year from the Civil List, and the Prince to have an extra £12,000 from the Duchy of Cornwall.

With all this on his mind, the news that this son was now in love with a young Catholic widow, whose name the King said he could not recall, was not thought, by comparison, to be a matter of prime importance. The Prince had a habit of loving today and leaving tomorrow; his father did not need to know the names of them all.

Sensibly, Mrs Fitzherbert did not take the Prince's attentions seriously either. Not at first. He was amusing and charming, went out of his way to please her, which was flattering, but his vows of love could only be taken lightly. Gently discouraging him, with kindness and good humour, seemed the best way of coping with a passionate young Prince. But His Royal Highness could not be discouraged so easily. He used all his charm and wit to divert and disarm her. He introduced her into Devonshire House, where the most brilliant circle in London gathered around Georgiana, the young Duchess. He made it clear that, with him at her side, all doors would open to her. In addition, he recounted stories of his sad childhood, the mother who didn't love him, the father who treated him harshly, and the loss of Frederick, his only friend. What he needed was someone like her: then he would change his way of life; then he would be happy. Mrs Fitzherbert, twice married but without the longed for children, may have been touched by the lost little boy she saw in the Prince. She also found him very attractive, as all women did. But, whatever her feelings, she had no intention of acting on them. She would never be any man's mistress. Dishonouring her good name, the name of her family, and the name of her late husband, was something not even to be thought of. The word 'dishonour', used in this connection, was very well understood in the eighteenth century, even by the Prince of Wales, and he began to murmur the word 'marriage'. But

Maria knew this to be impossible also: she was a commoner, six years older than him, and, much more significant, a Catholic. She may not have known exactly what constitutional crises such a marriage would cause, but she certainly knew it would endanger the Prince's whole future. He must turn his attentions elsewhere, she told him, because she could be neither his wife nor his mistress. Fox did not suspect, at this time, that the Prince had marriage in mind, and could not understand why Maria refused to be a royal mistress, the *maîtresse en titre*. Maria looked coldly on Fox from this time on.

The Prince persuaded his friend and confidante, Georgiana, Duchess of Devonshire, to approach Maria on his behalf. Reluctantly she agreed, and recorded their meeting: 'At last he engaged me to see her which I did at her own house but she agreed with me in the impossibility of his ideas; and her good sense and resolution seemed so strong that I own I felt secure of her never giving way.'[5] The Prince was, nevertheless, sure she would give way, and held a ball at Carlton House, at which he planned to make her the guest of honour, as if announcing her new role to the *beau monde*. Alarmed now, she declined to go. And when he drove to Park Street to beg her to come, her servants told him their mistress had retired for the night.

Maria no longer thought the Prince's vows of love could be gently turned away. She had made up her mind, as Lord Stourton put it, to resist, 'with the utmost firmness, the flattering assiduities of the most accomplished Prince of his age'. It was quite usual for ladies to go to continental watering places at the end of the London Season, and Maria decided to follow the custom, thus escaping from the Prince, and perhaps from her own emotions as well. The Duchess of Devonshire recorded the Prince's reaction:

> The Prince of Wales has been like a madman. He was ill last Wednesday and took three pints of brandy which killed him. He was confined three days to his bed – I fancy he made himself worse than he was in hopes to prevent the departure for Spa of a certain lady who goes in spite of all on Wednesday.[6]

The Prince could not bear to let the 'certain lady' go where he could not follow (he needed the King's permission to go abroad) and searched for some measure to prevent her escape.

Late on the eve of her planned departure, the surgeon Keate, Lord

Southampton, Mr Bouverie and Mr Onslow arrived at Mrs Fitzherbert's door saying His Royal Highness had 'fallen on his sword' (he had, in fact, stabbed himself), was refusing medical aid, and declaring he would bleed to death if Mrs Fitzherbert did not come to him. Mrs Fitzherbert said nothing would induce her to enter Carlton House at that time of night. Even when their stricken faces convinced her that they spoke the truth, she remained 'fearful of some stratagem derogatory to her reputation', and only agreed to go if they found a suitable lady to chaperone her. The Duchess of Devonshire was suggested and, when called on by Bouverie and Onslow, both 'pale as death', she agreed to go with them.

The sight of the Prince, blood-stained, pale and apparently half-mad, terrified both women, who genuinely thought him in danger of death. Keate admitted they had called Southampton to ask if the King should be informed. If the heir died without the King being warned of the situation, they feared a charge of treason. Amid this sort of talk, it is understandable that Maria agreed to do as the Prince asked, for fear a refusal would make his condition worse. He said he would accept treatment for his wound if Maria would agree to marry him. If she refused, nothing would induce him to live. The Duchess was against the very idea of such a marriage, knowing the dreadful damage it would do him. Only a conviction that the Prince's life was in danger could have made her take a ring from her own hand, and urge Maria to let the Prince of Wales place it on her wedding finger.[7]

The Prince then happily agreed to put himself in the hands of the doctor, and the ladies left for Devonshire House. There they recovered their composure, and drew up a statement covering the night's events:

> On Tuesday the 8 July 1784 Mr Bouverie and Mr Onslow came to me and told me the Prince of Wales had run himself thro' the body and declar'd he would tear open his bandages unless I would accompany Mrs Fitzherbert to him. We went there and she promised to marry him at her return but she conceives as well as myself that promises obtained in such a manner are entirely void.[8]

They signed it, and Maria left the country the next day, accompanied by Lady Anne Lindsay, as planned, having recovered sufficiently to write a strongly worded letter to Lord Southampton, 'protesting against what had taken place, as not being then a free agent'. She planned to stay abroad until the Prince's eyes had lighted on some other lady, or until his father had married him off to a suitable princess.

When the Prince heard that Maria had withdrawn her promise and gone abroad he wept for days. Mrs Armistead told Lord Holland:

> He cried by the hour … testified to the sincerity and violence of his passion and his despair by rolling on the floor, striking his forehead, tearing his hair, falling into hystericks, and swearing that he would abandon the country, forego the Crown, sell his jewels and plate, and scrape together a competence to fly with the object of his affections to America.[9]

Meanwhile, Maria, drinking the sulphur waters of Aix la Chapelle, was said by Lady Anne Lindsay to be, 'irresolute and inconsequential'. The Prince wrote passionate letters, delivered by couriers, begging her to take pity on him, interspersing his many vows of eternal love with threats of suicide. He sent gold bracelets, not as a suitor, he said, but as a husband. Lady Anne, though seemingly sympathetic to Maria, kept the Prince informed of their whereabouts.

Still believing he would forget her given time, Maria decided to visit The Hague. She probably had letters of introduction to the Stadtholder, Willem V, who liked to welcome English visitors, and who was hoping to marry his daughter to the Prince of Wales. Negotiations for the match had been opened, but had not proceeded far. The Stadtholder knew nothing of the Prince's desire to marry Mrs Fitzherbert, though he may have heard rumours that linked their names together, and would certainly have known that she had moved in Carlton House circles recently. She knew nothing, until she arrived, of a possible marriage, sometime in the future, with the Princess of Orange, who was still in her middle teens. The situation was potentially embarrassing, but, having no intention of marrying the Prince herself, and having frequently told him so, she decided she could encourage the Princess and answer her questions about the Prince. After all, it was in the hope of just such a marriage that Mrs Fitzherbert was travelling abroad. Lady Anne described the Princess as, 'pretty, pleasing and a good girl', and Mrs Fitzherbert agreed.[10] But when she heard that James Harris, a trusted confidant of both George III and his son, was due to arrive in The Hague as an attaché, she fixed her date of departure. Harris would know both of the proposed marriage with the Stadtholder's daughter and of the gossip regarding the

Prince and Mrs Fitzherbert. To meet at the Stadtholder's court would embarrass them both.

The Dutch royal family were sorry to see Mrs Fitzherbert leave. Willem V's mother had been a daughter of George II and, concerned at the French support for those who wished to replace the House of Orange with a republic, he wanted to maintain close links with Britain and welcomed anyone who was known at the Court of St James or who was part of the Prince of Wales's circle. He insisted she travel as far as Antwerp in the royal barge.

Back in France, the Prince's letters began to arrive in such numbers, and were delivered with such haste, that French officials arrested the couriers, taking them for spies. The Duke of Orleans, a friend of the Prince and greatly amused, intervened, explaining the messages were of romance, not politics. Maria's nerves were beginning to fray. She quarrelled with her French maid and dismissed her; and she wrote to a convent in Brussels asking if two English ladies could have apartments there, but then changed her mind. Lady Anne and her sister, Margaret, who had joined them, returned home at about this time, and eventually Mrs Fitzherbert crossed the border into Switzerland, and spent the rest of the winter there, joined for a time by her brother Jack.[11] The Prince's increasingly desperate letters followed her from one village to the next, and she became less and less certain how to respond, and grew increasingly unhappy and homesick. In the spring she returned to France and stayed in Paris for a time. But too many people knew her there, and were beginning to ask questions, and it was becoming difficult to explain why she stayed away from home for so long. She decided to leave Paris for Lorraine. In Plombière, alone and vulnerable, she met with yet another problem. The Marquis de Bellois, seeing a lovely, solitary and comfortably off young widow, was immediately attracted. A marriage to her would help his shaky finances, and give him considerable pleasure as well. Maria refused him out of hand,[12] and, in revenge, he put about the story that she had become his mistress. This distressed her beyond words. She had come to France to protect her good name, and she now found herself in a situation almost as full of danger as the one she had fled from, and there was no one to defend her.

The de Bellois story spread to London, where the Prince of Wales went into hysterics at the very thought that it might be true. His next

letter begged her to promise not to marry anyone else, even if she
wouldn't marry him. She was by now, in her own words, 'wrought upon
and fearful', and, as Lord Stourton later recorded 'was induced to promise formally and deliberately that she would never marry any other
person'.[13] This was the beginning of her capitulation.

The Prince, encouraged by this promise, began planning a marriage
that would satisfy Maria 's conscience. He had, he told her, assured her
mother and her uncle Errington that he intended to marry her as soon
as she returned. It seems he won over her mother, and, after protests,
her uncle as well. A letter to 'My dear Errington' dated July 1785, suggests that he had been in touch with Errington for some time, 'To you,
my dear Errington, I address myself first as I have always dealt most
openly with you in everything that related to Mrs Fitzherbert …'[14]

Worn out by his pleading, unwilling to wander on the Continent any
longer, and believing she had few other options, she began to consider
the marriage the Prince was offering. Her mother and her uncle
appeared to approve, the Prince had begun to hint that the King would
accept the situation and that one day the marriage could be made
public. She had only to trust him, he promised, and all would be well.
She agreed to return, but then changed her mind. The Prince's reaction was so agitated that she feared a further suicide attempt would be
made, which this time might be successful. He had insisted that life
without his 'dearest of wives, best and most sacred of women' was not
to be borne.

It is not certain when Maria definitely promised to return home
and marry him, but the Prince's last letter, a confused and emotional
forty-two pages, was dated 4 November 1785. In it he refers to her 'consent so lately given', so she probably agreed to marry him some time in
October. No one has ever suggested that she consulted a priest before
doing so, but Catholic families had always taken clerical advice if in
doubt about a proposed marriage, and it is unlikely that Maria, after
holding out for so long, would have agreed to a secret marriage without
first ensuring that her church would regard it as valid. If she did take
advice at this stage, she would have been told that the marriage laws
defined by the Council of Trent did not apply to England, and that,
especially in an unusual case like hers, the presence of a Catholic priest
was not strictly necessary, but that witnesses were. If this proviso was

met, and the couple were both free to marry, and had the intention of doing so, then the marriage would be valid.

She received the Prince's last letter as she waited at Ostend. In it, the Prince repeated what was surely a fantasy, that the King knew of the marriage, connived at it, and that, when the Prince had given up the succession of Hanover to Frederick, the King would agree to 'anything I choose respecting you, such as acknowledging you as my Wife or anything else I may please'. He seemed intent on making sure that she did not change her mind, and included a page of his usual threats of refusing to live in a world without her. This time he added an additional kind of emotional blackmail; he had confided his plans to a few close friends and family, and if she refused to come at the last minute, she would make him look like a liar.

> By coming you make me the happiest of men, by staying or doubting one instant you not only make me think that you are dead to feeling and to everything I have undergone for you but you stamp me with the epithets of a Liar and a Scoundrel. Do you think, my Maria, that were it possible to survive the losing of you, I would consent to live in the world with the slightest stain upon my honour, no I would not.

The letter ended:

> Come and for ever crown with bliss, him who will through life endeavour to convince you by his love and attention of his wishes to be the best of Husbands and who will ever remain unto the latest moments of his existence, unalterably thine.[15]

Reading through this long and excited letter, it is hard to see the Prince as anything other than a deeply self-centred man determined to get what he wanted. He dwells on his own suffering of the past year, but entirely fails to mention, let alone regret, that his Maria has gone through almost eighteen months of loneliness, embarrassment and painful indecision on his behalf. There is no mention of the cold and possibly dangerous winter sea crossing to be endured before she can arrive to fit in with his plans. He is full of anxiety in case she changes her mind, and suggests, almost insists, that they marry as soon as she arrives in London, and that she only tells her family of her arrival after the marriage has taken place. Were Mrs Smythe and Uncle Errington less enthusiastic about the marriage than he had suggested? Was he afraid they would dissuade her at the last minute? He mentions having to give up his claim to Hanover, but makes no mention of his having to give up the throne of England if his marriage to a Catholic ever became public knowledge. He must surely have known that the 1701 Act of Settlement made it clear beyond all doubt that, as the safety of 'this Protestant Kingdom' was inconsistant with being governed by a 'Popish Prince', should an heir become a Catholic, or marry a Catholic, he would become 'forever incapable to inherit the crown', which would then pass to the next in line, as if the heir were 'naturally dead'. The Prince was seeing only what he wanted to see (he never cared anything for Hanover), refusing to acknowledge the far more dangerous results of the marriage he was so desperate to celebrate. A year earlier, he had spoken of his willingness to give up the crown and to go to America with Maria; now he had convinced himself he only had to sacrifice Hanover.

If Maria recognised his selfishness and his refusal to face reality, she did not allow it to deter her. She had made a decision, given her word, and could stand no more uncertainty. She saw the long eighteen month wait on his part, with no change in his passionate devotion, as a sign that he did not regard her as he had regarded the others he had loved and left. She was probably as much attracted to him as he to her, and felt that her long period of refusal had been a good enough test for them both. She knew that in the eyes of her church they would be truly married, and seemed not to doubt the Prince's extraordinary claim that the King had accepted the marriage. But even so, it was not a happy smiling bride that stepped onto the boat at Ostend. She had written to Lady Anne, 'I have told him that I will be his. I know that I damage him and that my own tranquillity of mind is destroyed for ever.'[16] Nevertheless she was ready to go ahead. All her life she had been surrounded by honourable men on whom she could rely, and she now believed that the Prince was equally trustworthy. Perhaps most significantly of all, she believed he needed her.

The marriage did not take place immediately on her arrival, as the Prince had wanted. Arrangements for Maria's future had to be made clear first. She seems to have insisted on this herself,[17] and certainly her uncle Errington would have done so. It was agreed between the Prince, Maria, Henry Errington and Jack Smythe that, following the marriage, she would continue to be known as Mrs Fitzherbert, would live in her own house and keep her own establishment, but she would always have a place of honour at the Prince's table and act as his hostess at his entertainments in Carlton House, and that she would have an allowance of £10,000 a year. The Prince would always be welcome in any house of hers, but she would never spend a night in his house until the marriage was made public. A marriage certificate would be written and signed by the two of them and by witnesses. This would be kept by Maria, but she would never speak of it without his consent. The marriage would be announced to the world by the Prince as soon as the time was right. With the exception of the £10,000 a year, this was almost exactly the same arrangements that had been made by the Duke of Gloucester and Lady Waldegrave.

The Prince had found a Church of England clergyman willing to officiate at this secret and dangerous marriage. The Reverend Robert Burt was discovered in a debtor's prison and agreed to do so in return for £500 to secure his release, plus a living in Twickenham, and a promise of a bishopric when the Prince became King.[18] Because of the Royal Marriages Act, the presence of a clergyman could not make the marriage legal, but it helped to make it valid in the eyes of the Established Church. The presence of a Catholic priest was not necessary for it to be valid as far as Rome was concerned, Henry Errington and Jack Smythe were willing to act as witnesses at this illegal wedding; all concerned had agreed on the arrangements, and to the Prince's joy, the marriage would now take place.

4

Marriage

On 15 December 1785, the Reverend Robert Burt officiating and her uncle and brother witnessing, Maria Fitzherbert and George, Prince of Wales, exchanged their vows and were declared man and wife. The ceremony took place behind drawn curtains in the candlelit dining parlour in Park Street, while Orlando Bridgeman guarded the door with, it is said, a drawn sword (Bridgeman a Hampshire man, was a friend of the Smythes as well as one of the Prince's household).[1] The Prince wrote the marriage certificate himself and passed it round to be signed, before handing it to Maria, the lady who was, at last, his wife.[2]

The couple left for a villa near Richmond, possibly Ormley Lodge on Ham Common which Maria had begun to rent in 1784, for a few days of privacy. The others left under cover of darkness, well aware that by assisting at an illegal marriage they had committed a felony, which, if discovered, could have serious repercussions. But Mr Burt also knew, all being well, he would one day be a bishop, and Henry Errington and Jack Smythe knew they had secured Mrs Fitzherbert's good name by a marriage valid in the eyes of Christian churches, if not in English law.

The Prince and his bride returned to London before Christmas. They appeared together in public constantly, the Prince showing her every attention and courtesy. Speculation and rumour spread like wildfire. As early as 24 December, Lord Robert Hobart wrote to the Duke of Rutland, 'The lie of the day is that the Prince of Wales is to marry Mrs Fitzherbert, but, I believe, totally without foundation'.[3] Sir Gilbert Elliot passed on to his wife a story put about by Lady Palmerston (mother of the future Prime Minister), 'The report is that Mrs Fitzherbert is, or is to be, at Carlton House; that she was married by a Roman Catholic priest, is to have £6000 a year, and is to be created a Duchess'.[4] This was not true, but no one knew what to believe. The Earl of Denbigh demanded of Major Bulkeley, 'Is it to be believed or not?'[5] The Marquis of Lothian wrote to the Duke of Rutland, in Dublin,

> You ask me my opinion respecting the Prince's marriage. I think it has all the appearances of being true. I believe, when he has been spoken to on the subject he has been violent, but I cannot find out that he has denied it peremptorily. Most people believe it, and I confess I am one of the number ... I am very sorry for it, for it does him infinite mischief, particularly among the trading and lower sort of people, and if true, must ruin him in every light.[6]

Thomas Orde, also writing to Lord Rutland, made a comment which might have disturbed Maria, that 'the Prince denies the thing but at the same time drops hints of her belief in the connection and has wished therefore that their happiness might not be interrupted by conjectures and rumours'.[7]

Horace Walpole wrote to Horace Mann in Rome,

> Rumour, aye and much more than rumour, every voice in England to be credited, the matter somehow or other reaches even from London to Rome. I hope it is essentially void of truth and that appearances rise from a much more common reason.[8]

Mrs Charles Talbot wrote to Francis Fortescue Turville on 17 March,

> Mrs Fitzherbert makes a great deal of talk. I make no doubt but she is married to the Prince of Wales, he goes by my door every day at the same hour and seems very constant to her at present; it is said she is with child. After a while she will be a most unhappy woman.[9]

This is the first rumour of a pregnancy, but one that would be repeated.

Mrs Fitzherbert's reception in Society was mixed. The Seftons, who had been so kind in the past, ignored her. The Duchess of Devonshire avoided her. Lady Spencer, the Duchess's mother, asked anxiously:

> What will you do about going to the Opera with Mrs Fitzherbert? I wish it could be avoided ... She cannot be his wife. What then is she? ... At all events how much better it would be for you to stay out of town till people are become more accustomed to the thing, and till some respectable people, if any such will do it, have set you an example.[10]

The Duchess replied, 'I will never go to the Opera with her, I never have and never will and she knows it ... I search into nothing, I only wish to keep entirely out of it'.[11] The Devonshires were Whigs and agreed with Charles James Fox, who had written a serious and thoughtful letter to the Prince when Mrs Fitzherbert returned, warning him that the marriage he was suspected of planning was a 'very desperate step'. The Prince had replied on 11 December, three days before his marriage, writing calmly, in a letter meant to deceive, 'Make yourself easy my dear friend, the world will soon be convinced that there not only is not, but never was, any ground for these reports which of late have been so malevolently circulated'.[12] Fox took this as a denial of any intention to marry. Georgiana Devonshire was not sure, and wanted no part in it.

Lady Spencer need not have doubted that 'respectable' people would lead the way and receive Maria. Lady Salisbury welcomed Maria Fitzherbert to her house. She had known her for years and refused to believe she could do anything wrong. The greatly respected Lord and Lady Clermont invited her and the Prince to dine with them in Berkeley Square on several occasions, setting an example which many followed. Maria's public behaviour, in the midst of so much speculation, was impeccable; dignified and relaxed, her calm manner putting everyone at ease. The *beau monde* decided to accept her presence at the Prince's side without too many questions. Questions would be asked, eventually, by the King, by Parliament, in the newspapers and by the 'trading and lower sort', but in the meantime there was no reason not to be amiable.

Mrs Fitzherbert's fellow Catholics were certain she was the Prince's wife. Attending Mass at the embassy chapels, she continued to kneel with them to receive the sacrament on major feasts. This would be unthinkable if she was the Prince's mistress. But they were deeply uneasy, Lady Jerningham voicing their dismay, 'God knows how it will turn out – it may be to the glory of our Belief or it may be to the great dismay and destruction of it'.[13]

The Smythes were divided. Maria's mother, her brother Jack, her uncle Errington, her sister Frances and the latter's husband, Sir Carnaby Haggerston, all supported her, but her father and her brother Wat disapproved. Lady Forrester wrote, 'Mr Wat Smythe ... was much against his sister's marriage with the Prince and there was no great intimacy between them in consequence'.[14] The Welds and the Fitzherberts were cool.

Happily, Maria was not privy to the avid speculation in letters and diaries. But she must have been aware of the rash of cartoons, featuring herself and the Prince, appearing for sale in the print shop windows. Some came dangerously close to the truth, some were rude, and some cruel. *The Follies of a Day or the Marriage of Figaro* appeared in March, showing the Prince marrying a plump Mrs Fitzherbert, with Prince of Wales's feathers floating over her head as the wedding service was read by Edmund Burke from *Hoyle's Book of Games*. This was followed, a week later by *The Royal Toast: Fair, Fat and Forty*, portraying an over-weight, middle-aged looking Mrs Fitzherbert, who, in reality, was only twenty-nine. Those by Gillray, especially *Wife or No Wife: or A Trip to the Continent*, revealed some sympathy for Mrs Fitzherbert and the Prince by drawing them exquisitely, the Prince slim and handsome, and Mrs Fitzherbert looking delicate and pretty, full bosomed but tiny waisted, whereas Fox, giving away the bride, Burke as the priest, Sheridan standing by with bottles in his pockets, and Lord North as a sleeping coachman, look ugly, being obviously the villains of the piece.[15]

Cartoons were part of political life. Maria, learning quickly that no one connected with the Royal Family could expect privacy, probably tried to ignore them. But she could not have enjoyed the intimate details of her life being speculated over, and laughed at, by crowds around the print-shop windows. Unwelcome publicity did not, however, stop her from enjoying the entertainments at Carlton House, where fashionable Society passed, almost nightly, through the colonnades on Pall Mall to the gorgeous rooms beyond.

She sold the lease on the Park Street house and moved to St James's Square, where she, in turn, entertained the Prince and his friends in the lavish manner he thought fit for an heir to the throne. The Prince was unable to give her the promised £10,000 a year at this time, and her own income proved inadequate to meet the demands on it. The Prince agreed to allow her £3000 a year, but this was hardly enough. Work was still being done to embellish Carlton House; the expense was never calculated, and vast sums were spent. By April 1786, the Prince's debts had soared out of control, and he had no hope of paying his creditors. He was obliged to appeal to the King for help, even though they were barely on speaking terms. Abject and embarrassed, the Prince begged for assistance with 'the very difficult situation in which I find myself'. The King wanted a full breakdown of the Prince's liabilities, with assurances that the debts, if paid, would not continue to mount again. The Prince sent his father a 'Statement of Arrears' up to the end of the previous March: the total sum was a shocking £269,878 6s. 7¼d., of which nearly a third had gone to 'improving' Carlton House, and £50,000 on Mrs Fitzherbert's establishment. The King pointed out that many items were not adequately explained, and that he had been given no guarantees of better financial discipline in the future. He knew what was being said about his son and Mrs Fitzherbert. He asked no direct questions, but was deeply hurt that the Prince had not come and explained his situation – a situation that affected both family and constitution. The King's reluctance to pay off debts in these circumstances was hardly surprising.

The Prince was enraged by the apparent refusal of help and announced he would live in retirement, like a private gentleman. Building works were stopped, his stud and most of his carriages were sold, his household reduced, the handful of servants he retained agreeing to take a cut in wages. The chosen place of retirement was Brighton, the Prince travelling there, so the *Morning Post* told its readers on 11 July, as an outside passenger on the Brighton Dilly. Mrs Fitzherbert travelled later, when a small villa had been found for her, across the gardens from the Prince's rented farm house.

Mrs Fitzherbert's Brighton house was described as modest and pretty with green shutters, and may have been part of a terrace known as Marlborough Row which stood on the site of the present Royal Pavilion's north gate. The Prince's house was described by George Croly as, 'a singularly pretty picturesque cottage on a small piece of ground where ... the eye looked undisturbed over the ocean'.[16] Like all houses occupied by the Prince, it did not remain in its original state for long. By the following year, Henry Holland had been called in to transform it into a classical mansion. Later it was to change again, and again, ending as the exotic Pavilion. But that was all in the future; for this summer, true to his plan, the Prince lived simply; with Maria he drove on the Downs, walked on the Steine in the evening and dined modestly with a few friends, Richard Sheridan usually among them. Sheridan, who had given up the theatre in favour of politics, charmed Maria. Witty, and knowing how to please, he soon became a favourite. The Prince was happier than he had ever been, and his behaviour noticeably improved.

The Earl of Mornington commented to the Duke of Rutland, 'People talk much of the Prince of Wales's reform, particularly in this spot ... Mrs Fitzherbert is here and they say with child'.[17]

The rumour persisted. A cartoon appeared entitled, *Nine Months After*, showing the Prince and Mrs Fitzherbert with a baby, arousing further speculation. Earlier in the year the Duke of Gloucester had written asking if an ambiguous paragraph in a letter from the Prince had meant 'a son and heir was already on the stocks?' No one knows what the Prince had written to prompt the Duke's remark, and whether Mrs Fitzherbert did ever bear the Prince a child is a question that has echoed down the years, from this idyllic summer to the present day, but the rumours of 1786 were never followed by talk of a birth, nor hints of a child being brought up in secret.* Miscarriages and stillbirths were common, and being 'with child' did not always result in a living baby.

Nevertheless, it is strange that no questions seem to have been asked, and no comments made in letters and diaries about the end of this rumoured pregnancy. It seems to have been a rumour that simply faded, as time passed. The Prince had already fathered a number of illegitimate children, and probably expected Mrs Fitzherbert to have a child sooner or later, though what plans he had made for that event are not known, and at the beginning of 1787 he was much more concerned with the payment of his debts. The quiet months in Brighton had saved money; he had managed to pay off some of his smaller creditors, and to pay the interest on others, but he was still hard-pressed and knew a solution must be found soon. Newspapers and pamphlets were still full of questions about the marriage, and there was a danger of it being brought up in Parliament, should the payment of his debts be debated. The Whigs, though seen as 'The Prince's Party', were not keen to save him from his financial embarrassment if it meant the marriage question being raised. When Fox had made a plea for the settlement of the Prince's debts in the spring of 1786, there had been a cold silence from the Whig benches. Though mainly the scions of aristocratic families, the Whig Members relied for their votes on humbler sections of the community, who remained anti-Catholic. Rumours of the 'Catholic Marriage' had spread everywhere. As time passed and no denial was made, people began to

---

* See Appendix, 'The Question of Children', below, pp. 199–204.

believe the damaging gossip. Some of the cartoons implied that leading Whigs not only countenanced the marriage but had helped to arrange it. This was untrue, and they wished to have nothing to do with the Prince's debts until the question was clarified. The King was possibly of the same mind.

The Prince was growing desperate. Not a moneylender in the country would give even a small loan. If a debate on his affairs in the House of Commons was the only way to get the debts paid, then he would risk that; even if it meant providing some sort of answer to the marriage question. If the Whigs would not propose a motion to relieve his financial state, then a Private Member must be found to do so. Alderman Newnham, Member for the City of London, was asked to put forward a motion that the King should be respectfully requested to relieve the Prince in his embarrassed situation. Newnham announced that he would put forward the motion on 4 May.[18] William Pitt the Younger, now Prime Minister, tried to prevent any discussion of 'The Prince's Matter', and hinted he would have to to make certain 'disclosures' should a debate on the Prince's affairs take place. Everyone knew he had the Prince's marriage in mind, not his debts. To the astonishment of the House, John Rolle,[19] a west country squire, rose from his seat below the gangway and assured the Members, in his slow Devonshire accent, that, if Newnham's motion was put forward, he would bring up a question concerned with 'a danger to Constitution and State', which the Prince's situation made it necessary to ask. Again, every man in the House knew he referred to the rumoured Catholic marriage. Pitt was probably bluffing when he spoke of having to make 'disclosures', but Rolle was not. He would demand a blunt answer to the blunt question he intended to ask.

The words 'Marriage' and 'Catholic' were never uttered during any of these exchanges, but all knew what was at stake. The Prince knew, too, when word of these proceedings were brought to him. The payment of his debts was uppermost in his mind, but he knew the persistent talk of his marriage to a Catholic was making him increasingly unpopular, and, if a blunt question were to be asked in Parliament, then he must decide what answer should be given, and who should give it.

The second decision was easy to make. Only Fox, with his eloquence, commanded enough respect to carry it off convincingly. What instructions or guide lines, if any, were given to Fox has never been clear, but it is difficult to believe that no words passed between the two men at this critical moment. The Prince was desperate to have his debts paid, and also knew that Rolle and his supporters must be silenced. In the desperation of the moment (the Prince always lived for the day), he probably didn't care how he achieved these two aims. He saw, however, that the marriage, for which he had longed and schemed, must be denied. He had already denied it in private conversations. It was not a legal marriage; one could argue, therefore, that it was not a marriage at all in constitutional terms. So far as Rolle's question regarding 'Constitution and State' was concerned, the answer was there had been no marriage. The rumour could be denied. That, possibly, was the Prince's line of thought.

The problem was that Maria would never see it in that light. The last thing the Prince wanted was an argument with her over this delicate matter. He asked Sheridan to prepare her; to explain, to make her understand. Sheridan agreed to try. Maria could see the problem, knew questions might be asked, saw the dangers, but could not see that a denial of their marriage was justified. She said she was like a dog with a log tied round its neck, and that they, meaning Sheridan and the Prince, must defend her.[20] Unfortunately, defending his Maria, no matter how beloved, was not the Prince's first priority as he waited in Carlton House while the situation developed in the Commons.

It was on 30 April that Fox rose to tell the listening House, in his magical voice, that the rumours of the Prince's marriage were a 'base and scandalous calumny'. It was, he continued, a story 'unfounded and for which there was not the shadow of anything like reality'. He added that the Prince had authorised him to declare that he, the Prince, was ready to answer any questions on this matter in 'the other House' (meaning the Lords), and to 'afford His Majesty's ministers the fullest assurances of the utter falsehood of the fact in question, which never had, and common sense must see, never could have happened'.[21]

The denial could not have been more complete. The members were half incredulous, half relieved. Pitt urged Newnham not to force the House to debate the matter. Only Rolle was not satisfied. He wanted to know by what authority Fox spoke. The House waited. Fox rose again, 'By direct authority', he replied. Rolle said no more, and no debate followed.

Messengers rushed to Carlton House. The Prince was well pleased. Surely money would be forthcoming now. The denial of his marriage to Maria did not appear to worry him. At midnight he wrote to 'My Dear Charles', inviting him to call the next day and adding that he had already had 'a distant insinuation that some sort of message or terms were to be proposed ...', presumably regarding his finances. The letter was signed 'Ever affectionately yours,' and there was not one word of reproach for going too far in the denial. The Prince seemed euphoric with relief. Fox may also have felt pleased, but, entering Brooks' Club that night, he met Henry Errington, who said, 'I hear that you have denied that the Prince is married to Mrs Fitzherbert. You are mistaken. I was present at the marriage'.

Was this a total surprise to Fox? Had he believed everything he had said to the House? Or had he just known that only the strongest possible denial would save the Prince. He never reproached the Prince for deceiving him, just as the Prince never reproached Fox. Nevertheless, the two men saw little of each other during the rest of the year, and, when the parliamentary recess began, Fox, claiming to be disgusted with politics, went abroad with Mrs Armistead.

The Prince was left to consider Maria. Charles Bodenham later gave an account of how he approached her,

> Mrs Fitzherbert was on a visit with the Honourable Mrs Butler, her friend and relative, and at whose house the Prince frequently met Mrs Fitzherbert. The Prince called the morning after the denial of the marriage in the House of Commons by Mr Fox. He went up to Mrs Fitzherbert, and taking hold of both her hands and caressing her, said: 'Only conceive, Maria, what Fox did yesterday. He went down to the House and denied that you and I were man and wife! Did you ever hear of such a thing?' Mrs Fitzherbert made no reply, but changed countenance and turned pale.[22]

She was devastated. She believed herself to be dishonoured and disgraced by this public denial. She was silent when the Prince told her, but knew she had only one course of action. As she later told Lord Stourton, the public denial had 'compromised her character and religion' and she determined to break off all connection with the Prince.

The Prince could not believe she meant it, but he was shaken. He sent for Charles Grey, the cool, ambitious young Whig and future reformer, who already had a reputation in the House. The Prince admitted, uneasily, that a ceremony of a sort had taken place between himself and Mrs Fitzherbert, and that he hoped Grey might say something tactful in the Chamber to restore her reputation – without, of course, suggesting that Fox had been mistaken. Grey refused. Not pleased, the Prince sent for Sheridan, who readily agreed to speak in defence of Mrs Fitzherbert's good name. He made an elaborate and delicately vague speech on 4 May, drawing the attention of the House to 'another person ... on whose conduct truth could fix no just reproach, and whose character claimed, and was entitled to, the truest and most general respect'.[23] Her name was not mentioned, but everyone knew of whom he spoke. Daniel Pulteney wrote to the Duke of Rutland:

> What Mrs Fitzherbert can do in her present embarrassed situation I cannot pretend to guess, but Sheridan attempted, very foolishly, to repair the statement respecting the marriage by saying today in the House her situation was truly respectable, at which everyone smiled.[24]

Sheridan may have made some Members doubt the truth of Fox's statement, but nobody wanted the supposed marriage discussed a second time, and the speech in no way affected their plans to pay the Prince's debts, and was not enough, on its own, to change Mrs Fitzherbert's attitude.

Parliament voted £160,000 for the payment of the Prince's debts and £60,000 for the completion of Carlton House. The King increased the Prince's income by £10,000 a year, and the Prince promised to keep his affairs in good order in future. The King and Queen received their eldest son at the Queen's Drawing Room on 24 May, and harmony was restored within the Royal Family.

Maria, however, still refused to see him. As always when upset, the Prince became ill with fever and paroxysms, and had to be bled. As Thomas Orde told the Duke of Rutland on 28 May, 'He is better today but still in great danger'.[25] Some reports suggest the Prince threatened suicide again if Mrs Fitzherbert did not forgive him; if so, this was in keeping with his earlier behaviour when crossed. Her friends eventually persuaded her that, if there was a discrepancy between Fox's word and the Prince's, she was morally obliged to believe her husband. This was probably what she really wanted to do. Stifling doubts about the Prince's truthfulness, she decided the blame lay on Fox, to whom she never spoke again. Usually a forgiving person, her severe attitude to Fox shows how passionately she felt where her marital status was concerned. Having promised not to speak publicly of the marriage, refusing to speak to Fox was the only way she had of refuting his implication that she was a mistress and not a wife, and, as she saw it, of defending her honour.

The pair were publicly reconciled at a supper at Sir Sampson Gideon's, Maria sitting with the Prince at the head of the table, wearing white roses. She was probably every bit as happy to be reconciled as he was. In some ways, she had gained rather than lost by Fox's denial. The day after Fox's speech half the fashionable world called on her showing their sympathy and support. Looking back on that day, she told Lord Stourton that 'the knocker of her door was never still'. Sheridan's wife noted that 'Her behaviour has been perfectly amiable throughout'. The Duchess of Portland, having refused to do so before, now called on her, and invited her to her house, as did the Seftons. The old Catholic families ceased to be cool towards her, believing she had suffered on account of her religion.

There were still those who believed Fox's denial, and many delighted in the Gillray cartoon of 21 May. Entitled, *Dido Forsaken: Sic Transit Gloria Reginae,* it shows Mrs Fitzherbert seated on a rock out at sea holding up a crucifix as the Prince, Fox, Lord North and Edmund Burke sail away without her in a boat called 'Honour'. The Prince is saying 'I never saw her in my life', with Fox replying 'No never in his life, damn'. Beside her lie instruments of torture, 'for the conversion of heretics'. Catholics were not entirely wrong in thinking Mrs Fitzherbert's troubles were linked to her religion.

The Prince lost no time in reopening Carlton House and continuing to embellish it. Mrs Fitzherbert's new house, in nearby Pall Mall, was furnished with considerable style, as Mary Frampton recalled,

When Mrs Fitzherbert was living in Pall Mall within a few doors of Carlton House, we were at one of the assemblies she gave which was altogether the most splendid I was ever at. Attendants in green and gold beside the usual livery servants, were stationed in the rooms and up the staircase to announce the company and carry refreshments. The house was new and beautifully furnished. One room was hung with puckered blue satin from which hangings the now common imitations in paper were taken. Her

own manners ever remained quiet, civil and unperturbed and in the days
of her greatest influence she was never accused of using it improperly.[26]

This 'quiet, civil and unperturbed' behaviour continued to charm
London Society.

In July the Prince and Mrs Fitzherbert returned to Brighton, which
was rapidly becoming a fashionable resort, with the *Sussex Weekly
Advertiser* recording the diversions of visitors from the *beau monde*. On
25 July 1787, it reported, 'His Royal Highness accompanied by the Duke
and Duchess of Cumberland and Mrs Fitzherbert visited the Theatre in
Brighton'; and, on 6 August, 'His Royal Highness attended the races
with Mrs Fitzherbert and dined with her at the house of Colonel
Pelham'. A visitor from Ireland described a Brighton ball in August of
that year:

> The Duchess of Rutland was by far the fairest of the fair. Mrs Fitzherbert
> did not dance the first set but the second she danced with Isaac Corry and
> after dancing down she sat down with her partner and in a few minutes
> the Prince and the Duke of Cumberland came and sat beside her. The
> Prince expressed affection in his looks and the Duke esteem. She discov-
> ers strong sensibility and considerable dignity in her countenance and
> deportment.[27]

Queen Marie-Antoinette, who had once had serious doubts about
the respectability of Mrs Fitzherbert, decided that her alliance with the
Prince was quite proper after all, and gave approval for her friend
the Princess de Lamballe to visit Brighton that summer as one of the
Prince's guests.[28] The Princess was happy to dine every evening in Mrs
Fitzherbert's company.

One evening, during this summer of fine weather and restored
happiness, the Prince received word that his brother Frederick, Duke
of York, had returned from Hanover. Overjoyed, he left at once for
Windsor to welcome him. When the family parties were over, the
Prince brought Frederick to Brighton to present him to 'My Lovely
Fitzherbert'.

5

The Battle for the Regency

Maria had now turned thirty, still young by present-day standards, but not in eighteenth-century terms. The cartoons show her as distinctly plump, and even ladies who admired her, notably Mary Frampton, described her as 'elegant but too fat'. Portraits were beginning to emphasise the Smythe family's aquiline nose and show her golden hair darkening a little, but contemporary accounts insist that she still gave the impression of great beauty, and had lost none of her power to attract. A Brighton *habitué* wrote of her:

> I can recall her to mind at this time, radiant in her brilliant loveliness –
> her delicate features, her pure complexion, combining to produce a face
> that impressed every spectator with a delightful sense of aimiablity and
> tenderness; while her figure, set off to the best advantage by the costume
> of the time, was always distinguishable from those of the aristocratic beau-
> ties by whom she was generally surrounded, by its singular dignity and
> grace. Though nobody ventured to call her 'Princess', everyone of her
> innumerable admirers of both sexes enthroned her as a queen. She was
> recognised as the 'Queen of Hearts' throughout the length and breadth of
> fast-expanding Brighton ... They honoured her, they almost worshipped
> her.[1]

A Mr Shergold of Brighton, who was a very young man in 1787, had sim-ilar memories of her, and insisted, 'She was a woman who needed nothing but a diadem to make her a queen'.[2] The Duke of York was also much taken with her when they met, remaining a devoted friend for the rest of his life.

The royal brothers, happily reunited, fell back into the dissipated life they had briefly shared as youths, with heavy drinking, womanising and gambling. This distressed Maria, whose good influence on the Prince's life had been generally acknowledged. But he still treated her with such affection, and the Duke of York with such respect, that she decided to overlook their nightime amusements.

She no longer lived alone, Miss Isabella Pigot, daughter of Admiral Pigot, now acted as a cross between a companion and a lady in waiting. Mrs Fitzherbert and the Prince both became very attached to Miss Pigot, or 'Piggy' as he was sometimes known to call her. She was invaluable to them as a go-between, note-carrier and social secretary. Lady Forrester's autograph book describes her:

> Belle Pigot was a most singular person. She was very intimate with George IV and knew all the Court gossip. She made regular rounds of visits in the autumn and winter to the great houses in Staffordshire and Shropshire ... everyone was delighted to have her.[3]

Some of Miss Pigot's little notes to the Prince have survived, giving an idea of how indispensable she was. 'If you would have the goodness', she scribbled on one occasion, 'to hint to me what hour you would have Mrs Fitzherbert return home I am persuaded from her manner and conversation she will with the greatest of pleasure be punctual'; and again, 'Mrs Fitzherbert is dressing and begs you will have the goodness to allow me to say that she shall be very happy to attend you to Brighton tomorrow'; and 'Mrs Fitzherbert is just gone to Lady Harrington's and is to call me again. Therefore pray don't attempt to come here but rely on it I will meet you at home by one o'clock'.[4]

But life was not all little notes and pleasant arrangements. Lord George Gordon, leader of the riots of 1780, was in London in 1788. He was being prosecuted for libel, having circulated derogatory comments about the French Queen, and he introduced Maria's name into his defence, claiming that a conversation he had had with her, years before in France, was relevant to the case, having to do with an intrigue between the French and English courts. Maria, outraged and alarmed, refused to attend the Court. Gordon then called at her house, attempting to serve a subpoena, and was turned away by her servants. Her brother Walter, the coolness between them forgotten, warned Gordon never to come to his sister's door again. Gordon then wrote an extraordinary letter to Pitt:

> Sir, Mr Walter Smythe, brother to Mrs Fitzherbert, came to my house in Welbeck Street this morning accompanied by Mr Acton, to be present

whilst he informed me that he would call me to account if I went to Mrs Fitzherbert's house again, or wrote to her, or to him, or took liberties with their names in public, as Mrs Fitzherbert was very much alarmed when my name was mentioned. I answered that I looked on this as a threatening visit; but that I must yet apply to Mrs Fitzherbert, or himself, or Sir Carnaby Haggerston as often as I found occasion, till a written answer was sent to me concerning the proper title of their sister, just as if he had not called upon me. Some other conversation passed concerning the marriage; but this was the substance and result of the whole. I think it my duty to inform you as Prime Minister, that you may be apprised of, and communicate to the House of Commons, the overbearing disposition of the Papists. I have the honour to be, Sir, your most obedient and humble servant, G. Gordon.

4 o'clock Friday 4 May 1788.[5]

Pitt, who was at pains to avoid discussion of Mrs Fitzherbert's status, and who had nothing against Catholics, was unlikely to act on such instructions, but the affair caused Maria great unease, and shows how vulnerable her position was. In the same year her brother Charles had to take *The Times* to task for publishing 'scurrilous' articles about her[6]

While the Smythe brothers were defending their sister, the Prince of Wales and his brother were running deeper and deeper into debt. They carried Maria with them, as the lavish entertainments they expected to find in her house were beyond her income. The King had no sympathy for the Prince and Mrs Fitzherbert's financial embarrassment, but he was pained to see Frederick, his favourite son, drinking, gambling deep (and losing) and hopelessly in debt. Some wondered if the King's distress over Frederick had caused the violent bilious attack and abdominal pains and convulsions that lasted for several weeks in June 1788.

On recovery from the attack, His Majesty was persuaded to take the cure at Cheltenham, and agreed to spend six weeks there drinking the waters. 'The waters', he wrote to Pitt, 'are more efficacious than I possibly could have expected ... a general bracer to the constitution.'[7] He enjoyed Cheltenham and, according to Fanny Burney, had, 'a flow of spirits at this time quite unequalled'. The royal party returned to Windsor in August.

His two eldest sons, enjoying life in Brighton with Maria and their friends, showed little interest in their father's health. The King suffered various episodes of sickness, deafness and loss of vision during the early autumn and by late October it became apparent that control of his mind was slipping from his grasp. Profoundly concerned, the Queen and Court could only hope the condition would pass. By the beginning of November doctors had to be summoned and the Prince and the Duke called to Windsor. The evening of the Prince of Wales's arrival marked the beginning of the King's insanity. Halfway through dinner he seized the Prince by the throat and banged his head against the wall. He had to be forceably controlled and helped away to his room by the Duke and two pages, leaving the Queen in hysterics and his eldest son in tears.

The Prince regained his composure the next day, and, according to Fanny Burney, took charge of the situation: 'From this time as the poor King grew worse, general hope seemed universally to abate; and the Prince of Wales now took the government of the house into his own hands. Nothing was done but by his orders, and he was applied to in every difficulty.'[8] He brought in his own doctor, George Warren, for an additional opinion, even though Dr Warren, a strong Whig supporter, was a man the King disliked.

The King's condition was a distressing one: incessant, rapid and confused speech, abdominal pains, fever, a pulse rate of around 130, and an inability to sleep or stay still. These symptoms, combined with emetics, aperients and regular bleeding, the only medication the doctors could prescribe, reduced him to a state of such physical weakness that death seemed imminent.

Maria and the Prince's political friends returned to London to wait for news from Windsor. The Prince sat up all night, in court dress and full decorations, expecting any minute to be proclaimed sovereign. Captain Jack Payne, his equerry, hastened backwards and forwards to London with news. The Whigs dared to hope that a change of government, giving power to their party at last, was coming near. Maria, whom 'Jacko' Payne took care to call on, had hopes too. The Prince had repeatedly promised to make their marriage public as soon as he could, and, as King, she believed, he would find a way of doing so. Pitt, on the other hand, with no expectation of favours from a Prince turned King, feared his career was about to end.

But the King did not die that night. Yet it still seemed impossible that he could live, and Jack Payne's next message was one of postponement only: 'The last stroke as I hear, from the best authority, cannot be far off, it is what everybody in a situation to see, is obliged to wish as the happiest possible termination to the melancholy scene. The event we looked for last night is postponed perhaps for a short time.'[9]

London seemed to be holding its breath as everyone waited. To the surprise of the doctors, the King fell into a deep and natural sleep. When he woke his physical condition had improved, death was no longer expected, but his mental derangement was complete. Dr Warren wrote to the Countess Spencer, 'Rex noster insanit',[10] our King is mad, and was of the opinion that this was beyond cure. The King would live, but was not fit to reign. The scenario had suddenly changed, and the battle for the Regency was about to begin.

At first the Prince didn't realise there would be a battle. He had behaved with dignity when he thought his father was dying, but now spent riotous nights at Brooks' Club, celebrating his forthcoming power and being amusing about his father's condition. He planned and replanned his cabinet with Sheridan and his fellow Whigs, while Maria waited at home in Pall Mall. Only Gilbert Elliot, the most thoughtful of the Whigs, saw difficulties ahead, and wrote to his wife, 'I do not much relish this triumphant sort of conversation, especially before the battle is won, or even fought'.[11] The Prince had assumed that he would automatically be made Regent. Only when Parliament met on 20 November and was prorogued until 4 December to give the King's condition time to change did he realise things might not be so straightforward. Pitt knew that if the Prince became Regent, with full sovereign powers, the Whigs would take office, and he, Pitt, would go into the wilderness. Playing for time, he hoped the King would begin to recover before December. He and the Queen agreed that only if the King were no better would new arrangements be made. The Tory government was no friend of the Prince of Wales, and would not pass a Regency Bill on the nod, bringing about their own destruction. A coldly determined Pitt threatened the Prince's euphoric dream, and at this point Maria ventured, for the first and last time, into the political arena. Fresh plans were laid and secret meetings held, Maria attending most of them. Fox, the only man who could match Pitt in debate, was travelling on the Continent with no forwarding address. Even Maria had to agree that Charles James Fox was needed now. Eventually he was found in Bologna, and, seeing the

urgency of the situation, travelled home immediately, doing the journey
in a record nine days. He arrived, ill and exhausted, at the end of
November. When he entered the Commons, on 12 December, he was
barely recognisable. Could this sallow-faced, emaciated figure, walking
with obvious difficulty, be the exuberant Fox they had always known?

Perhaps it was his weakened state that caused him to blunder. When
doubts were voiced about the Prince as Regent, Fox rose to claim that
George, Prince of Wales, the heir and fully of age, had a clear 'right' to
be Regent with full sovereign powers, just as if the King had died.[12] At
this, Pitt smiled. The Whigs, and Fox in particular, had always pressed
the rights of Parliament against the rights of Kings. What was Fox doing,
pressing the 'right' of a Prince against the power of Parliament to
appoint?

Pitt had reason to smile. 'Rights', he claimed, would now have to be
examined, along with precedents from previous regencies. He set up
committees to do this, which took a further two weeks. He eventually
conceded that the Prince of Wales, though having no 'right', had a
strong 'claim', but that certain restrictions to the Regent's powers were
necessary in this case. Outrage ensued among the Whigs, as Pitt had
known it would, and angry exchanges delayed proceedings into the New
Year. All this was relayed daily to the Prince and Maria, and Fox was
blamed for the waste of precious time. The battle lines were drawn. On
one side stood Pitt, Dr Willis (a specialist in 'mad' cases), now the King's
chief doctor, and the Queen, furious at her son's callous treatment of
his father. On the other side stood the Prince, backed by his brothers
and uncles, the leading Whigs, Dr Warren and Maria. The latter's active
role did not go unnoticed, Lady Eleanor Butler commenting on 5 February, that 'Mrs Fitzherbert is determined to assert her claim'.[13] It was
said that she was responsible for the Duke of Portland being won over
to the Prince's cause, George Selwyn telling Lady Carlisle, 'The Duke [of
Portland] now sups every night with His Royal Highness and his brother
at Mrs Fitzherbert's'.[14]

Meanwhile the King's suffering increased. Dr Willis believed in treat-
ments that now seem unbelievably barbaric. He lay tied to his bed,
strait-jacketed, head shaven, blistered, bled and dosed with bark, but
fully aware of what was happening to him. One night, despairing of help
from anyone else, he cried out, pathetically, for his daughter Amelia,

aged only five, begging her to come and release her father.[15] But his sons, the town, and Parliament seemed concerned only with the political outcome. At balls and assemblies and at the opera the Whig ladies wore 'Regency caps' (three white feathers with 'Ich Dien' inscribed on the head-band), to show their allegiance to the Prince, while the Tory ladies wound red white and blue ribbons around their arms and in their hair. Feelings ran high, Lord Sidney writing to the Marquess Cornwallis, 'Never before, has it been so necessary to separate parties in private company. The acrimony is beyond anything you can conceive'.[16]

The Prince and his party thought it outrageous of the Queen to side against them. Sir Gilbert Elliot wrote of her, 'She is playing the devil and has all this time been at the bottom of the cabals and intrigues against the Prince'.[17] The Prince himself took a tone of grieved surprise, claiming his mother showed 'a degree of passion which I have never witnessed before'. In general, public opinion ran with the Queen and Pitt. The Prince was extremely unpopular, both for his extravagance and for his 'papist wife', whose influence was believed to be great. Fox's denial of the marriage had been largely discredited, and though anti-Catholic prejudice might have died in high society, it lived on in the country. Letters, calling for stringent restriction to the Prince's powers as Regent, poured in from the shires. Confident of support, Pitt proposed a regency with restricted powers. The Regent would not have the power to create peers, nor the right to give pensions and honours, or posts in the King's household. Control of the King's person and household would be given to the Queen, and the Regent would have no right to touch crown property. In addition, it was made known to the Prince that, should he find these restrictions unacceptable, the Queen was happy to become Regent herself. This left the Prince humiliated but with little choice. He could become Regent on Pitt's terms, or not at all.

Pitt's Bill was then presented to Parliament. At this point Fox left for Bath, to be treated for various ailments. Some said that he also wished to avoid any further questions from the irrepressible Squire Rolle, whose mind was still on the Prince's alleged marriage. Throughout the Regency debate, Mrs Fitzherbert and the 'Marriage Question' was in everyone's mind. Many Whigs now saw her as a serious handicap. The Bill stated that the Regent must resign if he married a Catholic; Rolle introduced an amendment adding the words 'or should be proved to have already married a Catholic'. The amendment was not carried, but the threat of it was enough to bring both Grey and Sheridan to their feet to deny all possibility of such a marriage. Grey knew some ceremony had taken place, but was prepared to claim that the mere rumour of such a marriage was 'false, libellous and calumniatory'.[18]

Maria's reaction to this second denial of her marriage is not recorded. Was she beginning to realise that a denial was necessary before the Prince could ever be either Regent or King? Or was he still able to reassure her, whatever he said elsewhere, that one day he would present her to the world as his wife? She could not have known that Lord Harcourt had just written:

> I find it is a measure of the Party to say that the Prince from his amiable character retains a friendship for Mrs Fitzherbert; but that she has not the least remaining influence; that he is quite tired of her, and is in love elsewhere, and therefore the Public need have no further alarm on her account.[19]

That particular 'measure of party' would not have been mentioned in her presence, but the Prince certainly supported it, and might even have suggested it himself, in his desperation not to lose his chance of power.

Lord Harcourt went on to tell his wife that 'The report of H.R.H. being tired of Mrs Fitzherbert gains ground. The old Duchess of Bedford said at a party she had the other day, she knew he [the Prince] could not stand the unpopularity occasioned by his connection with a Catholic, and that he entreated her to go to France or anywhere abroad and he would give her £10,000 per annum. She, however, refused'. Lord Harcourt said he doubted the truth of this. It was almost certainly untrue, but it shows what the gossip of the day was like, and suggests what fears may have begun to grow in Maria's mind.

The Regency Bill passed through the Commons and was sent to the Lords, but, on the day of its third reading, a medical bulletin announced the beginnings of His Majesty's recovery. Pitt had for some time been receiving reports from Dr Willis saying the first signs of improvement were appearing, even while Dr Warren continued to say the insanity was irreversible. A few days later, the King's condition was said to be so stable that no further bulletins would be published.[20] 'There appears this morning to be an entire cessation of His Majesty's illness', the last bulletin informed the waiting world. The Regency Bill was put aside. The nation rejoiced in the recovery of 'the good old King', and the Prince and his supporters hid their bitter disappointment as best they could.

If any of the Prince's friends had secretly hoped the King might suffer a relapse, they were disappointed a second time. By April, though still weak, he was well enough to take part in a service of thanksgiving for his return to health, held in St Paul's. The Prince and Frederick were obliged to attend, but sat whispering and laughing together, and openly eating biscuits during the sermon. The knife was twisted in the Prince's wound when he learned his father had told the Duke of Gloucester he would have retired to Hanover, leaving the Regent in charge, if the Bill had been passed before his recovery.[21] Pitt and the Queen had won, but by how small a margin.

On 29 April Gillray's cartoon, *The Funeral Procession of Miss Regency*, made a final comment on all the lost hopes. It showed a coffin being carried, with the Prince's coronet, a dice box and an empty purse on top. Behind walked Mrs Fitzherbert, Fox and Sheridan, and the other disappointed men.

6

Lady Jersey

Among all the Prince's disappointed supporters only Maria gained something from the lost Regency. Had the Prince become Regent with limited powers, his denials of their marriage would have become more emphatic. Desperate to gain full powers, he would have distanced himself from her in public, and probably in private as well. As it was, the Prince turned to the domestic comfort of her houses, the only real homes he had ever known.

The last ball of the Season was at Hammersmith, and the Prince, the Duke of York, Maria and the Sheridans attended. Sheridan's sister, Betsy, described the evening:

> Mrs Fitzherbert was also at the Prince's table, dressed simply in a white dress and black veil. When the supper was over there was music with some excellent catch singers and immediately afterwards the Prince, who enjoyed his music, called to the catch singers and suggested that one of them should join himself and Mrs Sheridan in singing a trio. Eliza was much taken by surprise at his request and though she had not practised for months immediately agreed. They sang two or three songs and then gave over for fear of tiring Mrs S. He has a good voice, and being so well supported, seemed to me to sing very well.[1]

Sheridan's wife had been a professional singer, but had given no concerts since her marriage. Maria was happy to listen when the Prince sang.

The years following this pleasant evening were difficult for Maria. 'Few were the happy hours that she could number even at that period',[2] wrote Thomas Raikes. Her active role in the Regency battle had been heavily criticised in newspapers and pamphlets, one being so libellous that a court case was brought against the writer, who was fined £50 and imprisoned for a year.[3] Some believed that the suspiciously prompt arrival of the bailiffs at Maria's house when she had owed, for a very short time, a mere £1580, and their determination to stay in the house until the debt was paid,[4] was part of a plan to make life so difficult for her that she would go and live on the Continent again.

If this was so, it was ill-timed. Disturbing news was coming from France. Louis XVI had summoned the Estates General to deal with the crown's chronic financial position, but part of it, the Third Estate, declared itself to be the real authority in the land, not the King. When an armed mob stormed the Bastille on 14 July 1789, killing the guards and the governor, Charles James Fox hailed it as the 'greatest event ever', but Elisabeth Vigée-Le Brun, the French Court portrait painter, wrote in her memoirs, 'The dreadful year 1789 was upon us and fear had already seized the minds of wise men and women'.[5] One suspects that fear seized Maria's mind too, for she had many friends in Paris. In October a mob marched on Versailles and came close to entering the Queen's apartments. At this point, Maria's sympathies were definitely with the French royal family, not with the cause of liberty. Robert Fitzgerald, the Chargé d'Affaires at the British Embassy, wrote to Lord Leeds claiming that the Duke of Orleans was behind the riot,

> In short, my Lord, the general idea here is that the Prince [Orleans, part of the royal family, was often referred to by this title] was chief promoter of all the disturbances here, of the expedition on Monday 5th of this month to Versailles, that his designs against the King were of a very criminal nature, that he aimed at the Regency of the Kingdom for himself, and proposed to bring his own Party into power.[6]

Orleans's arrival in London a short time later was rumoured to be an exile imposed on him by the French King, and George III was distinctly cool towards him. French *emigrés* had already begun to arrive in England, and sympathy, not just of the *beau monde*, but of the whole country, was with them.

In 1791 the Duke of York's debts had become alarming and he went to his father for help. The King was sympathetic. Debts would be settled if Frederick married a Protestant German Princess. The Duke agreed immediately, possibly feeling he had no other options. A marriage with Princess Frederica of Prussia was arranged and the pair were married in Berlin in September. The younger brothers, all of whom (with the exception of Adolphus, later Duke of Cambridge) also had

substantial debts, but do not seem to have been offered financial help
in return for marriage to a suitable princess. Instead they were kept out
of England, well away from the influence of the Prince. William, Duke
of Clarence, had been a successful, if over strict, naval officer, but had
regularly shocked his father by his drinking, debts, brawls and women.
The speeches he made in the House of Lords on the war with France
and in favour of slavery were considered irresponsible, and his father
thought is wiser not to let him return to sea. Eventually he found a
long-term mistress in the actress Dorothea Jordan who, over the years,
bore him five sons and five daughters. Edward, Duke of Kent, similarly
outraged his father by his debts and rackety behaviour and also chose
a long-term mistress, Thérèse-Bernardine Mongenêt, known as Mlle de
St-Laurent (or later Madame de St-Laurent). She was an excellent
choice and stayed with him, sharing his interests, his love of music and
his chronic shortage of money, in Gibraltar, Canada and England, for
twenty-five years. Ernest and Adolphus both fought with the Hanovar-
ian army and both were wounded, Ernest losing an eye. Augustus,
whose health was not good enough for him to continue as a soldier,
was kept in unhappy exile in Rome. In 1795, Ernest was allowed to
return to England, and, as something of a war hero, Parliament gave
him an annual income of £18,000. He was seen to be growing embittered and strange, if not sinister; so much so that when Princess Sophia,
the prettiest of his sisters, gave birth to a son, in great secrecy in Weymouth in August 1800, rumour had it, probably erroneously, that he
was the father.

The Prince of Wales had been consulted about the match between
Frederick and Frederica, and in his formal agreement he inserted what
Sir Gilbert Elliot, writing to his wife, called a 'saving clause':

> He has put in a saving clause for himself in case he chooses to marry which
> he thinks possible if he sees his brother happy with his wife, and told the
> King that, had he permitted him to go abroad at the time he asked leave
> to do so [in 1784] he meant to have looked out for a princess who would
> have suited him as he was too domesticated to bear the thoughts of mar-
> rying a woman he did not like.[7]

This indicates how far the Prince had moved away from Maria, even
while very much with her in their shared life. It also reveals the distor-
tions of which his mind was capable when he viewed his own past. Far

from looking out for a princess in 1784, he was desperate to marry Maria and wished to go abroad only to follow her. He could no longer distinguish between what had actually happened, and what, at a later date, it suited him to believe had happened. Maria may or may not have been aware of his state of mind, but Frances, Countess of Jersey, who had known him for years, and with whom he had once been in love, was shrewd enough to see that, given the burden of his debts and his passionate desire to be Regent or King, a break with Maria Fitzherbert would one day be inevitable. In 1782 she had discouraged him, thinking him still a boy, and claiming 'it is impossible for anyone to give another less encouragement than I have'. But the Prince was older now, and Lady Jersey could see an advantage for herself when the parting she anticipated came.

Maria was presented to her new sister-in-law at the Duchess of Cumberland's ball, and the entire company looked on to see how the two ladies behaved. Miss Dee wrote to to Lady Harcourt, 'The Duchess of Cumberland presented Mrs Fitz. Both ladies squeezed their fans and talked for a few minutes, and that was all'.[8] The new Duchess of York, who had been reared in the etiquette of a Prussian court, believed morganatic wives should be kept at a distance. This was not how Maria expected to be treated, and, indeed, it was not how she had been treated by London Society, including the Royal Dukes, for the past six years. The Prince took the Duchess's attitude as an insult, and the two brothers became less intimate as a result.

It was during this year, 1791, that a second Catholic Relief Act was passed. The Mass was no longer illegal, Catholic churches could be built (provided they had neither spire nor peel of bells), and most of the remaining penal laws were removed from the statute book. Maria must have been pleased, but she never showed that enthusiasm for the Catholic cause displayed by others. She practised her religion quietly, aware that the Prince found having a Catholic wife increasingly awkward.

But no matter how politically awkward the marriage might be, Maria was always included in the Prince's party, and still sat in a place of honour at his table. With debts increasing, they spent much time visiting friends in the country, or staying at his hunting lodge at Kempshot, where he lived like a country gentleman, with Maria occupying a cottage nearby. She laid out the Kempshot gardens and arranged the rooms, creating the comfort and elegance that even modest living required.

Although her Fitzherbert in-laws spent little time in London, and were never a part of Brighton Society, she never lost touch with them, and she and the Prince sometimes stayed at Mains Hall, Claughton, with her brother-in-law, William Fitzherbert-Broccles, and were godparents to one of his sons.[9] They were also godparents, by proxy, in January 1792, to the daughter of Barbara, the youngest Fitzherbert sister, living in Nice with her second husband.

Among the Prince and Maria's friends, a special place was given to Lord Hugh Seymour and his wife Horatia. Lord Hugh, as well as being a naval officer, was part of the Prince's household as Keeper of the Privy Purse, and was a valued friend. The Seymours had a large family, the first four being boys, known as 'the four jolly boats'. Mrs Fitz, as they called her, was very fond of them all, and they of her.

The year 1792 saw the Prince and Maria back in Brighton, where the French *emigrés* were arriving in large numbers. As boats arrived they waited on the beach, often finding friends from happier times among the exhausted passengers. On one occasion Maria recognised her school friend Catherine Dillon, with three other nuns from the convent at Montargis, which they had been forced to leave by republican officials. They were on their way, by a roundabout route, to Flanders. Catherine begged Maria to look out for the remainder of the sisters who would arrive later. Maria gladly agreed and began a subscription for them, suspecting they would arrive penniless. They eventually landed, after a long and stormy crossing, down the coast at Shoreham. Maria took the Prince's carriages as well as her own, and set off to meet them, bringing them to the Old Ship Inn, where arrangements had been made for their shelter. The Prince came to welcome them, and persuaded them to stay in England, warning that Flanders would soon become as dangerous for them as France.[10]

Other religious orders were housed in England as more and more priests and nuns fled from the guillotine. Trappist monks found a home at Lulworth, Benedictines at Acton Burnell and Swynnerton, and Poor Clares at Haggerston Hall, home of Maria's sister. Thomas Weld offered his estate at Stoneyhurst to the Jesuits of Liège Academy. Maria could only watch, perhaps wistfully, as the members of her extended family opened their doors to refugee communities.

One of the *emigrées* Maria was most pleased to welcome in Brighton was the Princess de Lamballe, who escaped from France in 1791, expecting the French royal family to follow. But, on hearing they had been intercepted and imprisoned, she returned to France to support and comfort the Queen in prison. She was called on to take the Oath of Detestation of the Monarchy, and refused. As she left the courtroom, she was attacked by a waiting mob and literally torn to pieces. Maria shared the disbelief, horror and grief of everyone who had loved this charming and courageous woman. The Duchess of Noailles was luckier. She escaped from Dieppe disguised as a boy sailor and stepped, wet and penniless, still wearing a seaman's jacket, onto the Brighton shingle. She was aged twenty-one and pregnant. Maria took her straight to her house, where she stayed until recovered from the ordeal.[11]

On 21 January 1793 King Louis XVI was guillotined, and shock waves spread through Europe. In England public opinion strengthened against the revolutionaries. In February, the new republican government of France declared war on Britain. The Prince was made Colonel of the 10th Light Dragoons, and became a soldier at last. In an embarrassingly tight uniform, the now portly prince led his troops to camp in Hove, and spent the summer in manoeuvres on the South Downs, the delight of it leaving him faint with joy. He could not claim to have shared the hardships of campaigning, his tent being sumptuously equipped with a green and lilac draped divan and chairs costing a thousand pounds each, but he did thoroughly enjoy himself.[12]

His enjoyment was dimmed only by his debts. He owed £400,000 and had tried to raise money all over Europe, with little success. The banks could not afford to lend any more, Thomas Coutts writing with exquisite courtesy, begging the Prince not to ask for further loans from his bank, as it would grieve him to refuse.[13] In 1793 he turned, with unfeigned despair, to his father. The King's answer was that given to the Duke of York: marry a Protestant German Princess and I will help you; if you do not wish to do that, I will see that Parliament does not help you either. The Prince knew then that his options had run out, but Maria seemed unaware both of the sword hanging over her head, and of Lady Jersey laying her plans.

Maria based her life on the belief that she and the Prince were man and wife, joined by vows that would last till death. Like all couples, they had had their quarrels, but these had always ended in happy reconciliation. The Prince still signed himself 'ever thine', and addressed her as 'Dearest Love', and became jealous if she was seen talking with other men, as Lady Lucy Fitzgerald noted in a letter home to Dublin:

Bye the bye have you heard of the piece of work at the Opera the other night? It was this. The Prince found Charles and Mr Lascelles in his box with Mrs Fitzherbert. They immediately withdrew, but he flew into the most dreadful passion called them all sorts of names and scolded Mrs Fitzherbert so loud that all the House heard it.[14]

Nevertheless, gossip said the relationship was over. As early as 1791 Edward Jerningham had written to his niece, 'The tittle tattle of the town is of the separation of the Prince and Mrs Fitzherbert'.[15] The Duke of Gloucester seemed to think their relationship had changed since the days when he, Gloucester, had said she loved His Royal Highness more than herself. He now told Mrs Harcourt that the Prince 'had his amusements elsewhere', but had 'much consideration' for Mrs Fitzherbert, even though she was 'sometimes jealous and discontented; her temper violent, though apparently so quiet'.[16] (It should be remembered that 'temper', in eighteenth-century usage, meant state of mind rather than a fit of anger, and 'violent' meant very upset.)

The Prince had come to realise that the only way out of the 'total ruin' of his debts was to marry a German Princess and gain his father's help. He would hardly have spoken of this to Maria, but she must have seen that the debts had brought him to a desperate state of mind, and that only his father could save him. She should also have known that the King would insist on certain conditions, just as he had with the Duke of York. Though still outwardly united, tension certainly existed between the couple. This was unintentionally increased, in 1793, by the Prince's brother Augustus, Duke of Sussex. Living in Italy because of poor health, Augustus met and married Augusta Murray, the daughter of Lord Dunmore. They returned to England and were married a second time, without using their titles, in St George's, Hanover Square. Augustus then informed his father. The King was furious at this breach of his Royal Marriages Act, and got the Court of Privileges to declare the marriage null and void, and any children illegitimate. Lady Augusta was

Protestant, descended from royalty on both sides of her family, and the Duke of Sussex was the sixth son. The King's severity towards this couple revealed the strength of his feeling over 'suitable' marriages for Princes of the Blood. What chance then had Maria Fitzherbert, if her marriage was ever made public, as a Catholic with no royal blood, who had dared to marry the heir to the throne? She must have seen that the precedent created by the Court of Privileges weakened her position, but may have refused to see how it influenced the Prince. He could argue, now, that if a marriage without the King's consent could be found 'null and void', that is not a marriage at all; then he was not married, and was free to choose a bride to suit his father.

In the past, the Prince had always reassured Maria with fresh promises of eternal devotion whenever she was troubled, swearing that she was his dearest love without whom he could not live. But it was doubtful if this state of affairs could continue. The Prince would agree to almost anything if it meant that his devastating debts could be paid; and Lady Jersey now saw a chance to step in and win the Prince's affections for herself.

One year older than Maria, Lady Jersey was undeniably attractive, well-groomed and vivacious. Sir Nathanial Wraxall bore witness to her 'irresistible seduction and fascination',[17] but she was also described as 'the type of a serpant – beautiful, bright and glossy in its exterior – in its interior poisonous'.[18] Her husband, much older than her, was a courtly, exquisitely dressed gentleman who had held various posts in the Prince's household. She had provided him with two sons and seven daughters, but their relationship was now politely formal. It has been suggested that the Queen encouraged Lady Jersey's bid for her son's affections, believing that if enticed away from Maria Fitzherbert he would quickly settle for a suitable marriage. Most of the Royal Dukes and their sisters believed the Prince to be married to Maria, treating her *en belle soeur*, but the Queen and King knew that no marriage between them could be legal. Lady Jersey's brief was to captivate the Prince and urge him towards a marriage pleasing to his father. As a reward, she would have an important place in the Prince's enlarged establishment after the marriage.

The Prince proved all too easy to entice away, probably believing that he could return to Maria and her loving forgiveness any time he liked. But Lady Jersey convinced him that his unpopularity with the people was due to Mrs Fitzherbert and her religion. Without her, he would be as well loved as his father. If he married suitably, and fathered an heir, as the Duke of York had noticeably failed to do, his future would be free of worries. She also told him that Maria had been heard to say she was only interested in his rank, not in his person.

Maria did not know what Lady Jersey chose to say to the Prince, but she did know that they were spending a great deal of time together, and so did the rest of Society. She had forgiven his previous amours, notably with Lucy Howard, whose child was said to be the Prince's son, and with the actress Anna Maria Crouch, famed for her performance as Polly Peacham in *The Beggars' Opera*. His affair with Lady Jersey, however, was a public humiliation. The rumour that the Prince would now leave Maria began to spread.

The Duke of York appeared to change his mind about her, and also spoke of her 'unfortunate temper', advising the Prince 'not to bear with it any longer', and that he would be better, 'out of her shackles'.[19] It is possible that stories of Maria's 'temper' were being put about by the Prince himself, to justify the parting he knew must come, and to shield himself from too much criticism when the parting became public. Maria was quite capable of outspoken anger in private, but it is impossible to imagine her doing so in public. She was too well trained in good behaviour, and had too much natural dignity; accounts of how she behaved when they were alone could only have been circulated by the Prince himself. If this was so, it might explain York and Gloucester's comments, they being the ones most likely to hear, and believe, the Prince's version.

Seemingly unaware of the talk of separation, Maria left London for Richmond shortly before the end of the Season in 1794, expecting the Prince to join her later. She had begun to rent Marble Hill House, the little Palladian villa elegantly designed in white stone, with gardens running down to the Thames, originally built for Henrietta Howard, the mistress of George II. Of the many houses Maria occupied, this was by far the most beautiful.

The Prince instead went to Brighton, where Lady Jersey joined him. On 24 June Maria received one of his usual little notes:

My Dearest Love, I have just received a letter from my Sister by the Coach this evening, desiring me to come to Windsor, which though exceptionally inconvenient to me at this moment, in particular, owing to my being [committed] to give my annual Regimental dinner on Wednesday, I mean to comply with [it] and to set out tomorrow morning early, having put off my dinner with all my Company to Friday. I therefore mean to pass Wednesday in London and return here on Thursday ... Adieu, my dear love, excuse haste. Ever thine G.P.'[20]

An affectionate note, showing how good the Prince had become at dissembling, and explaining why Maria, frequently receiving these loving messages, went on believing their marriage was secure. She was dining with the Duke of Clarence at Bushey that evening, and was seated at his table, when a second message from the Prince was delivered. It told her, with appalling brevity, that he would never enter her house again.

She was quite unprepared for this abrupt dismissal. She rose from the table, refusing all offers of assistance, and returned to Marble Hill. She seems to have destroyed the second note, or for one reason or another it has not survived, but across the note received that morning she wrote, 'This letter I received the morning of the day the Prince sent me word he would never enter my house again'. Then, as if it explained everything, she added, 'Lady Jersey's influence'.[21] Lord Stourton claimed the dismissal 'came upon her quite unexpectedly'. The warning signs, however, had been there, but Maria had believed too firmly in the indissoluble nature of marriage to read them correctly.

She withdrew from Society, and for some days no one knew where to find her. She did not communicate with the Prince, who, though far from changing his mind, found he needed her forgiveness. He needed to know that she understood, and that they were parting as friends. But no one could find her. As always, when unable to get what he wanted, he became ill, feverish and excitable, and had to be bled.

Towards the end of July, Jack Payne, now an admiral, and newly home from victories at sea, located her, and arranged a meeting at Hambledon, in Hampshire, near Portsmouth. This spot, though convenient for a sea going man like Payne, seems a surprising place for Maria to be, as she was now thought to be on her way to Margate. A possible explanation is that she had been in Hampshire, acquainting her family with her separation before the gossips did so for her. If she planned to spend the rest of the summer in Margate, Hambledon was a reasonable place to spend the first night of the journey. From there, on 28 July, Payne informed the Prince that, 'Mrs Fitzherbert arrived here late this night and heard with great concern that you are unwell', adding that she would have written herself to express her concern, had she not been fatigued by a tedious journey and was 'incapable of doing it'.[22] The next morning he was still trying to get Maria into 'a tranquil enough frame of mind' to write to the Prince. She was obviously upset and afraid that any letter she wrote might be shown to Lady Jersey, and news of it passed round the Town. (The Town had already begun to talk. Lord Mornington had written to his brother Arthur Wellesley, on 15 July, 'I heard last night that a treaty of separation and provision is on foot, if not already concluded, between His Royal Highness and the late Princess Fitz').[23]

Payne's letters hint at a special requirement of the Prince's to which he, Payne, believed Maria would now agree. On 30 July he wrote from Hambledon, 'I am in hopes that in the temper she left this [place] and the effect the idea of your illness had upon her … that something may be hit upon to accomplish the wish Your Royal Highness has so much at heart'. Later he reported that she was 'in the happiest disposition to conform to every wish of yours'. Was the Prince only anxious to part good friends, or was the wish he had at heart something more concrete? Payne's letters are unclear; he was obviously writing in haste and bent on pleasing his master, and some of his remarks can be interpreted in more than one way. He had clearly been sent to persuade Maria to agree to something. The Prince was not just enjoying an affair with Lady Jersey; he was planning to marry, and there was something he needed. The marriage certificate, which he had so obligingly written in his own hand nine years ago, had to be kept secret. Maria had promised never to produce it without his consent, but that was before he had abandoned her. It was necessary to be sure that she would still keep her word. Was the phrase, 'to conform to every wish of yours', a coded message meaning she gave that assurance? The Prince replied immediately with his thanks 'for all the pains trouble and vexation' Payne had endured to secure his master's happiness, 'and all I can say is that I shall ever be happy to contribute everything that lays in my power to render Mrs Fitzherbert's situation as comfortable as possible … *mais tout est fini.* I think it perfectly needless to say anything more upon it'.[24]

Three days later he informed his father that all was over between himself and Mrs Fitzherbert, and that he wished to marry a suitable princess.

7

Caroline of Brunswick

The King, overjoyed, wrote to Prime Minister William Pitt, 'I have this morning seen the Prince of Wales who has acquainted me with his having broken off all connection with Mrs Fitzherbert and his desire of entering into a more creditable line of life by marrying; expressing at the same time the wish that my niece, the Princess of Brunswick, may be the person'.[1] To his credit, George III had urged his son to take time to choose a Princess he could be happy with, but the Prince, of the opinion that 'one damn frow was as good as another', had already decided on Princess Caroline of Brunswick-Wolfenbüttel. Perhaps he thought the choice would please his father, or that a quick decision would hasten his release from 'total ruin'.

The King was certainly pleased. 'Undoubtedly she is the person who naturally must be agreeable to me', he confided to Pitt. The Queen thought differently: 'There is a woman I do not recommend at all', she wrote to her brother. Queen Charlotte had never liked her sister-in-law, Princess Caroline's mother, but she had also heard certain rumours concerning the Princess of Brunswick's 'indecent conduct',[2] which she revealed to her brother but not to the King. Caroline herself was proud and delighted to have been chosen, and her father was honoured to accept on her behalf. James Harris, now Lord Malmesbury, duly arrived in Brunswick to arrange the details of the match and a ceremony of betrothal, before escorting the Princess to England. He saw at once that the Prince could not have chosen a bride less compatible to his taste. She was not unattractive: though short and plump, she was graceful, had nice eyes, good hands, abundant fair hair, and a cheerful disposition. But she seemed to have no idea of what was generally regarded as correct behaviour, and her conversation tended towards improper innuendo, even to lewdness. There were rumours that she was never trusted out of sight of a chaperone when men were in the company. She was now twenty-six years of age and her father showed considerable relief that she was to be married.

Malmesbury noted that she was careless about dress and personal hygiene, and was obliged to tell her that the Prince was most particular about cleanliness of both clothes and person, and that underlinen must be changed daily. Her mother had obviously given no guidance in these matters, so Malmesbury did not blame Caroline, but had to make sure her maids understood that certain rules, concerning washing and changing of clothes, must be kept.

Malmesbury did his best to train Caroline in the ways of the English court, but, though she was eager to learn and willing to accept correction cheerfully, he was fearful of the effect her gauche and immodest manners would have. His instructions, however, were not to see if she were suitable but to escort her to England. He had done his best to prepare her, emphasising that facetious conversation, vulgar jokes and flirtatious looks would shock the English royal family. She was kind-hearted and entirely without malice, and Malmesbury could not dislike her, but he doubted if her conversation and manner could ever be sufficiently schooled to be acceptable to a fastidious Prince.

Arriving at Greenwich, at noon on Easter Day, they found there was no one to greet them. The royal carriages, and an escort of the Prince's Light Dragoon Guards, were an hour late, delayed, so Malmesbury heard later, by Lady Jersey, one of the party to meet the Princess, who had failed to be ready on time. Caroline already knew that Lady Jersey was the Prince's current *chère amie*, but must have been a little surprised to find she had to share a carriage with her on the drive to St James's Palace.

Maria might have sympathised with Caroline if she could have seen and heard Lady Jersey doing her best to be disagreeable throughout the drive. Though living in seclusion at Marble Hill, Maria had, like the rest of the country, known of the proposed wedding for months, the *beau monde* speculating on her possible reaction. Horace Walpole wrote to Miss Berry, 'The Princess arrived at St James's on Sunday nor do I believe Mrs Fitzherbert will forbid the Banns'.[3] Maria secretly doubted if banns would ever be called for nuptials she could not believe would take place. She was not alone in this; wagers were being placed, for and against, in all the London clubs. But London was illuminated for the

Princess's arrival, and, according to the *Sussex Weekly Advertiser*, 'The house of Mrs Fitzherbert in Pall Mall was among those illuminated in honour of the Prince's nuptials'.[4] She would remain at Marble Hill, but had no wish to draw attention to her odd position by letting her house in Pall Mall be the only one in darkness. The Prince had not forgotten Maria: at the time of his betrothal to Caroline he had asked his father to promise to continue the payment of her income of £3000 a year should the Prince die. George III pointed out that the Prince was unlikely, in the 'natural order of things' to die before his father, but agreed to the request, assuring his son that he 'had no reason to entertain any uneasiness on this account'.[5]

Princess Caroline's welcome to St James's was not what she had expected. When the Prince came into the room to greet her she stepped forward to kneel, as instructed by Malmesbury, but was lifted to her feet ('gracefully enough', Malmesbury noted) by her future husband, who then turned away, saying he was unwell and asking for brandy. Malmesbury, knowing him well, suggested water instead, but, saying he was going to the Queen, the Prince departed. Caroline, watching her future husband lurch from the room, asked if the Prince always behaved like that, adding that he was rather fat and not nearly as handsome as the portrait he had sent. She was determined to make a success of her new position, however, and appeared at dinner with the royal family hoping to make a good impression. In this she spectacularly failed. 'I was far from satisfied with the Princess's behaviour', wrote Malmesbury, 'it was flippant, rattling, affecting raillery and wit.'[6] Lady Jersey was present at the table and Caroline could not resist 'throwing out coarse and vulgar hints' about the former's relationship with the Prince. The 'giddy manners' of the young woman he was committed to marry clearly appalled the Prince, and the King and Queen were hardly less dismayed.

Later, the Queen was heard to say: 'George, it is for you to say whether you can marry the Princess or not'.[7] The King offered to take responsibility for cancelling the arrangements if his son felt unable to go ahead with the wedding. The Prince refused the offer, but his father instructed the Duke of Clarence to stay with his brother night and day until the wedding took place. Perhaps he feared the Prince would simply run away.

Maria may have half expected the same thing. The night before the

wedding, glancing from her windows at Marble Hill, she saw the familiar figure of the Prince on horseback, riding to and fro beyond her gates.
She made no signal, and sent no servant to invite him in, and eventually he galloped away.[8] When, years later, Lord Stourton asked if she had
known what he was doing there, she said 'I had no idea'. But his appearance that night must have strengthened her belief that he would not,
could not, exchange the solemn vows of marriage with someone else,
and that the bigamous wedding would never take place.

Take place it did, however, though everyone present in the suffocat-
ingly hot chapel in St James's Palace held their breath until the vows
were exchanged. Caroline, in diamond-strewn white satin, was the only
one who looked relaxed. The Prince was extremely drunk and hardly
seemed to know what he was doing, swaying at the altar between two
bachelor dukes. 'The Prince was like a man doing a thing in desperation, it was like Macheath going to execution; and he was quite drunk',
commented Lord Melbourne later.[9] The Archbishop of Canterbury
repeated the words 'any person knowing of a lawful impediment ...'
twice, looking hard at the Prince and the King, then waited for anyone
to speak. No one did. At one point the Prince rose to his feet, and the
King, still fearing his son might make a bid for freedom, walked over
and ordered him to kneel again. Eventually the Prince of Wales led his
newly-wedded wife from the chapel and the bells of London rang out,
while Lady Mary Stuart remarked quietly, 'What an odd wedding'.

Maria, at Marble Hill, was too far away to hear the bells. Orlando
Bridgeman, who had stood guard while the Prince married Maria in
Park Street ten years before, galloped out to Richmond as soon as the
ceremony was over and told her the marriage had taken place. She
refused to believe him, until he said, gently, that he had been present
and witnessed it. At that, he maintained afterwards, she 'fainted away'.[10]

Maria had always found excuses for the Prince's behaviour and possibly understood that the burden of nearly £400,000 debts, and the need
to please his father before they could be paid, plus the calculated wiles
of Lady Jersey, had been too much for him. Nevertheless, her hurt was
profound.

For a time she remained in retirement at Marble Hill, as if beginning
a third widowhood. She may have been grieved to hear that the Prince
had taken his new bride to Kempshot, to the small house where he and

she had spent some of their best times together. A more tactful choice could have been made, but the Prince intended no offence to first or second wife. He simply wanted some hunting, and Kempshot was where he always went for that. He took a band of male companions with him, and the only lady in the company, apart from Caroline, was the now openly malicious Lady Jersey. According to her own account, it was a far from happy experience for the Princess, who hated Lady Jersey, and deeply resented having no female companion but her. She described the men as, 'very blackguard companions of the Prince, who were constantly drunk and filthy, sleeping and snoring in boots on the sofas'.[11] The stay at Kempshot may, in fact not have been as bad as she later made out. The young Cornet Brummell of the Prince's Dragoons (later the famous 'Beau' Brummell) was among the company, and his comment was, that the young couple seemed 'perfectly satisfied with each other, particularly the Princess ...' Whatever the truth of the Kempshot weeks, soon after returning to London Caroline announced herself pregnant, though, she claimed, much to her surprise. She was later to tell the story of her marriage night, which the Prince, completely drunk, spent in the grate 'where he fell, and I left him', and to imply that when the marriage was finally consummated, it was in such a manner that she could not believe a child could be the result.[12]

But the pregnancy, however surprising, raised her stock considerably with the royal family, and the news delighted the Prince, who felt his duties were being accomplished faster than he had expected. His attitude to Caroline seems to have been quite amiable at this time; she was allowed other ladies in waiting as well as Lady Jersey, and he took her to Brighton, where she found the air beneficial.

Maria had deserted Brighton for Margate, where Miss Berry had observed her the previous September and told Horace Walpole, 'Mrs Fitzherbert is at Margate driving away sorrow in a phaeton and four'.[13] She had given up the lease of Marble Hill, and had taken instead Castle Hill Lodge, Ealing. In place of the grand mansion in Pall Mall, she bought 6 Tilney Street, close to Hyde Park, a house that remained her London home for the rest of her life. Lady Clermont had persuaded her to remain 'in Society', urging her to rise above her feelings and, as Lord Stourton put it 'open her house to the town'. This she did and 'all the fashionable world, including all the Royal Dukes, attended her parties'.

She was supported by the Duke of York, with whom she was 'united in the most friendly and confidential relations'. The renewed friendship of the Duke of York may suggest that he now thought his brother had exaggerated when he spoke about Mrs Fitzherbert's 'temper' before the separation, or just that he admired the way she had taken her blunt dismissal; in any case, he clearly wanted to keep her friendship.

It wasn't only the Royal Dukes and Lady Clermont who supported Mrs Fitzherbert at this time. Many others chose to remain her friend rather than the Prince's, a fact that angered him. He found it hard to believe that Mrs Fitzherbert's company could be sought above his own. Their closest friends, Lord Hugh and Lady Horatia Seymour, were shocked by the Prince's behaviour. Lord Hugh, arriving home from a personal triumph against the French fleet on the 'Glorious First of June' 1794 could hardly believe that the Prince had deserted their beloved 'Mrs Fitz'. He told the Prince, to his face, that he thought his conduct dishonourable. This was something the Prince could not forgive, and Lord Hugh was told of his dismissal from the Prince's household after he returned to sea. Lady Melbourne, whose lover the Prince had once been, also told him she would go on inviting Mrs Fitzherbert, in spite of his disapproval.

The desertion of his friends was not the Prince's only disappointment. His allowance had been sizeably increased, but his huge debts were to be paid 'out of income'. This disgusted him. Things were not turning out as he had expected. But his spirits rose when, on 7 January 1796, Princess Caroline gave birth to a healthy child. He sent a note to his mother giving her the good news: 'The Princess after a terrible hard labour is this instant brought to bed of an immense girl, and I assure you not withstanding we might have wished for a boy, I receive her with all the affection possible'. To his father he wrote, 'Thank God mother and child are quite well and likely to remain so. The Princess has had a very severe time indeed, having been upwards of twelve hours in constant labour'.[14]

It had been necessary for the Prince, along with a selected number of statesmen, to be present at the delivery of an heir to the throne, and he had been up for two nights running, as the Princess struggled through her labour. No doubt exhausted, he became suddenly and violently ill, as he so frequently did in moments of strong emotion. On recovery, his mood swing to depression was extreme. Believing he was about to die, he sat alone in his rooms and wrote a long and hysterical will. It began, rather wordily, by addressing the Almighty,

> To Thee oh ever merciful and Almighty God do I in these my last moments with truest fervour and devotion and with all humility address myself to unveil my whole soul, and before my eyes are for ever closed, to speak that truth and to render that justice to others as well as to myself before my Creator as well as before the whole World, without which, when brought before Thy great Tribunal I could never expect that mercy and justice to which all Christians are taught to look forward ...

He went on to 'bequeath, give and settle' all his worldly property on 'My Maria Fitzherbert, my wife, the wife of my heart and soul'. To make doubly sure, he listed everything he included in his 'property': monies; all the land and houses that were his own, including the Pavilion at Brighton, but not Carlton House, which he did not own; all the furniture, plate, paintings ornaments, silver and jewels, and even all the wine in his cellars. He spoke of his burial, and left instructions that it should take place 'with as little pomp as possible', and that the miniature of 'my beloved wife' be tied around his neck with a ribbon and laid above his heart. Then he made a further request:

> I likewise wish and desire and entreat of my adored Maria Fitzherbert to permit that, whenever she quits this life and is interred my coffin should be taken up and placed next to Hers, wherever she is to be buried, and, if she has no objection, that the two inward sides of the two Coffins should be taken out, and the two Coffins then be soldered together, as the late King's and Queen's were ... therefore I wish to be buried not in my Family Vault, but anywhere, as privately as possible, in order that my Ashes may repose in quiet, until they are placed next to hers or united with hers.[15]

This strange document raises many questions. Was the Prince of Wales suffering from some terrible guilt at having left Maria and married again? Guilt made worse by the belief that he was about to die? Was he really professing his abiding love for the woman he had treated so badly, or was the whole strange document motivated by a sudden hatred of Caroline of Brunswick? By insisting that Maria Fitzherbert was his wife in the eyes of God, was he trying to prove that 'she who is called the Princess of Wales', to whom he left 'one shilling', was not, and never had been, his wife?[16]

What could Caroline have said or done, in the brief time between his writing of her with such kindness to his parents, and taking up his pen, only days later, to write of her with such hatred? Had she been talking again of her amazement at finding herself pregnant, perhaps being more explicit, with a crudeness that came naturally to her, about the Prince being 'incapable' as a husband, something she certainly implied later. Whatever caused him to write the will, when fully recovered the Prince did not destroy it. He placed it among his papers, and began to plan a formal separation between himself and the woman he now called 'the Fiend'.

The christening of Charlotte Augusta, the Prince's daughter, outwardly a family and national celebration, was marred by the antagonism between her parents, and soon afterwards, on 30 April, the Prince sent the Princess of Wales a letter of dismissal almost as abrupt as the one he had sent to his first wife. He wanted a complete separation, but Carlton House was big enough for husband and wife to have separate apartments and communicate, when necessary, by sending notes. This was the Prince's proposal. Caroline thought she was being treated very badly, and felt entitled to make some terms of her own, one of which was that Lady Jersey should no longer be a part of the household. The Prince conceded this point and Lady Jersey resigned her position.

Maria knew nothing of the Prince's plan to live apart from the Princess, but she knew, of course, about the birth of Princess Charlotte. In a letter to Thomas Coutts, her banker and friend, she wrote of the three of them, 'they will ever have my sincerest wishes for every happiness. Whenever I can fix on my own plans and settle myself I cannot but hope I shall feel my mind tranquil from a consciousness of having neither remorse nor reproach to make myself, having invariably considered and wished *their* interest and welfare more than my own'.[17] She felt no ill will towards Princess Caroline, and no bitterness towards the Prince, but she saw no reason why she should be generous to Lady Jersey. Especially when she learned that the Prince was having the mansion next door to Carlton House refurbished for Lady Jersey's family, and that he had taken houses in Bognor so that they could spend time together there. Whatever regrets the Prince may have had about abandoning

1. Maria Fitzherbert by Sir Joshua Reynolds. (*National Portrait Gallery*)

2. George Prince of Wales, portrait by H. P. Bone, 1805. (*Ashmolean Museum, Oxford*)

3. Caroline of Brunswick. (*National Portrait Gallery*)

4. The Pavilion, Brighton, in 1778.

5. A View of the Steine, Brighton, about 1815.

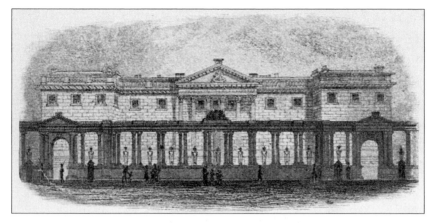

6. Carlton House, facing Pall Mall.

7. George IV, driving at Windsor.

8. Minney Dawson Damer.

9. Marianne Smyth.

10. Maria Fitzherbert in 1836, aged eighty.

Mrs Fitzherbert for Caroline of Brunswick, and whatever he had written in his will, he saw no need to give up Lady Jersey as a sign of devotion to the 'wife of my heart and soul'.

Always believing, however, that he could have his cake and eat it, the Prince was soon sending secret envoys, his brothers, Jack Payne and Miss Pigot, to discover if Mrs Fitzherbert would consider resuming their former relationship, as his connection with 'she who is called the Princess of Wales' was now only a formal one. Maria's answer was no. She was willing to excuse, and even forgive, but to take the Prince back on the old footing, as if his marriage to the Princess had never taken place, was out of the question. She should have known that the Prince never took 'no' for an answer. He began putting pressure on her to relent, and became hysterical and despairing each time she refused. He broke completely with Lady Jersey.

Maria was uncertain where correct behaviour lay, and unsure of her own feelings. In the autumn she went to take the waters at Bath, and while there she received a letter from Lady Horatia Seymour with the good news that she had safely given birth to a daughter, her seventh child, named Mary. As Lady Horatia was suffering from tuberculosis, this survival of both mother and child was something no one had dared to hope for. She had been told that she must live for a time in a warmer climate if her health was to improve. Lord Hugh was serving off Madeira, and he had arranged to take her there when the next ship was ready to sail. Lady Horatia was desperately eager to take the new baby with her, but the doctor insisted the delicate child would never survive the journey. Full of sympathy, and aware that temporary homes would have to be found for all seven children, Maria wrote offering to take any one of them into her household. There were plenty of aunts and uncles on both sides of the family, all apparently willing to divide the young Seymours between them, but Lady Horatia wrote back to Maria inviting her to meet them at Portsmouth saying, 'The letter I received from you on Monday was just like yourself, everything that is kind, good, friendly and comfortable to one's feelings ... I know exactly what you feel about taking care of one of them and nothing would be greater relief to my mind than leaving little Mary with you'. Then, knowing how easily her friend gave way to anxiety, she added, 'But I know very well that the instant her little finger ached you would be frightened and make yourself ill, therefore as I cannot ensure her perfect health I think she had better be at Hambledon with Phillips who will have no alarms. We will talk all this over at Portsmouth'.[18]

Maria set out for Portsmouth immediately, and found the Seymours waiting to sail, having left 'Little Mary' with her nurse at Brompton. There is some confusion over what was arranged at that meeting, but certainly Maria went back to Bath believing that she was to have the care of the baby. This was confirmed in a letter Lady Horatia wrote the day before she left England, 'I have written to Lady George Seymour to tell her that little Mary is to be your child. There never was anything so kind and good as yourself'.[19] But Lady Horatia's sister, Lady Euston, who had also been in Portsmouth, always insisted that, when Mrs Fitzherbert confided that she might return to the Prince, Lady Horatia was so upset at the very idea of her doing something so mistaken, and wrong, that she left the arrangement deliberately more open, apparently saying that Maria should only take charge of Mary if none of the family could have her.

Whatever the arrangements were, two events took the matter out of everyone's control. On returning to Bath, Maria became seriously ill with a 'severe chill'. Her mother was sent for, and for a week or more her life was in danger. When well enough to return to town, Maria found that 'little Mary' was being cared for by Lady George Seymour, who intended to keep her. That seemed to be the end of the matter. Measles, however, broke out among Lady George Seymour's elder children, and Maria was begged to take Mary at once to get the delicate child away from an infected house. Maria gladly agreed, had a nursery hastily made ready, and sent for the child and her nurse. When the door of 6 Tilney Street opened to receive the infant, Maria Fitzherbert's life changed for ever.

At first she felt only concern for the child's survival. 'I could not feel', she wrote later to Sir Robert Seymour, 'for so young a child of a month or two anything more than the natural anxiety attending infants of that age, and had no other idea than that of returning her to her parents as soon as they came again to this country.'[20] To her own surprise, however, Maria became enchanted with the child, who entirely won her heart, and her devotion to 'Minney', as she called her, soon knew no bounds.

But even Minney could not divert Maria from anxiety over the Prince of Wales and his pleading to be taken back. Predictably he had become ill again, with fever and abdominal pains. The Queen and his sisters saw, with dread and anxiety, a similarity to his father's symptoms. The Princesses added their entreaties to those of their brother, hinting that it was Maria's 'duty' to return to him. Her indecision deepened. She was still the Prince's wife; perhaps she did have a duty to return. According to Lord Glenbervie's diary, the Queen added her own plea: 'Mrs Fitzherbert showed Lady Anne Barnard [formerly Anne Lindsay] a letter to her in the Queen's own handwriting pressing her to be reconciled to the Prince and written at the time of his rupture with Lady Jersey and when he affected to be or was very ill and told his sisters that he was sure he would die if a reconciliation did not take place between Mrs Fitzherbert and him ...'[21]

When Maria had spoken to Horatia Seymour about the Prince's pleading, and admitted to still loving him, Lady Horatia told her sister that for Maria to feel love for the Prince now, in the present circumstances, 'would hardly be excusable in a girl just escaped from the nursery'. Maria was aware of her friend's disapproval, and knew almost everyone would share it. But passionate letters continued to be delivered to her door by the Prince's messengers. In a moment of weakness, she agreed to return, then changed her mind. At this, the Prince sent an almost incoherent letter, delivered by the Duke of Cumberland:

> Save me, save me on my knees I conjure you from myself. What! After *a solemn promise given, pledged to my brother* to be mine again, is there truth, is there honour in this world, and is it not inherent in you, Oh my friend, my friend Payne, what will you say? Was it only to *trifle* with my feelings that my *hopes were to be raised, that fortune, prospects, the only ones of life and happiness to me were to be held out to me, because the agonies I had already suffered were not sufficient ... reiterate your promise or recollect you sign yourself my doom.*[22]

Maria must have been used to these cries of doom and death, but a note added to the letter, at 4 a.m. the next morning, contained a new threat. If she did not return to him, he wrote, 'My Father and the rest of my family, shall be acquainted with my situation ... on my knees I have sworn it, and on my knees do I write it to you'. He had already written the letter to his father, and had it ready to despatch if she refused him. He signed himself 'thine unalterably thine' but could not resist adding a few more lines. 'Think not that Payne or any advice whatever, will make me change my purpose, or forswear my oath, thank God my witnesses are living, your Uncle and your Brother.' It was these last words that alarmed her most. If the Prince named her uncle and brother as witnesses of their marriage they could be accused of felony, stripped of their possessions and exiled. She would not risk that. There had been a time when she had hoped her marriage would be made public one day, as the Prince had promised, but that was when she had believed that both King and Parliament would accept it, and laws be changed. She now knew better. The royal ladies did not have a proclamation of her marriage in mind when they urged her to return to the Prince.

The threat of proclaiming the marriage had not been kept secret. In March 1799 Lord Glenbervie wrote in his diary, 'Is it that there is a foundation for what is generally whispered, viz. that the Prince of Wales is going to declare his marriage with Mrs Fitzherbert?'[23] Maria hoped to dissuade the Prince from such a declaration by saying she would consult her church: if the validity of their marriage was confirmed, and it was deemed proper for her to return to him as his wife, then she would do so. Difficult marriage questions were always referred to Rome, and local priests, if asked for an opinion, would have seen this particular question as far too delicate to be commented on by them. Unfortunately for Maria and the Prince, events in Europe that year made an appeal to Rome impossible.

8

Reconciliation

Napoleon Bonaparte had led a French army into the Italian peninsula in 1796, taking Milan and marching south. Pope Pius VI agreed to pay tribute money to keep the French from entering Rome and huge sums were demanded. The Pope gave his paintings and jewels cut from his vestments, leading Roman families gave all they possibly could, and Cardinal York, younger brother of Charles Edward Stuart, gave their mother's Sobieski jewels and most of the family's silver plate, leaving himself virtually penniless; all in an attempt to save the city. Nevertheless, the French found a pretext to enter Rome in 1798. The Cardinals and senior clergy fled, but the Pope, a man over eighty, refused to leave, and also refused to give up his claim to rule the Papal States. He was led away a prisoner, and eventually held in Valence, where he died on 29 August 1799.

Maria heard of his death along with the rest of the Catholic world, adding to the common grief a personal sense of dismay, knowing a decision on her marriage could be endlessly delayed. Some writers believe that she had sent a message to Pius VI in 1797, and that the Prince, willing to agree to almost anything so long as she would take him back, promised to leave her in peace until the Pope's reply came. This would fit with Lord Stourton's claim that she spent a few weeks in a quiet resort in Wales while she awaited Rome's decision. If this was the case, the French must have entered Rome before a decision was made or, perhaps, as travel was slow, before her messenger arrived. Announcing the death of 'the former so-called Pope', Napoleon declared that the Church of Rome had met its end, and there would be no successor to Pius VI. Ignoring this, Cardinals began to travel, slowly, by land and sea over war-torn Europe, to hold a conclave in Austrian-held Venice. In the cold mists of a Venetian winter a quorum assembled in the Benedictine monastery on the island of San Giorgio to elect a new pontiff.

Weeks passed without a successful ballot. As the Catholic world awaited the outcome, news reached Pitt that Cardinal York (who, since the death of his brother, liked to be called Your Majesty rather than Your Emminence, having a better hereditary claim to the throne of England than the Hanoverians) was now old, sick and impoverished. Pitt passed this news to George III, who, deeply shocked to think of a grandson of a King reduced to poverty, sent word to Venice that he, personally, would pay the Cardinal a pension for the rest of his life. For the only time in papal history a messenger from outside was allowed into a conclave, and word of George III's generosity was delivered, amid surprised but happy congratulations. Maria had always believed the Prince's father to be a kind and good man, and this story, when she heard it, confirmed her belief.

In March 1800 Cardinal Chiaramonte became Pope Pius VII, and Napoleon, realising he must after all make terms with the Church, allowed him to return to Rome. 'We have a Pope!' wrote Lady Jerningham joyfully,[1] and John Nassau, a priest at the Warwick Street Chapel, accompanied by a layman, Gregory Stapleton, discreetly left England to seek the new Pope's decision on the marriage of Maria Fitzherbert and George, Prince of Wales.

Maria, knowing it might still be months before they reached Rome, and months again before an answer came back, had already decided what she must do. In June she would hold a grand breakfast, to which she would invite the whole of fashionable London 'To meet the Prince of Wales'. This would be her public announcement that she and the Prince were together again, putting an end to speculation and letting everyone see that there was nothing clandestine in their relationship. Until then she would continue to see the Prince only when other people were present. Lady Jerningham observed their behaviour with dismay, and wrote to her daughter on 17 March:

> The affairs of Mrs Fitzherbert and the Prince, have become very incomprehensible. It is a fact that he meets her whenever he can and a conversation ensues which takes them both out of the company. On Saturday Lady Kenmare tells me that Mrs Fitzherbert, Mrs Butler and the Prince were in a high box all night in conversation, the Princess at the Opera, and also Lady Jersey. I comprehend it no longer for I had thought Mrs Fitzherbert a woman of Principle.[2]

Invitations to the breakfast at Tilney Street, on 16 June, were sent to nearly four hundred people, Lady Jerningham included. It may seem strange that, having sent John Nassau on a long and hazardous journey to seek the Pope's advice, she should have gone ahead with her plans without waiting for his reply. It can only be assumed that, like the Queen, she now believed that the Prince's physical and mental health would break if she did not accept some form of reunion at an early date. Lady Anne Barnard supplies what may be the key to the situation, claiming Maria had told her, after the reunion, 'we live like brother and sister. I find no resentment though plenty of regret that I will have it on this footing and no other, but he must conform to my stipulations or I will have nothing to say to him. I did not consent to make it up with the Prince to live with him as his wife or his mistress'.[3] If Lady Anne was right, a compromise had been offered, and the Prince had accepted it.

Facing London Society, in this new situation, was difficult for Maria She did not enjoy hosting the famous breakfast, as Lord Stourton confirmed: 'She hardly knew how she could summon resolution to pass that severe ordeal'. The Town may have disapproved of her behaviour, but nearly all of them went to the breakfast. Carrying a few of her favourite white roses, and making a supreme effort, Maria greeted them all with her accustomed grace. No matter how much gossip and speculation took place afterwards, the breakfast was a huge success, some guests not departing until 5 a.m. According to Lord Stourton, it marked the beginning of the happiest years of Mrs Fitzherbert's chequered relationship with the Prince of Wales.

In the meantime, Pius VII was travelling, by slow and difficult stages, to Rome. He arrived in early July and had a meeting with John Nassau a few days later. Bishop Douglass's account of it survives:

Mr Nassau had his audience of the Pope on the eighth of July: His Holiness received him with great condescension and good nature, bade him sit down and harkened to the narrative of his business with familiar attention. The conversation was in the Latin language and closed with the Pope's directing him to state the case in writing ... His Holiness delivered the statement of the case to Monsignor Pietro and his confidential counsellor ... The answer of the two divines was approved by the Pope on the eighth August. The decision was given to Mr Nassau as being the decision of His Holiness.[4]

The marriage was found to be canonically valid, and Maria Fitzherbert was therefore free to return to the Prince of Wales as his wife, provided the Prince was suitably penitent, which he no doubt claimed to be. John Nassau did not reach London until the following November, when a papal bull outlining Rome's decision was handed to a grateful Maria, who now knew she could live as the Prince's wife with an easy conscience, regardless of public opinion.

Public opinion was very much against the Prince returning to his first wife; or, rather, to his old mistress, that being the way the majority preferred to see the situation. No one wanted to believe that the Prince, no matter how unpopular, was a bigamist; that his marriage to Princess of Wales was null and void; and, worse still, that the young Princess Charlotte, on whom hopes for the future were already being built, was illegitimate. Princess Caroline remained well loved by the people of London, and was loudly cheered wherever she appeared. The hatred the people had conceived for Lady Jersey at the height of her affair with the Prince was now transferred to Mrs Fitzherbert. Society, however, continued to receive her no matter what their doubts, and it was noted that the Dukes of York and Kent called almost daily at Tilney Street, and, although Maria never went to the Drawing Rooms, the Queen was believed to look with approval on the reunion.

Maria moved with surprising serenity into this new phase of her life, believing that, in yielding to the Prince's frenzied pleadings, she had followed the right, and, indeed, the only possible course. A course probably dictated by her heart, as much as her conscience.

The Prince was a happy man again; by pleadings, illness and threats he had got what he wanted. In the calm of Maria's drawing room he could forget how unbearable the Princess of Wales had been, and how he would rather have had toads crawling over his food than share a table with her. He could also forget how deeply unpopular he had become with the people he would one day rule. With Maria regained, all was now well. His good humour was boundless. He smilingly took up again with those he had shunned for staying friends with Mrs Fitzherbert when he had abandoned her. Having refused to speak to the Melbournes for six years, he walked into their Whitehall mansion one day and resumed the friendship without a word of explanation, as if there had never been a coldness between them.

The Prince's euphoria is understandable. Much more surprising is

Maria's obvious happiness, and her claim that June 1800 marked the start of her best years with the Prince. He had behaved so badly in the past, hurt and humiliated her so publicly, told so many lies, surely she would have been wary of trusting him, and doubt he was capable of change. But he seems to have convinced her that he had changed. She told Lady Anne Barnard that the Prince was 'so much improved, all that was boyish and troublesome before is now become respectful and considerate'.[5] Happiness brought back all the Prince's wit and charm, and, in spite of his ever-increasing weight (seventeen stone and tightly corsetted) Maria saw in him the disarming and lovable young man she had agreed to marry fifteen years before; only now he was more mature. The Prince of Wales's charm should not be underestimated. Few could be as gracious and delightful, when in good humour and seeking to please, as he was now.

In addition to being charmed, Maria felt, as a wife, that her place was back with her husband. Trained from girlhood in the art of pleasing, she liked to have a man to care for, to fuss over and soothe, chat to and laugh with. As a woman on her own she had kept her place in the fashionable world, attended assemblies and breakfasts and given her own entertainments with dignity and style, but how much more pleasant to be escorted by someone as attentive and thoughtful for her wellbeing as the Prince now was. He had once pursued every woman who caught his eye; now, at the age of thirty-nine, he seemed to have lost interest in casual loves and had eyes only for her, or so she believed. Supported by the royal family, who gave her credit for the huge improvement in the Prince's state of mind, she felt increasingly confident that she had been right to rejoin the Prince. The tensions and disagreements that had spoiled their earlier years seemed to have gone. Only the old money problems remained.

Maria probably had no idea how much the Prince owed his tradesmen, many of whom faced bankruptcy due to his failure to pay. Incapable of purchasing in normal amounts, he had boots, breeches, pantaloons, wigs and side curls, powders and creams and coronet-embroidered handkerchiefs delivered to Carlton House by the tens of dozens. He rarely bought less than twenty-five waistcoats at a time, and gloves by the three dozen. Once, in a single day, he bought thirty-two walking sticks. There was hardly a hatter, boot-maker, or jeweller who was not owed a substantial sum, which the Prince had little hope of paying. But these debts were paltry compared with what he owed for the building works, furnishings and fittings of Carlton House and the Brighton Pavilion. Repaying his debts out of his increased income had not worked, and he now owed £600,000,[6] a devastating sum when judged by the value of money at the time.

Even if she had guessed at the size of his debt, there was little Maria could do about it, and the Prince seemed to make light of the problem to her. Looking back on this time, she told Lord Stourton that they had very little money to spend but were 'as merry as crickets.'

The Town did not know what to make of the new situation. Puzzled to see the Prince and Mrs Fitzherbert meeting again at parties and theatres, Lady Jerningham was alarmed by their reunion, and, as she confessed to her daughter, had been glad of an excuse to avoid the Tilney Street celebration, even though the rest of the fine world went along with it. 'Yesterday I was dreadfully ill all day, a bad cold and I believe a storm in the air. It has dispensed me with going to Mrs Fitzherbert's breakfast this morning.'[7]

The last event of the Season was an even more spectacular breakfast, given by the Duchess of Devonshire at Chiswick House. Her eldest daughter had been presented at court that year, and all the Devonshires' entertainments were especially grand to celebrate her 'coming out'. Lady Jerningham described the scene for her daughter:

> I am returned living from the breakfast. I found it extremely pleasant and was very much amused. We got there a little after three, and were told the Duchess was in the Pleasure Ground. We accordingly found her sitting with Mrs Fitzherbert by an Urn … The Prince … stood almost the whole time by his band with Dr Burney ordering different pieces of music. Lady Jersey was casting around the spot where he stood with her daughters. The Prince was quite annoyed with her and eyed her askance, but she is resolved to plague him.[8]

Maria could remain serene. She had no cause to fear Lady Jersey now, and the Duchess was too well bred, and too eager to keep the Prince as a friend, to be anything other than courteous when they met. But this did not mean the Duchess approved of the situation. The Devonshire House set was far from enchanted to see the Prince of Wales reunited with Mrs Fitzherbert. They had little against her personally, but she was the 'Popish Wife' the voters in the shires still talked of. If that dangerous question: 'Has the Prince of Wales married a Catholic?', were to be raised again in Parliament it could do untold harm. They had been waiting a long time for the Prince to come to power and return the Whigs to government. With the King growing older and weaker, they would have preferred Mrs Fitzherbert to remain apart from the Prince, and out of the public eye. The Duchess claimed Society was 'thrown into disarray' by the reunion, but, a shrewd judge of situations, she seemed to think their relationship less than it appeared, and confided her doubts in a note to Lady Melbourne, 'I cannot quite believe his entire reconciliation with Mrs F. – I think it certainly is in a way – but not complete, at least she certainly takes great pains to persuade the contrary'.[9] Was she delicately hinting that they were friends again but not lovers? Had she heard rumours of Lady Anne's 'brother and sister' comments? Or was she saying she didn't think it would last? Whatever she meant to imply, there was nothing ambiguous about the Duchess's final comment: 'He certainly never appeared more calm and contented'.

Lady Holland recalled that 'every prude, dowager and maiden' had visited Maria before, and asked why the Town should now cry shame for her doing as she did five years ago? And a more detached Madame de Cogney observed that the relationship was, 'a rondeau in which variations are made *ad libitum*, but the return is to the first air'.

When the Season ended, Maria involved herself for several months with housing arrangements. She bought the house next door to number 6 Tilney Street and had the walls knocked through to make a mansion large enough to accommodate the entertainments the Prince would expect. She enjoyed creating elegant and comfortable interiors almost as much as the Prince. The Duke of Kent obligingly bought Castle Hill at Ealing, which she had long wished to sell. The Prince had continued to pay her £3000 a year allowance during their separation (her uncle Errington insisting that she accept it) and he now increased it to £4000.

Although deeply contented to be back with the Prince, she could not disguise from him that the centre of all joy and happiness, so far as she was concerned, was little Minney Seymour, now aged almost three. The Prince, far from minding that his Maria doted on someone other than himself, soon became almost as devoted to the child as she was. Nearly every day he called on Maria at a time when Minney would be brought down from the nursery, and a close friendship grew up between the two, Minney and 'Prinny', as he instructed her to call him. He was good with children when he chose to be. He may have been the future King of England, but to Minney, running joyfully across the drawing room to meet him, he was just a large friendly man whose knee she could jump on, who joined in her chatter and her games. The Prince, in contrast, took little notice of his daughter Charlotte, and was not at ease with her in the way he was with Maria's vivacious but carefully-reared darling.

In the autumn, the Prince and Maria travelled to Hampshire to stay with the Smythes, and in December they were with the Haggerstons at Grantham. According to Lord Stourton's memoir, the only thing marring Mrs Fitzherbert's serenity at this time was 'the Prince's bitter and passionate regrets and self accusations for his conduct, which she always met by saying: "We must look to the present and the future and not think of the past"'.[10] She was happy with the present, but how did she envisage their future? Perhaps the Prince's changed behaviour, and his family's support, led her to believe that her position was permanently secure. If this was so, events at the beginning of the New Year may have reminded her that, politically speaking, nothing was secure.

The Duchess of Devonshire once said that the Prince had an 'inclination to dabble in politics',[11] and in January his interest in the doings of his father's government was rekindled. Pitt's Act of Union, uniting the Parliaments of Westminster and Dublin came into force on 1 January 1801. Pitt intended to follow it up with Emancipation for Irish Catholics, giving them a voice in government, and was quietly preparing the way for this change. The King, hearing of Pitt's plan, announced at a crowded levée on 28 January that not only would he never give royal consent, but that anyone who introduced a Bill for Catholic Emancipation, or voted for it, or even brought up the 'Catholic Question' in Parliament, would be regarded as the King's enemy. Pitt was not present at the levée, but there were plenty of people to pass on the message. He had virtually promised Emancipation to the Irish. Seeing that his hopes of privately forcing the King's hand were now pre-empted, he offered his resignation, which the King did not hesitate to accept. Half Pitt's cabinet resigned with him. To everyone's surprise, the King

offered the premiership to Henry Addington, the somewhat undistin-
guished Speaker of the House of Commons, who, after some persuasion,
agreed to try and form a government.

George III had nothing against Catholics, many of whom, like Lord
Petre and Thomas Weld he visited and regarded as friends. He had been
more than generous to Cardinal York, he had gladly signed the earlier
Catholic Relief Bills, and Catholics were welcome at Court. It was only
the electing of Catholics into Parliament, with the possibility of their
entering into government, that he felt obliged to oppose. Not to do so,
he believed, would break his coronation oath, an oath which required
him to defend the Protestant Religion, and to keep from places of government those who shared the religion of James II.

The Prince had little interest in his father's views on Emancipation,
but the sudden departure of Pitt, his hated enemy, excited him a great
deal. Like most people, he could not see Addington being up to the job
and believed he would fail to form a government, leaving the King with
no option but to turn, however reluctantly, to the Whigs, giving the
Prince's friends their chance. Maria was his 'Dearest Love', but it was
Georgiana, Duchess of Devonshire who understood politics, and it was
to Devonshire House that he rushed with the news that Pitt was 'out'.
The Duchess was expected back from the country that day, and the
Prince was awaiting her in the courtyard when her coach drove through
the gates. Barely waiting for her to alight, he told her that Pitt had gone,
and, tired though she was with travelling, they went inside to begin
planning a Whig government.

Most of the Whigs, largely from aristocratic backgrounds, found it
hard to see Henry Addington, the son of a Reading doctor, with no min-
isterial experience and little influence, as a man able to form a lasting
government, and were tempted to believe their hour had come. When
the King's distress over the 'Catholic Question' brought on all the old
symptoms of stomach cramps, delirium and coma, they saw, in the
words of the Duke of Buckingham and Chandos, 'a brilliant prospect'
before them. The royal family were alarmed by the King's symptoms
and the Duke of York called in Willis and his brother (another doctor)
in addition to the royal physicians. The King did not respond to treatment at first and for over a week seemed close to death. Once more talk
of a regency spread fast, and the Prince of Wales was at meetings and

late suppers at Devonshire House, planning his government. No one thought, this time, of including Mrs Fitzherbert.

The King's bout of madness occurred before Pitt had had time to hand in his great seal of office, so he was, technically, still Prime Minister, even though Addington had been appointed to the post. Luckily the two men were prepared to work together. Pitt made it very clear to the Prince that the old Regency Bill from 1787 would be brought into the House again as soon as it was necessary, and that the Prince would do well to accept it, with all its restrictions. In the meantime the Prince, 'should forbear to advise with those who had for long time acted in direct opposition to his Majesty's Government'.[12] No political capital was to be made from the King's distressing situation, and no Regency crises was to be built up this time. The Prince, longing for power, listened to Pitt's stipulations, and distanced himself from Devonshire House.

The Duchess blamed Mrs Fitzherbert for the Prince's sudden coolness towards their plans. 'The reason is', she noted, 'his fear of disobliging Mrs Fitzherbert, who never has forgiven and never will hear of Fox.'[13] It was true that Maria did not care for Fox, but it is unlikely that her old resentment was strong enough for her to wish to ruin his political career, even if she could have done so. Many others, including Sheridan and Grey, and the Prince himself, had denied the marriage since Fox's famous speech. Fox remained at St Anne's Hill throughout all the excitement. Having had more than enough of the Regency crises last time, he refused to come to Town. It is unlikely that his name was mentioned between Maria and the Prince, and even more unlikely that the Prince told the Duchess that, on this occasion, he had been influenced by Pitt, not by Mrs Fitzherbert.

In the end it did not matter who influenced whom, for, to the relief of many but the disappointment of a few, the King recovered physically and mentally. By March he was able to understand and sign the important papers, and Addington, with a government in place, was confirmed as Prime Minister, while Pitt sat on the back benches.

The disappointed Prince did not believe his father was as well as he seemed, and accused his mother of disguising the seriousness of his condition to prevent a regency. His father continued in a weak state for some time, and the Willises refused to leave him. The Prince saw his father in April and, using the third person, as was usual, left a written memorandum of the meeting. He noted that, 'He [the King] continually and repeatedly talked of himself as a dying man, determined to go abroad and ... to make over the Government to the Prince'. These were the words the Prince had longed to hear, and he reported the conversation the Lord Chancellor, Lord Eldon, asking him to initiate the necessary steps for an abdication in the Prince's favour. Once again he recorded the interview: 'The Prince told his Lordship that it was the intention of his Majesty ... to devolve the Government on him, the Prince; that he wished therefore the Chancellor would consider the proper mode of that being carried into effect; and that it was the King's intention to retire to Hanover ...'[14]

Did the Prince's desperate activity to gain the Regency make Maria wonder about her future position? If so her worries were postponed this time. Lord Eldon, understandably, could take no action on the Prince's word only, and the King appears to have said no more about handing over his powers; he got rid of the Willises and left to recuperate in Weymouth. His son, once more frustrated, turned to Tilney Street for comfort. But Maria, though understanding as always, was suddenly facing a loss of her own. Lady Horatia Seymour was returning home, and Minney's happy days in Tilney Street looked about to end, leaving Maria bereft.

9

Minney

It was in the spring of 1801 that Maria learned of Lady Horatia's imminent return. She imagined, or perhaps had been told, that her friend's health had improved enough for her to return to England and take charge of her family again. While rejoicing at her friend's recovery, she was utterly desolate at the thought of losing Minney. She had always known the child was to be hers for only a limited period; but she had looked after her almost from birth and the thought of life without this enchanting little person, who adored her in return, seemed unbearable. Minney, now aged three, was more dear to Maria than she could find words to say. Unable to face the thought of parting with the child, she consoled herself with a fantasy: perhaps Lady Horatia was coming home to give birth again, and, if it were another daughter perhaps she, Maria would be allowed to continue caring for Minney.[1]

A house in Charlotte Street had been taken for Lady Horatia and her children, but it was agreed that Minney should stay in Tilney Street for the time being. Lady Horatia arrived at the end of May or the beginning of June but, clearly, had not come home to give birth. With that last hope taken away, the reality of losing Minney could no longer be avoided. Holding back her tears, Maria took Minney to Charlotte Street, writing later, 'The instant poor Lady Horatia came to England (and I acknowledge I went with a heavy heart) I took my little charge to deliver her up to her mother'.[2]

It was Lady Horatia who shed tears. As well as pitying Maria for her distress over losing Minney, Lady Horatia was amazed by the little girl's obvious health and happiness. The child's composure, naturalness and good behaviour delighted her, and she could not thank Maria enough for taking such care of the daughter she had not been able rear herself. 'Do not think,' she said 'that I would be so unfeeling as to take her from you. You are more her Mother than I am.'[3]

In gratitude, Maria arranged for Minney to be taken every day to spend time with Lady Horatia. Minney was alone with her mother on the day the Prince called. He wished to be reconciled with Lady Horatia, and through her with her husband, healing the rift that had opened between them when he had abandoned Maria to marry Caroline. He also wished to put in a word of his own regarding Minney's future care.

Lady Horatia was growing daily weaker, and Minney must have been confused by the situation she found herself in, and by the overheard conversations of grown-ups she did not know, using words she could not understand. At the sight of Prinny's familiar figure, she ran across the room and jumped up onto his knee. Lady Horatia was touched by the affection between the two, and saw the Prince as a powerful friend and protector of the little girl for whom she had been able to do so little, and to whom she must very soon say goodbye. She almost certainly did ask the Prince to do all he could to ensure Minney's future well being, but the dramatised version which the Prince gave at a later date, of Lady Horatia begging him to listen to the prayer of a dying mother, and to take a solemn vow to be a father to her child, was coloured by his imagination.

By the end of June, Lady Horatia's condition was rapidly deteriorating and her grieving sisters took her to Clifton, outside Bristol, where the air was better. Maria was planning to go to Brighton in July, but offered to change her plans if Lady Horatia wanted Minney to be near her. Lady Horatia refused the offer, saying again, 'Oh no, pray keep it and do with it as you please and as you have done'.[4] Though grieved to see that her friend was almost certainly dying, Mrs Fitzherbert clung tightly to Minney, and took her with her to join the Prince in Brighton. It was eight years since she had been to Brighton, but she had not been forgotten and a cheering crowd greeted her. On 12 July Lady Horatia died, and in September Lord Hugh died in the West Indies, before the news of his wife's death reached him.

The Seymour children were now orphans, and Lord Hugh's will appointed his executors, Lord Euston (his brother-in-law) and Lord Henry Seymour (his brother), as his children's guardians. All his sons, and his daughter, Horatia, were mentioned by name, but there was no mention of Minney, born after the will had been made. The executors, however, believed their guardianship did extend, by implication, to 'little Mary', and requested that the child be handed over to Lady Waldegrave, one of Horatia's sisters, as soon as convenient.

Maria was devastated. She begged that the little girl be left with her for some time longer, for the child's own sake, until she was of an age to understand what was happening to her. Reluctantly, the guardians agreed to leave Minney where she was until July 1803. This gave Maria time to take advice about her next move. The Prince had no intention of letting Minney be handed over to Lady Waldegrave. He assured Maria that when the time came he would make arrangements with the two executors and that the child would remain with her.

In the meantime, Prime Minister Addington had made a shaky peace with France in 1802. Brighton was now gayer than ever, with visitors coming and going by sea as well as land. Balls and assemblies at the Pavilion had never been so crowded, and the Prince was full of plans for rebuilding on an ever larger scale. Land surrounding the existing Pavilion Gardens had been bought and a new house for Maria had been started. Amid all the gaiety she tried to put aside her fears over Minney. There were many new faces at the Pavilion, but old friends, including Sheridan, continued to come. The days were full of diversion, and the Prince continued to assure her that he would never allow Minney to be taken away.

In February 1803 he wrote to Lord Euston and Lord Henry Seymour saying that the child would suffer terribly if removed from Mrs Fitzherbert, the only mother she had really known; that he, too, had become deeply attached to the child, and that, to secure her future, he would settle £10,000 on her, if she remained in Mrs Fitzherbert's care.[5] Though they replied to the Prince with every courtesy, the executors made it clear that there was no question of leaving their niece with Mrs Fitzherbert beyond the date agreed, and that there was enough family money set aside for the little girl's future. Further, it was pointed out, Mary had many blood relations, aunts and uncles, maternal and paternal and 'of the half blood', all interested in her welfare. This being so it was hardly suitable for Mrs Fitzherbert, 'a stranger in blood', to care for her much longer. Maria was frantic when she heard this reply. So far as she was concerned the child had been entrusted to her care by the mother and father, and it was her duty to go on caring for her, but she hardly knew what to do next. The Prince, with a lifetime's practice of never taking no for an answer, decided to take the matter to court.

He consulted the ex-Chancellor, Lord Thurlow, who in turn advised him to instruct Samuel Romilly, a gifted lawyer who later became Solicitor General. Romilly took the line that the executors' claim to the custody of Minney was unfounded. Lord Hugh Seymour's will appointed them as co-guardians with Lady Horatia in the event of his death and her second marriage. Lord Hugh had made the will before Lady Horatia's illness, at a time when, aware of the dangers of his job, he expected to die first. The situation he envisaged, his own death being followed by his wife's remarriage, was quite different from the one that existed now, even leaving aside the fact that Mary Seymour had not been born when the will was made.[6]

Instead of Minney being handed over to her uncles in July 1803, the case went to court. A bill was filed in the Court of Chancery against Lord Euston and Lord Henry Seymour and their claim to guardianship over Mary Seymour. The case was argued at enormous length and reported in all the papers. London Society watched and waited, agog to know the final outcome. and it became the talk of the town for the *beau monde*, and a source of anguish for Maria.

The Seymour Case was hard fought; both sides sincerely believing they represented the true wishes of Lord Hugh and Lady Horatia, and both equally concerned for Minney's future well-being. Mrs Fitzherbert had made her position clear in a letter to Lord Robert Seymour in 1802:

> I don't presume to doubt Lord Henry's reasons for thinking himself bound in conscience to take my little charge from me. Indeed I never heard what they are ... The child was placed with me by both the parents, in confidence that I should treat it as my own. This confidence I accepted, and had occasion to renew the promise to her poor mother whilst she was sinking fast into her grave ...[7]

In an earlier letter she had made no secret of her attachment to the child:

> I am perfectly certain no person can feel for her as I do or be actuated by such real love and affection as I have for her. I fairly own to you that I am so totally wrapped up and devoted to that dear child that if I lose

her it will almost break my heart. The whole occupation of my life is centred in her.[8]

She also promised to meet any conditions Lord Henry Seymour might make: 'There is no one earthly thing he or any of the family can point out to me that I am not willing to subscribe to, or that I would not do to secure this darling child.'

Minney's uncles believed that they had, by Lord Hugh's will, the moral right to guardianship of all the children, including Mary, and that Lady Horatia had never intended the child to remain with Mrs Fitzherbert permanently. Determined though they were to take the child back, they were not insensitive to the pain they were causing Mrs Fitzherbert, as a letter from Lord Euston to Lord Henry, in November 1801, shows:

Lady Waldegrave has proposed taking care of the two little girls, Horatia and Mary, as soon as it may be convenient to Mrs Fitzherbert to wean herself from the latter, of whom she has at present the care, as she has had ever since the child was born. I am aware that it may be an unpleasant proposal to make to Mrs Fitzherbert, who, I really believe, is much attached to the child, but perhaps it may be fortunate that there is so good a reason for removing her from what hereafter might be thought an improper education.[9]

Four years later Lady Euston wrote to Minney's eldest brother:

being obliged to act with an appearance of harshness towards Mrs Fitzherbert is extremely painful to my feelings ... though I may and must feel for Mrs Fitzherbert I must not allow such feelings to interfere with my duty to any of the children of the the two people I ever had the most reason to love in this world.[10]

The concern of the Seymours was not just that Mary should be brought up by her own family; they wished to rescue the child from the influence of Mrs Fitzherbert's questionable relationship with the Prince of Wales. To grow up in an improper household would damage her morally, and a girl brought out into Society by a lady in Mrs Fitzherbert's uncertain position would find it difficult to make that 'good marriage' on which the future of all young females depended.

Mrs Calvert, an Irish lady, and part of Brighton society at this time, summed up the situation. 'Lord Hugh's family and also Lady Horatia's have objected to her living with Mrs Fitzherbert for many reasons. They very naturally consider the Prince's mistress (for what else can one call her, he having a wife?) not the most respectable protectress.'[11] This was what lay behind Lord Euston's delicate reference to 'what might hereafter be seen as an improper education'. Such an argument was never mentioned in court. It would have caused too much offence to the Prince, and might have raised old questions of the 'Catholic Marriage', which were best avoided.

If Maria herself was aware of this unspoken objection, she gave no sign of it in any surviving letter or reported conversation, and made no mention of it in the account of the case she left with Lord Stourton. The court went into the case in detail. Long affidavits were called for and carefully considered. Perhaps the most interesting and important was Lady Euston's.[12] She had spent a lot of time with her sister in the weeks before her death, and maintained that, though Mrs Fitzherbert had been given charge of the child, Lady Horatia had regretted it afterwards, but loved and pitied her friend too much to demand the child back. There is no reason to doubt Lady Euston's sincerity and truthfulness. Lady Horatia was very ill, in a weak and distressed state, and it is quite likely that she was in two minds about her decision regarding the child. Having promised to leave Minney with her beloved Mrs Fitz, she might easily have doubted the wisdom of the decision when she heard the views of her sister, whom she also loved. It was Maria's return to the Prince which worried both sisters, and, though Lady Euston did not say so, the court was left with the impression that Lady Horatia had thought it unwise to leave her daughter permanently in Mrs Fitzherbert's household.

The Prince's affidavit gave a very different picture.[13] Though made on oath, it is the one most likely to be inaccurate. He claimed that Lady Horatia had nothing but praise for Mrs Fitzherbert and for all she had done for Mary, and that he was asked to listen to the words of a dying mother and to 'solemnly swear to be a Father and Protector to her for life'. It was, he claimed, his willingness to swear this solemn oath which enabled poor Lady Horatia to die in peace. He was almost certainly exaggerating both the manner and the matter of Lady Horatia's last request to him. It is certainly true that she hoped the Prince would take a special interest in Minney, but she had agreed to see him and repair their friendship so that he might give help to her sons as well.

It is unlikely that anyone in court set much store by the Prince's affidavit, and his emotional contribution to Mrs Fitzherbert's case was not helpful. He made no secret of his own great affection for Minney, and some suspected that he not only passionately wanted to be the father of such an enchanting child, but that, in his strange way, he had almost convinced himself he was the father. Spencer Perceval, later to be Prime Minister, appeared for the two guardians. Though careful to acknowledge that 'Mrs Fitzherbert merited everything that could be said in her praise', he went on to add, 'but whatever amiable qualities she might possess, the religion she professed excluded her from the right to retain the custody of a Protestant child'.[14] Sir Samuel Romilly, acting for Mrs Fitzherbert, assured the court that the child's religion would not be influenced by Mrs Fitzherbert's own beliefs. Mrs Fitzherbert had herself gone to great lengths in her affidavit to promise Protestant instruction for Minney. She had already consulted the Bishop of Winchester, who had recommended a London clergyman who was already instructing the child, who would from time to time be examined by the Bishop to ensure that instruction was being properly given. The Bishop's affidavit affirmed that Minney, in so far as anyone of her age could be, was determined to remain faithful to her religion, and was well advanced in knowledge and understanding for one so young. Doctors were called, who spoke of the trauma and danger to health the child would suffer if torn away from Mrs Fitzherbert's care against her will.

The Master in Chancery, however, decided in favour of the guardians. Near to despair, Mrs Fitzherbert appealed to a higher court, where Lord Chancellor Eldon again decided against her. All that was left was an appeal to the House of Lords. The Prince canvassed Mrs Fitzherbert's case shamelessly among the peers, causing angry protests both from the Lords themselves and from Spencer Perceval, and was in danger of damaging Mrs Fitzherbert's chance of success. However, when she called on Lady Hertford to beg for her help, the Prince, unknowingly, became a significant asset to her cause. The second Marquess of Hertford was the eldest of Minney's uncles and head of the Seymour family. His main interest was his collection of fine French furniture, on which he was an expert. He had been kept informed of the various stages of the Seymour Case, but so far had taken no active part. Lady Hertford, a formidable woman, never very popular in London Society, was a committed supporter of the Tories, and may have hoped to become to them what the Duchess of Devonshire was to the Whigs. When Maria sat in her Manchester Square house begging for her help, the Marchioness saw a way of turning the malleable Prince into her friend, and weaning him away from his Whig allegiances. Famously described by Mrs Calvert in 1807 as the 'most forbidding, haughty and unpleasant looking woman', she might not have expressed sympathy for Mrs Fitzherbert, and agreed to persuade Lord Hertford to intervene, had she not seen an advantage for herself. Maria Fitzherbert's gratitude meant little to her, but the gratitude of the Prince of Wales was a different matter, and Lady Hertford agreed to do what she could.

The case came before the House of Lords at the beginning of 1806. The oft-repeated arguments on both sides were heard again for three days, but, before a division was called, Lord Hertford rose and offered to take charge of the child himself. If the Lords agreed, he and his wife would act as her guardians. Relieved at not having to vote on someone else's family dispute, the Lords were pleased to accept this solution. The Seymour clan assumed that he would hand 'poor little Mary' over to Lady Waldegrave, who was all ready to receive her. Great was their disbelief and dismay when they heard that Mrs Fitzherbert was to remain in charge of Minney, with the Hertfords' blessing.

Lady Euston wrote to Minney's brother, and not so kindly this time: 'The prospect for your poor little sister's moral and religious education is a melancholy one ... Mrs Fitzherbert must feel that she will be answerable to us all for any misconduct of your poor little Sister and has in fact (to indulge her own inclinations) run the risk of being called to a very severe account if this child fails in any moral or religious duty'.[15]

The Seymour Case had lasted three years, and caused enormous public interest. Gillray produced one of his best-known cartoons, showing an ample Mrs Fitzherbert flying upwards towards a Catholic altar with Minney Seymour in her arms.[16] When the case was over, Edward Jerningham wrote to Lady Bedingfield:

> I am perfectly glad the Lords have checked the literal application of the law to this cause. It would have been the actual death of the child. She is so fervently and exclusively devoted to Mrs Fitzherbert. And Mrs Fitzherbert having manifested her unequivocal intention of rearing her little orphan

in the Established Doctrine, it would have been a cruel persecution for the Lords to have acted otherwise.[17]

Maria, whose nerves had been shattered by this long drawn out affair, could not find it in her heart to be charitable towards Lady Waldegrave, whom she referred to as 'a horrid creature'. To Lady Hertford she had overwhelming gratitude. Lady Hertford had only to ask, and there was nothing Mrs Fitzherbert would not do in return. The Prince was grateful to the Hertfords as well, and visited Manchester Square to say so, and returned often, ostensibly to consult Lord Hertford about French furniture, but gazing, rumour soon had it, with passionate admiration at the Marchioness.

Tilney Street was in a flurry of letters and callers as all the fine world came to share Maria's relief and joy. An excited Minney could sometimes be seen dancing down the nursery stairs to make her careful little curtsey to the guests, secure in the knowledge that Tilney Street, or any house Mama, as she had called her since Lady Horatia's death, might occupy, would now be her home for ever. One of the first to send congratulations to his 'Ever Dearest Mrs Fitzherbert', was the Duke of Kent, 'Accept then assurance of my best wishes on this, as well as on every occasion', he wrote, adding, 'Pray give my love to your little Angel'.[18]

Maria sent a note to Lord Thurlow's daughter, Mrs Caroline Brown, dated 17 June 1806:

Words cannot do justice to the happiness I enjoy at the thought of my darling child secured to me, after the long series of misery and anxiety I have endured. The good news of my having gained my case so completely so over set me that I have scarce been myself ever since ... thank your dear Father from me a million times, and tell him I shall not feel my happiness complete till I and my child in person make our acknowledgements and bless him for all the interest he has taken ... excuse this hurried scrawl, as I have a hundred notes and letters to write. God Bless you.[19]

When her last letter was written and her last call paid, an exhausted Maria set out with Minney for a stay in Brighton. She was within a few weeks of her fiftieth birthday, and her health, never robust, had been affected by the years of 'misery and anxiety' while the Seymour Case dragged on. There had been other problems to face as well during these

years, and, looking back over all that had happened, she may have wondered how she had coped with so much and still behaved as calmly as
she did. Mrs Calvert, intrigued by Mrs Fitzherbert, had observed her
closely when in Brighton, and had noted a few cracks in her composure
on Pavilion evenings, writing in the summer of 1804:

> Her manners are good-humoured (though I think I can at times discern
> a look of ill-temper glide across her countenance), unaffected and pleas-
> ing but very absent and I often have thought she was not happy, for she
> heaves such deep sighs sometimes in one of those fits of absence that I
> have actually started. There does not seem to me to be any brilliancy about
> Mrs Fitzherbert no powers of captivation, but captivation there must be
> about her, though I don't perceive it, as she has captivated His Royal
> Highness for so many years.

Arriving in London Society too late to have heard the gossip of 1786,
Mrs Calvert had always thought Mrs Fitzherbert's position odd. 'She
lives in a house communicating with the Pavilion till one she is building is finished. She lives entirely with the Prince and in a manner does
the honours of his house', she had noted in puzzlement. She went on to
describe Mrs Fitzherbert as she appeared then:

> She is now, I believe, about fifty, very fat but with a charming counte-
> nance, her features are beautiful, except her mouth which is ugly, having
> a set of not good false teeth, but her person is too fat, and she makes a dis-
> play of a very white but not prettily formed bosom which I often long to
> throw a handkerchief over.[20]

Mrs Calvert was mistaken about the false teeth: but even Mrs Fitzherbert's admirers could not deny that she was too plump to be
fashionable. The cartoonists had always exaggerated her size, especially
the cruel *Brighton Breakfast: or Morning Comfort*, appearing in *Fashionable Follies* in 1802, showing a gross Mrs Fitzherbert eating a substantial
breakfast and drinking brandy. Mrs Fitzherbert had not appeared to
worry about putting on weight, but there had been plenty of other
things, in addition to the threat of losing Minney, to make her sigh and
look 'absent'.

The Prince, though unfailingly supportive during the Seymour Case,
had become less 'captivated'. He had had several lovers during those
years: the dancer Louise Hilliston, the French wife of the second Earl of

Massareene, and a Madame de Meyer whom he had established in an apartment in Duke Street. He had accepted the paternity of the sons of Mrs Crewe, Mrs Davies and Elizabeth Crote. Maria had not been in total ignorance of all this, and, though choosing to ignore his *petits amours*, the thought of these women and their babies might well have caused that look of unhappiness that had made Mrs Calvert wonder.

Mrs Calvert was not the only newcomer to know nothing about the talk of a marriage that had once buzzed all over London. Elisabeth Vigée-Le Brun, though received in all the best houses between 1802 and 1805, had heard nothing to suggest that Maria was the Prince's wife. A gifted portrait painter (and a beautiful woman),[21] Madame Vigée-Le Brun had arrived in London following the Peace of Amiens, and had stayed on after the peace ended in 1803, meeting the Prince several times. Her memoirs give the garbled version of the Prince's relationship with Maria picked up in the London drawing rooms:

> As he had been the the most handsome man in the three kingdoms, he still saw himself as the darling of the ladies. His first Mistress was a Mrs Robinson; then, a little while later he had a more serious affair with Mrs Fitzherbert, who was older than the Prince and a widow, but extremely beautiful. His passion for her was so great that there was a moment when everyone feared he would indeed marry this woman, who was a daughter of one of the first Catholic families of Ireland. Her natural inconsistency retrieved this potentially dangerous situation and many women have since followed in the footsteps of Mrs Fitzherbert.

A strange version of the story; but she went on to note what she had observed for herself:

> A little before my departure I painted the portrait of the Prince of Wales, I depicted him full length and in uniform ... As soon as the portrait was finished, the Prince gave it to his old friend Mrs Fitzherbert, she, in turn, placed it in a portable frame, as they do with the larger dressing mirrors, so that she could wheel it into whatever room she happened to be in; I thought this very ingenious of her.[22]

It is possible that the Prince had given Madame Vigée-Le Brun the impression that he and Maria were just old friends. This version suited the needs of a Regent-in-waiting better than the earlier talk of a Catholic wife. Perhaps Maria had sensed a shift in the Prince's attitude, but she loved the Vigée-Le Brun portrait of him, which, much later, she gave to Minney.

The new house mentioned by Mrs Calvert was being built on land adjoining the Pavilion estate, bought by Maria in 1803. William Pordon, the Prince's architect, had begun to build a mansion 'in the Egyptian style', but it had been destroyed in storms the following year. Maria's distress at this misfortune is easily imagined, but Pordon had soon designed and built a second house on the same site. Facing the Steine, the open area used as a promenade, and separated from it by a small strip of garden, the new house had been planned with large south-facing windows giving onto a covered veranda on the ground floor and small balconies at the upper windows, all with views of the sea. The entrance was at the side and led to ground floor reception rooms, a double staircase leading to the drawing rooms and Maria's bedroom and boudoir, with a number of other rooms above and at the back. After its completion in 1806, Lady Jerningham described it as 'a beautiful little residence'.[23]

When the Seymour Case went to court in 1803, Addington's peace with France had just ended, and for the next few years the fear of invasion by Napoleon's Grand Army was very real. Of a worrying disposition, whenever in Brighton Maria's eyes had searched the horizon for the black shapes of French warships as nervously as anyone's, knowing the Prince would be among the first to be targeted if Napoleon's army landed. The Prince had been desperate for high military command. With troop carriers gathering along the French coast, and Napoleon crying 'Let us be masters of the Channel for six hours and we will be masters of the world', it was ludicrous, he raged, and humiliating, for the Prince of Wales to be a mere Colonel of the 10th Hussars. Letter after letter had been sent to his father. The King had explained that, if an invasion took place, he would expect his eldest son to ride at his side to meet the French, but that it was not appropriate for the heir to the throne to have a military command. The King had become so exasperated by the endless pleading that he had threatened to take the Prince's regiment away from him if he didn't forget the matter.

The Prince refused to forget: he wanted the people to know that he was willing to go to war for them, wanting more than anything to regain his long lost popularity. Hoping to achieve both, he had published his correspondence with his father for everyone to read. *The Times*, always against the Prince, had refused to have anything to do with the letters, but the full correspondence had appeared in the *Morning Chronicle*, the *Morning Herald* and the *Sun* on 7 December 1803. The King was outraged, repeating in disbelief, 'He has published my letters!' The newspaper-reading public had simply been amused. The episode had done the Prince no good, but had caused a deep rift between him and his father. This grieved Maria more than it did the Prince. Ever since their reunion in 1800, she had kept in touch with the royal family through the Dukes of York and Kent, but there was nothing she had been able do to heal this bitterness between father and son.

In January 1804 the Prince had fallen ill with another of the violent episodes of pain and fever which punctuated his adult life. He was feared to be dying, and surgeons had been rushed from London to Brighton. Maria had moved into the Pavilion, Glenbervie noting in his diary, 'Mrs Fitzherbert, contrary to her rule, took up her lodgings at the Pavilion in order that she might be nearer the Prince, and she nursed him night and day with unremitting devotion'.[24] For forty-eight hours his life had hung in the balance, but a change for the better followed quickly, and Sheridan was able to write to his wife, 'the Prince has just recovered from an illness in which his life was despaired of for two days ...'[25]

Maria, who acted as go-between for the Prince and the royal family during these years, passed on the good news to the Duke of Kent, who replied on 4 February, showing how they depended on her for news of the Prince:

> I cannot find words sufficient to express the joy I derived from your most kind letter of last evening by which I have received so comfortable an account of the dear Prince. It has relieved me from an immense weight, as yesterday I must confess I felt quite broken-hearted about him. Pray say everything most affectionate from me and that nothing could be more kind than the intent expressed both by the Queen and all our sisters about him.[26]

10

Lady Hertford

The King had been taken ill again in 1804, all his old symptoms returning, and Malmesbury believing him 'in immense danger'. The Prince
had begun to hope, once more, for crown or regency, and his friends
for political power. Charles James Fox had been in town and Creevey
had commented that the Prince 'loaded Fox with caresses'. But by the
end of March the King had recovered sufficiently to resume, in a limited way, his royal duties, robbing the Prince of his hopes and leaving
him with little to do but plan his social arrangements for the London
and Brighton Seasons.

His Brighton entertainments followed a regular pattern. Guests were
summoned to dine at the Pavilion, usually about eight or ten men, and
one lady to keep Maria company. Later, other guests would arrive for
cards, music and whatever entertainments the Prince had planned. The
temperature in the Pavilion had always been kept much too high for
comfort, Sheridan being heard to say that this was just as well as it prepared them all for the place they must occupy in the next world. Maria
and all the ladies found it trying, Mrs Creevey writing to her husband
in 1805, 'My head is very bad, I suppose with the heat of the Pavilion last
night. We were there before Mrs Fitzherbert came and it almost made
her faint, but she put on no airs to be interesting and soon recovered'.[1]

Sheridan was still playing his practical jokes at the Pavilion as if he
were a boy, not a man of fifty-five. He had begun to drink more than
ever, and had perhaps lost some favour with Maria as a result. But she
had been amused when, disguised as a constable, he had come into the
room to arrest the dowager Lady Sefton for playing illegal games. And
she had laughed with everyone else when, the room in darkness for a
phantasmagoria show, Sheridan had sat on the knee of a Russian guest,
Madame Grebotzoff, and remained there, even though the lady had
'made enough row for the whole town to hear'.

The Prince celebrated his forty-third birthday in Brighton in 1805 with an ox roasted on the Steine for the people and entertainments for his guests until the early hours. According to a local paper:

> Soon after six His Royal Highness in his carriage left the Pavilion to dine with the Marchioness of Downshire at Westfield Lodge ... The dinner was of the most brilliant and inviting description. About nine o'clock the Prince, the Marchioness and the whole of her guests removed to the Pavilion where a most splendid entertainment, consisting of a Ball and a supper was given by the Prince.[2]

Minney had had her own share of festivities, reported in the same paper, 'On the night following ... the little interesting protégée of Mrs Fitzherbert, Miss Seymour, gave a ball and supper to a party of juvenile nobility at the Pavilion'.

Though popular in Brighton, Maria had been persistently blamed by Londoners during these years for the Prince's treatment of the Princess of Wales, to whom they remained devoted. The Princess had left Carlton House in 1801, moving to a house in Blackheath, where she had begun to live in what was seen by Society as an improper manner, enjoying the company of a strange mixture of friends, most of them men, and gaining a very doubtful reputation. It had been decided that Princess Charlotte should live in Carlton House, or in one of the houses nearby, when her father was in town, and join her grandparents whenever he left London. The Prince had never shown her the love he showered on Minney, and her childhood had not been happy. Her governess in these early years of the century had been the Dowager Lady de Clifford, one of Maria's friends, and for a time Maria had seen Princess Charlotte rather more often than her mother did. The lonely child had one day flung her arms round Maria begging her to ask her father to receive her with greater kindness. Maria later told Lord Stourton that she 'could not help weeping with this interesting child'. Any child who came into Maria's life was assured of affection and concern.

During 1805 a friendship had grown up between Maria and Mrs Creevey, wife of the Whig MP. When news of the Battle of Trafalgar reached the Pavilion in November of that year Maria had sent her a note:

> Dear Madam, The Prince has this moment received an account from the

Admiralty of the death of poor Lord Nelson, which has affected him most extremely. I think you may wish to know the news, which upon any other occasion might be called a glorious victory – twenty of three and thirty of the enemy's fleet being entirely destroyed – no English ship being taken or sunk ... Poor Lord Nelson received his death by a shot of a musket from the enemy's ship upon his shoulder and expired two hours after, but not till the ship was struck and afterwards sunk, which he had the consolation of hearing, as well as his complete victory before he died. Excuse this hurried scrawl. I am so nervous I scarcely can hold my pen. God bless you.[3]

Mrs Creevey called on Maria two days later, and wrote to her husband:

The first of my visits this morning was to my Mistress ... I found her alone and ... she gave me an account of the Prince's grief about Lord Nelson and then entered into the domestic failing of the latter in a way infinitely creditable to her and skilful too. She was all for Lady Nelson and against Lady Hamilton, who, she said (hero as he was) overpowered him and took possession of him quite by force. But she ended in a natural good way by saying: 'Poor creature! I am sorry for her now, for I suppose she is in grief.'[4]

Creevey, though a Whig, did not approve of the Devonshire House set, and Mrs Creevey had passed on Maria's view:

there her opinions are all precisely mine and yours and what is better, she says they are now the Prince's; that he knows everything – above all, how money is made by promises, unauthorized by him, in the event of his having power: that he knows how his character is involved in various transactions in that House and that he only goes into it from motives of compassion and old friendship when he is persecuted to do so. In short, he tells Mrs Fitzherbert all he sees and hears, shows her all the Duchess's letters and notes and she says she knows the Duchess hates her.[5]

The Duchess had always included Maria among the guests at both Devonshire House and Chatsworth, but there was an understandable element of jealousy on both sides. It is most unlikely that Georgiana, Duchess of Devonshire was ever the Prince's mistress but they had been close friends, addressing each other as 'sister' and 'brother', for years. He had always gone to her for advice, and she was one of the few who dared to give it honestly. Passionately interested in politics, she was awaiting the Prince's coming to power with an eagerness that matched his own. But she had begun to suspect a certain 'unsteadiness' in the Prince where allegiance to the Whigs was concerned, and feared that Mrs Fitzherbert could still cost the Whigs their return to government. The comments on money are harder to explain. The Duchess had been deep in debt for some time due to an uncontrollable gambling habit, and she had often asked the Prince for loans, which he had been happy to give when he could. Perhaps she had used the Prince's name to quieten some of her more threatening creditors. Perhaps the Prince had told her she could. Saying one thing to the Duchess and another to Mrs Fitzherbert would have come naturally to him, and the latter's information about Devonshire House may not have been accurate if it had come from the Prince.

Mrs Fitzherbert, rather isolated in society, and sometimes lacking a close woman friend to talk to and confide in, had become fond of Mrs Creevey and had, apparently, confided something of her life to her, Mrs Creevey had once again told her husband:

> Mrs Fitzherbert came before 12 and has literally only this moment left me. We have been all the time alone and she has been confidential to a degree that almost frightened me ... telling me the history of her life and dwelling more particularly on the explanation of all her feelings and conduct towards the Prince. If she is as true as I think she is wise, she is an extraordinary person and most worthy to be beloved.[6]

What had Maria said? Having kept silent for so long, perhaps she felt the need to hint that her long relationship with the Prince had been both more special, and more respectable, than many supposed. But even so, her 'history' must have been carefully edited, for the Prince's sake, if for no other reason. Mrs Creevey possibly made her letters as dramatic as possible. She did not always exaggerate, however, and recorded, also in 1805, a conversation between herself and Mrs Fitzherbert which reads like unadorned reporting, and echoes hauntingly down the years:

> We talked of her life being written. She said she supposed it would sometime or other but with thousands of lies: but she would be dead and it would not signify. I urged her to write it herself but she said it would break her heart.[7]

In January 1806, an unexpected event had brought the Prince back to politics once again. William Pitt, who had become Prime Minister again in 1804, suddenly died. He had held office for seventeen years, but was mourned only by the few who knew him well. These had not included Mrs Fitzherbert, who had seen him as the Prince's enemy. Among Pitt's political opponents only Charles James Fox had grieved sincerely. The House would never be the same, he had said: 'I think I will pair with Pitt'. Pitt's government had been replaced by a coalition, the 'Ministry of All the Talents', and the King had accepted Fox as a Minister. Both Prince and Duchess had rejoiced. But in March, after an agonising illness, Georgiana, Duchess of Devonshire died. All Society mourned the passionate and talented woman who had charmed them for so long. 'The most amiable and best bred woman in England is gone', had been the Prince's public memorial to her, and in private he had wept for the loss of a friend. Maria would never have wanted Georgiana Devonshire to suffer as she had, nor wished her to die at only forty-three, but she was not able to share the Prince's great grief.

By May of that year, Princess Caroline's life had become even more notorious. Lady Douglas had claimed that a child living in the Blackheath house was the Princess's son, and that Caroline herself had confided this to Lady Douglas. For a Princess of Wales, this was a desperately serious accusation and the King had felt obliged to have it investigated. A committee of Privy Councillors had been set up to do so. The proceedings, known as the 'Delicate Investigation', had filled the Prince with hope of a divorce, freeing him from 'the Fiend' for ever. Maria had always been careful never to comment on the Princess of Wales; she did not do so now. Caroline, likewise, had never spoken ill of her husband's first wife, her lady-in-waiting, Lady Charlotte Bury, noting, 'The Princess of Wales speaks highly of Mrs Fitzherbert. She always says: "that she is the Prince's true wife. She is an excellent woman"'.[8] But Maria, like many excellent women, was shocked by loose behaviour, and the Princess of Wales's behaviour had become very loose indeed.

On 1 June 1806, Fox had risen in the House to propose the Abolition of the African Slave Trade. He carried the day by 114 votes to 15. This had been his greatest moment, the one of which he was most proud. It was on the same day that the Lords had begun debating the Seymour Case, and four days later Mrs Fitzherbert had won the charge of her 'darling child'. Both had been well pleased. But Fox's strength was running out, and Maria was soon to find there was a price to pay for her joy.

Lady Jerningham wrote to her daughter from Brighton in August 1806, describing the Season there as she found it:

> On Sunday last, after I had closed my letter to you, arrived on foot Mrs Fitzherbert and little Miss Seymour, a pretty child not quite eight years old and a little taller than Agnes. Mrs Fitzherbert was very pleasing and conversable, and said she imputed her late ill health to the uneasiness she had undergone for this little girl; that she was particularly fond of children, and should have liked to have had a dozen of her own.

Later she added:

> About eight o'clock I had a note from her [Mrs Fitzherbert] saying she was ordered by the Prince to desire we would go that evening to the Pavilion, so we put ourselves immediately in proper attire and went at ten o'clock the usual hour. It is really not to be described how amiably polite and fascinating his manners are – on his own ground ... On Pavilion nights, two rooms are open, there are card tables in the long room, and the Prince's band of German musicians playing in the next ... Mrs Fitzherbert usually is at cards ... the other ladies walk about or converse softly.[9]

The Prince's birthday festivities that year, on 12 August, were reported by the *Sussex Weekly Advertiser:*

> This being the natal day of the Heir Apparent, the morning was ushered in by the ringing of bells and the flag was hoisted on the tower of the Church ... At half past twelve the Prince of Wales, habited as a Field Marshal, a star at his breast, accompanied by his royal brothers and mounted on a grey charger, splendidly caparisoned, left the Pavilion for the Downs where ... Regiments were drawn up in line ... Lady Haggerston and Miss Seymour, the Lord Chancellor, Lord Headfort, Mr Sheridan and Mr Smythe were in the Prince's Landau. Mrs Fitzherbert was detained at home by indisposition.[10]

Nothing significant should be read into the last statement. There was no suggestion of a serious illness, still less of a quarrel between her and the Prince. All other sources suggest their summer in Brighton was idyllic.

But there was more to life than seaside summers and their problems had not gone away. The publicity given to the Seymour Case had fanned anti-Catholic feeling. The cartoon showing Mrs Fitzherbert rising to heaven with Minney in her arms was reprinted, with Minney replaced by Charlotte, implying that she hoped to turn the Prince's heir into a Catholic.

The result of the 'Delicate Investigation' had cleared the Princess of Wales of the worst charges against her. The claim that the boy in her household was her son was dismissed through lack of proof, and, though she was found guilty of extremely indecorous and loose behaviour, no grounds for a divorce, which might have changed Maria's position in some eyes, were proven. The Prince was outraged, but the Princess's popularity with the people did not diminish. They regarded her sexual vagaries as no worse, even if as bad, as his.

Maria had learned to ignore cartoons, but the pamphlet published by Nathaniel Jefferys, the Prince's jeweller, could not be ignored. When Maria had run into debt the Prince, being financially embarrassed himself, had borrowed £1600 from Jefferys, later taking Maria to thank him in person. Jefferys claimed she wore an expression of 'mortified pride' and showed insufficient gratitude. He also complained that the Prince's failure to pay his bills had ruined his business, though others said that Jefferys had made a large profit from the Prince's custom. Most of his accusations against Maria were unjustified. He claimed she was responsible for the Prince's treatment of the Princess of Wales and for the breakdown of their marriage, which was not true. But it was his strong hints that she was married to the Prince herself, which of course was true, that posed the greatest danger. He maintained that 'She a third time entered into the married state, according to the ceremonies of the Romish Church with an Illustrious Personage of the Protestant Religion: for this reason the marriage was kept secret'.[11]

London booksellers refused to handle the pamphlet, and Edward Jerningham wrote in her defence: 'The Pamphlet is a libel and can make no impression but upon the minds that are actuated by a malignant disposition'.[12] Jefferys then wrote a public letter, addressed to Mrs Fitzherbert, making further accusations. The public, he claimed, felt disgust when they saw that she was treated like a Queen while the Princess of Wales was snubbed, and that their taxes supported her extravagance. He added that:

When the Prince of Wales was married to the Princess it was agreed that you should retire from that intimacy of friendship you had so long enjoyed, and your houses in Pall Mall and at Brighton were given up accordingly. Yet viewed in a retrospective light, the necessity of such a retreat (accompanied as it was by a pension of several thousands per annum ... and a retention of very valuable plate, jewels, etc., given to you by the Prince) did not, in the opinion of the world, add much good fame to your reputation.

He went on to maintain that, with her 'intimacy' now resumed, she lived on a still more extravagant scale:

> A noble house in Park Lane, most magnificently fitted up, and superbly furnished; a large retinue of servants; carriages of various descriptions ... your separate residence at Brighton; and the Prince more frequently in your society than ever. When, Madam, your friends pretend that your feelings are hurt, let me ask you (and them) if you think the people of moral character in this country have no feelings! I am sure they must relinquish all claim to any, if they could view with indifference, such a departure from decency as this conduct exhibits in you.[13]

Letters defending Maria and calling Jefferys a misinformed liar, appeared immediately, but she felt her good name had been tarnished.

She and Minney remained in Brighton throughout the summer, and in September the Prince left for an extended tour of the north of England. It was while staying with the Staffords that he learned Charles James Fox had died on 13 September 1806. He wrote to Fox's nephew, saying his tears flowed so fast he could not see what he was writing,[14] and for once he was not exaggerating. He went immediately into black clothes, hardly ate, and gave up drinking. He cut short his visits and returned to London. Maria was once again in an unhappy situation. Charles James Fox, like the Duchess of Devonshire, had never been her friend; avoiding his company, she had not seen enough of him to be aware of his charm, wit and ability. Now she had to leave those who had loved him to mourn with the Prince, grown thinner and old-looking in his grief.

The year 1807 started badly for Maria. On 26 January her mother died. Mother and daughter had been close, and in the many uncertainties of her life she had always confided in her, and received in return a love and understanding she would now have to live without. In February the unpopularity of both the Prince and Maria, and the anger of the London mob, caused the Duke of Carlisle to write to the Prince:

> Though I do not only believe, but know, how innocent Mrs Fitzherbert is of all that may be imputed to her ... yet I solemnly declare I consider her

situation as becoming more perilous. Measuring, as I fancy I do, the feelings and dispositions of many of the lower classes of the people, I hardly
doubt that, with half the mischievous ability of a Lord George Gordon,
Mrs Fitzherbert might at any hour be liable to insult and danger not only
in the streets, but also in her own house.[15]

Maria knew her situation was 'perilous'. She had not forgotten Lord
George Gordon. The 'Ministry of All the Talents' had fallen, and
Spencer Perceval, who had led against her in the Seymour Case, was
now part of a Tory government which she distrusted. She destroyed the
papal document regarding her return to the Prince and cut the signatures of her uncle and brother out of her marriage certificate.

On the 5 June, she gave what was to be the last of her large assemblies, Mrs Calvert recording in her diary, 'My sister and I went late to
an Assembly at Mrs Fitzherbert's where were all the Fine World'. On 25
July she recorded what 'all the Fine World' was beginning to notice.
'Last night we went to a ball at Lady Headfort's. The Prince was in high
spirits and looks better. I think poor Mrs Fitzherbert much deserted by
him now. He has taken it into his head to fall desperately in love with
Lady Hertford ...' In Brighton, later that year, she continued to note
Lady Hertford's ascendancy in the Prince's affections: 'The Prince and
Mrs Fitzherbert are expected here either today or tomorrow ... The
Prince going to Cheltenham to be near his beloved Lady Hertford. Alas
poor Mrs Fitzherbert!'[16]

Ragley Hall, the country seat of the Hertfords, was a short journey
from Cheltenham. The Prince did stay in Brighton long enough, however, to celebrate his forty-fifth birthday, and returned to Brighton in
November for Minney's birthday, as the *Sussex Weekly Advertiser*
reported, 'The Prince arrived here in order we understand to celebrate
the birthday of the Hon. Miss Seymour the interesting protégée of Mrs
Fitzherbert'.[17] Minney was now the main link between the Prince and
Maria as it became more and more clear that Lady Hertford dominated
his thoughts and emotions.

Lady Euston, who in spite of losing Minney to her, never held any
grudge against Maria, wrote to Sir George Seymour:

I know not what Mrs Fitzherbert does in all these confusions as the World
says it is all owing to Lady Hertford's influence that the Prince is put in a

way to become a good Boy ... Mrs Fitzherbert looks remarkably well but she appears in public in an odd situation having few people to converse with, the Prince often not speaking to her at all and at other times she appears indignant with him when he does.[18]

If invited to dine with the Prince, Lady Hertford insisted that Maria be there too, to avoid any gossip. The Prince still visited her in Tilney Street, but largely to have the pleasure of seeing Minney, who was happily unaware that anything was amiss between Prinny and Mama. When in Brighton, Lady Hertford now occupied a house next door to the Pavilion, but, again, only dined with the Prince if Maria was present, acting as a reluctant chaperone. Years later, when Maria dictated her memoirs to Lord Stourton, she remembered the pain of these evenings:

> Lady Hertford, anxious for the preservation of her own reputation, which she was not willing to compromise with the public even when she ruled the Prince with the most absolute sway, exposed Mrs Fitzherbert at this time to very severe trials, which at last almost, as she said, ruined her health and destroyed her nerves.[19]

In addition to the humiliation by Lady Hertford and the insults of Jefferys, Maria was hurt in other ways. Her Fitzherbert sister-in-law, Barbara, had died leaving an only daughter, Mary. When the girl's convent education had finished, Maria, her godmother as well as her aunt by marriage, offered to introduce her into English Society. Barbara's grand-daughter, recounted the story:

> When she [her mother] was seventeen years old her godmother wished to take charge of her and present her in society, but this intention was frustrated. Her father who had been for long a *détenu* at Verdun and without means of ascertaining how far the reports, unfavourable to Mrs Fitzherbert's character, which casually reached him while in durance, were true, preferred to accept his brother's title-tattle version and forbade all intercourse between his young daughter and her aunt.[20]

Maria had kept in touch with the Fitzherbert family, and had genuinely wanted to help Barbara's daughter. It was one of the many hurtful episodes in a year full of distress. But nothing in the world could hurt her as much as the Prince's total defection to Lady Hertford.

Lady Hertford had not expected the Prince to fall 'desperately in love'. She wished to gain influence over him, and coax him away from the

Whigs towards the Tories, but his display of passion took her by surprise. Mindful of her reputation, she refused all his amorous advances, reducing him to fits of weeping and depression. Thomas Creevey observed, 'When he was first in love with Lady Hertford, I have seen tears run down his cheeks at dinner and he was dumb for hours'.[21] The Prince became ill, constantly demanding to be bled, until reduced to a weak and pathetic state, and wrote passionate, tear-stained letters begging her to come to him, Lord Holland observing: 'Those ... who had made a study of his gallantries, recognised his usual system of love-making in these symptoms. He generally it seems, assailed the hearts which he wished to carry by exciting their commiseration for his suffering and their apprehension for his health'.[22] When Lady Hertford was out of town his letters became longer and more desperate, just as his letters to Maria had once done. Lady Bessborough, Georgiana Devonshire's sister, commented, 'He writes day and night almost and frets himself into a fever ...' His letters were often ignored by Lady Hertford. Longing for sympathy, and apparently not knowing what he was doing or saying, he went one night to Lady Bessborough, who wrote to her lover, Lord Granville Leveson Gower:

> I really believe that his father's malady extends to him, only it takes another turn ... such a scene I never went through. He threw himself on his knees, and clasping me round, kissed my neck before I was aware of what he was doing. I screamed with vexation and fright; he continued, sometimes struggling with me, sometimes sobbing and crying ... then over and over and over again the same round of complaint, despair, entreaties and promises ... and attempting some liberty, that really G. had not my heart been breaking, I must have laughed out at the comicality ... of that immense, grotesque figure flouncing about half on the couch and half on the ground.[23]

Lady Bessborough had known the Prince when he was young and was grieved to see him in such a state. The town was buzzing with gossip over this latest grand passion, and sympathy for Mrs Fitzherbert was on everyone's lips. It must be hoped she knew as little as possible about the Prince's ludicrous behaviour, arising from a passionate love she once thought was only for her. The Prince dreaded displeasing Lady Hertford, as Lord Stourton later recorded: 'When at Brighton the Prince, who had passed the mornings with Mrs Fitzherbert on friendly terms at her own house, did not even notice her in the slightest at the Pavilion the same evening, and she afterwards understood that these attentions would have been reported to her rival.'[24] She was not in a position to complain as her attendance at the Pavilion was 'extorted by the menace of taking away her child'. The Hertfords, as Minney's legal guardians, could remove her at any time.

When, in spite of this, she began to talk of obtaining a separation from the Prince, the Duke of York, acting for the family, dissuaded her. According to Lord Stourton, 'She was frequently on the point of sepa-ration ... but was prevented by the influence of the Royal Family'. They believed the Prince still needed her calming influence.

In addition to all this, Maria was in financial difficulties, writing to the Prince in 1808:

> Not withstanding every precaution on my part Mr Pordon has thought proper to outrun the estimate he undertook to build my house at Brighton to the amount of near £300. It is a peculiar hard case, as I had scraped every farthing I could collect, and had frequently deprived myself of many comforts to enable me to pay him the sum he asked to build my house, which, to the amount of £6000 – the price he undertook it for – was paid to him before I ever took possession of my habitation ... I had piqued myself that neither my House in Town or at Brighton had ever cost you one farthing.

He had, she reminded him, 'voluntarily and unsolicited pledged your-self, not only to Mr Errington but several others, from the beginning of my acquaintance with you, to give me an income of £10,000 per annum, instead of which, till very lately, I have subsisted upon an allowance of £3000, now increased to £5000'. But she was quick to add that she did not blame him:

> I mean no reproaches to you sir, for not having kept your word, for I should have felt more gratified and happy giving up to Y.H. what I had than in receiving the sum alluded to, could it on any occasion have con-tributed in the smallest degree to your comfort ... I would rather have lived in beggary than to have distressed you, or by any mean dirty tricks have taken advantage of you ... which I know I might easily have done had I been disposed.

Returning to Pordon, she continued: 'I know that it is quite impossible for me to pay Mr Pordon ... It is no debt of extravagant folly, but a circumstance that will happen now and then – that of being deceived by those we place confidence in.'

In July, anxious both to economise, and to escape from London where she felt threatened, Maria had bought the lease of a house at Parsons Green, and she ended the letter by explaining: 'Several of my friends have with the greatest generosity and kindness assisted me to procure the place above mentioned, which I am sure I shall find great comfort to myself and advantage to my child, which has been the primary object of a small place in the country, and being so near Town she will have the same advantage as if in London'.[25] No reply to this letter has survived, but the extra £300 was paid and Maria spared further embarrassment.

It is unlikely that the Royal Dukes were among the friends who helped to buy to the Parsons Green house. They were nearly always in debt themselves, and looked to her for sympathy over their many troubles. The Duke of York was in serious trouble. His current mistress, Mary Anne Clarke, had been making money for herself by taking what amounted to bribes in return for recommending men for commissions. It was suspected that the Duke had shared the profits. He denied all knowledge of it, and was eventually found not guilty, but, nevertheless, had to resign as the army's Commander in Chief. This was bad news for the army as well as for the Duke, as he was good at his job. Maria's sympathy was real; though found innocent, there were those who thought him guilty, and she knew what it felt like to be unjustly, and publicly, accused.

The same year, 1809, Maria's patience with the Prince ran out. Mr Bloomfield, the Prince's Secretary had been intolerably rude to her at the Pavilion one evening. On 18 December she wrote:

> I trust your Royal Highness will permit me to explain the reasons why I could not possibly accept the honour of your invitation to the Pavilion for yesterday and for this evening. The very great incivilities I have received these two years just because I obeyed your orders in going there was too visible to everyone present and too poignantly felt by me to admit of my putting myself in a situation of again being treated with such indignity, for, whatever may be thought of me by some individuals it is well known your Highness four and twenty years ago placed me in a situation so nearly connected with your own that I have a claim upon you for your

protection. I feel I owe it to myself not to be insulted under your roof with impunity. The influence you are now under and the conduct of one of your servants I am sorry to say has the appearance of your sanction and support, and renders my situation in your house, situated as I am, impossible any more to submit to. Something is due to my character and conduct, both of which will bear the strictest character scrutiny particularly with regard to everything that concerns Your Royal Highness, for after all that has passed between Your Royal Highness and myself I did not think human nature could have borne what I have had to undergo.

Her final words were of Minney, 'The disappointment to my dear little girl mortifies me very much'.[26] The Prince replied the next day, but with a mildly pained air, as if he were the injured party: 'In whatever time, my dear Maria, that you may be pleased to write to me or in whatever way you may think proper to act by me, deeply as I may feel and lament it yet that never can nor shall make me deviate from or forget those affectionate feelings I have ever entertained for you ...'[27] No apology, no begging for pardon, no plea for for reconciliation as in the past. The rest of the letter was about Minney and how his feelings for 'the dear Child' would never alter.

The Prince's unpopularity was thrown into sharp contrast with the affection felt for his father when the King celebrated his Jubilee on 25 October 1810. Fêtes, fireworks and illuminations were held all over the country, and vast London crowds turned out to cheer the 'Father of the Nation'. The King's pleasure in the celebrations ended abruptly a few weeks later when he learned that Amelia, his youngest and favourite child, had not long to live. The Prince of Wales, who could still behave well when it suited him, visited Amelia daily towards the end, and was her greatest comfort. To her, he was the 'Dear Angelic Brother', her 'Beloved *eau de miel*', and his regular visits were her 'greatest happiness'. She died in November, leaving everything she had, which was not much, to General Charles Fitzroy, one of the King's equerries with whom she was deeply in love. This was a potentially embarrassing situation for the royal family, but according to Lady Holland, 'The Prince behaved throughout with the greatest tenderness ... with the utmost circumspection'.[28] The Prince was often at his best with his sisters, all of whom loved him.

The King could not accept that Amelia was dead, and before long all the now familiar symptoms returned and the doctors were called in. They hoped he would recover physically, but knew he could not continue to act as King. In December Spencer Perceval, now Prime Minister, felt it was time to bring Pitt's Regency Bill before the House. When visiting the King in one of his lucid moments, he told him that arrangements for a regency were being made, and the King agreed it was for the best. The Prince of Wales, aged forty-eight, would be Regent at last.

11

The Prince Regent

The news soon spread to Brighton but Mrs Fitzherbert stayed in her house on the Steine, not expecting any change in her circumstances from the coming of a Regency. Long gone were the heady days of 1785, when an ardent young Prince had promised to repeal the Royal Marriages Act, and even the Act of Settlement, and announce their marriage to the world when he came to power. He had forgotten those rash promises, and thought it quite reasonable, in 1811, to cast Mrs Fitzherbert in the role of 'old friend'.

To her great surprise, however, the Prince called her to London. As her coach bowled along the familiar London road, she may have wondered if, after all, her long and chequered relationship with the Prince might have a new beginning with this Regency. If so, hope vanished on arrival. According to Lord Stourton, 'He told her that he had sent for her to ask her opinion, and that he demanded it from her, with regard to the party to which he was about, as Regent, to confide the administration of the country'. She reminded him that the Whigs were his friends of many years and 'urged him in the most forcible manner' to stay with them. 'Only retain them, Sir, six weeks, if you please, you may find some pretext to dismiss them, at the end of that time; but do not break with them without some pretext or other'.[1]

The Prince's position was more complicated than she realised. The King had agreed to a Regency but had not abdicated. The Queen was reporting daily improvement in his condition, and, should he find his son had called the Whigs to government, he might still return to the exercise of power. But if he saw his own ministers retained, and policies continuing as before, he was likely to remain in retirement in spite of improved health. Britain was still at war with France, and feeling in the country was that peace without victory was unacceptable; but the Whigs were in favour of an early settlement with Napoleon, a point of view the

Prince did not share. The present Whig leaders were not his friends in the way Fox and Sheridan had been, and he felt less obligation now to the party once known as 'the Prince's Friends'. In addition, Lady Hertford, the stern governess, more amenable to his advances now that he was about to be Regent, was in favour of retaining the Tories. There was another factor also that may have influenced him even more strongly. Lord Glenbervie had noted in his diary that Mrs Fitzherbert visited London, spending 'the greatest part of the day' with the Prince, and then added something the Duchess of Gordon had told him: 'some of the adherents of the present Ministry intended to have called on the Prince to declare, before he should take the oath for the Regency, whether he was not married to a Papist'.[2] The Duchess of Gordon was a Tory hostess, and in a good position to hear that kind of talk. If the Prince had heard the same talk, it might have been more than enough to persuade him to keep the Tories in power. It is no wonder the Prince told Mrs Fitzherbert that following her advice was 'impossible, as he had promised'.

He had 'promised', as he put it, before Mrs Fitzherbert arrived in London, possibly before he sent for her; so why had he called her to town? Was he worried that the anger in her recent letters, full of reminders of their long association as husband and wife, and of the promises he had made but not kept, would eventually drive her to speak in public? Did he need to be told again that she would always guard the secret that could ruin him?

Thomas Creevey met her by chance, and arranged to call on her the next day. He already knew of the Prince's decision regarding a government and, though a Whig, was not angered by the Prince's abandonment of his party. The Prince, in his opinion had every right to choose what party suited him best, and he wrote in his diary for 2 February, 'I went ... to Mrs Fitzherbert at twelve today, an opportunity I made with her yesterday in the street, and she and I were agreed on this subject'. He also noted that Mrs Fitzherbert was 'evidently delighted at the length, and forgiving and confidential nature of his [the Prince's] visits'.[3] Creevey's comment suggests that the Prince had called more than once at Tilney Street, that he had gone out of his way to be charming, and that they had talked, in confidence, of something more than which party to call. But the only other subject mentioned in Lord Stourton's account was the treatment of Princess Charlotte. Maria may have been shaky on politics, but she knew about young girls. According to Lord Stourton:

> She then urged upon him, as strongly as she was able, the disadvantages which must accrue to his future happiness from treating his daughter the Princess Charlotte, with so little kindness. She had warned him, 'You now Sir ... may mould her at your pleasure, but soon it will not be so; and she may become, from mismanagement, a thorn in your side for life'. 'That is your opinion, Madam', was his only reply.[4]

Maria returned to Brighton. The King's ministers were retained, the Prince of Wales took his oath as Regent, and a new era began. He and Lady Hertford planned a grand fête, to outdo all previous royal celebrations. Open celebration of the new Regency might look in bad taste, as it had only come about by his father's sad decline, so members of the exiled French royal family were invited, and, ostensibly, the banquet was to be in their honour. Lady Hertford, as a leading society hostess, knew who should be invited and who should sit, strictly according to rank, at the Regent's table. Two thousand invitations were sent out for 19 June 1811 at Carlton House. Maria received hers, but it did not offer a place at the Regent's table. When she asked him where she would sit, she was told, 'Madam you know you have no place'. Meaning no place at his table.

The Regent's table was to be in the great Gothic conservatory, but the majority of the guests would be seated at tables in marquees, where flower-painted trellises and mirrors created galleries and promenades. Among these would be a seat for Mrs Fitzherbert. But this she could not accept. If no place was given her at the Prince's table, where she had always sat, quietly assuming the role of a wife, then she would not attend. If he denied her this position, it would appear to all the fine world that she was, and always had been, his mistress. The greater part of her adult life had been spent in being a loving and dutiful wife to the Prince; in spite of their many quarrels, she had been obedient and totally faithful,[5] and had put his interests first. She had departed in silent dignity when he dismissed her; and returned, against her friends' advice, when he called her back. To take a place at one of the garden tables, no matter how many of her friends sat with her, would be a public denial of everything her life had been about. She had been hurt and angered before, but, to her, this was the last insupportable injustice. The Duke of York tried to persuade the Regent to be less rigid about sitting according to rank, but he was adamant.

Maria sent her excuses for not attending, and wrote, on 7 June, to explain her reasons, thinking, she told him, 'it more candid and open to lay my reasons before you'. Her letter made her position very clear:

> After the conversation Your Royal Highness held with me yesterday I am sure you will not be surprised that I have sent my excuses for not obeying your commands for Wednesday next. Much as it has ever been my wish during a period of near thirty years to save you from every embarrassment in my power yet there are situations when one ought not to entirely forget what is due to oneself ... by excluding her who now addresses you merely for want of those titles that others possess, you are excluding the person who is not unjustly suspected by the world of possessing in silence unassumed and unsustained a rank given her by yourself above that of any other person present ... I cannot be indifferent to the fair, honourable appearance of consideration from you, which I have hitherto possessed and which I feel I deserve, and for which reason I can never submit to appear in your house in any place or situation but in that where you yourself first placed me many years ago.[6]

The Regent did not reply to this letter. She kept a copy, and labelled it 'Written June 7th 1811 when the Prince was persuaded by Lady Hertford not to admit me to his table'. In her distress, Maria did not seem to see that seating her well away from his table, both at this fête and at subsequent dinners, was a way of reducing the chance of their marriage endangering his claim to regency and crown. She preferred to blame Lady Hertford, just as she had blamed Lady Jersey for their first parting, years before.

The fête went ahead in all its splendour, and was reported in all the papers. Maria could not have avoided hearing that the Regent, well corsetted and attired in a field marshal's uniform, looking older than his forty-eight years, in false side whiskers and long, curled wig, had greeted Louis XVIII and the French royals with elegant grace; that he sat with the Duchess of Angoulême on his right and the Duchess of York on his left, but that the Queen, all her daughters, the teenage Princess Charlotte, and, of course, Princess Caroline, were absent; that those present said with Thomas Moore, 'Nothing was ever so magnificent', but those who were not there called it a shameless extravagance. But she was possibly too wounded to care.

A few days later she attended an assembly at Devonshire House. By this time the Duke had married again, and it was the new Duchess, the former Lady Elizabeth Foster, who greeted her. Lord Stourton, recorded the event:

> The Duchess of Devonshire, taking her by the arm, said to her: 'You must come and see the Duke in his own room, as he is suffering from a fit of the gout, but he will be glad to see an old friend.' In passing through the rooms, she saw the Prince and Lady Hertford in a *tête-à-tête* conversation, and nearly fainted under all the impressions which then rushed upon her mind, but, taking a glass of water, she recovered and passed on.[7]

Even years afterwards, Maria thought this little episode important enough to repeat to Lord Stourton. The pain it caused her strengthened her resolution to ask for a formal separation from the Regent. The Duke of York and the Queen felt they could no longer ask her to go on being humiliated. The Prince raised no objection, and it was agreed that an income of £6000 a year, paid from a mortgage on the Brighton Pavilion, should be hers for life,[8] and that she should in future live as a private person. From that time on, she and the Prince never spoke.

The 'ill-starred connection' was over. As she had an income of £6000 a year, plus jointures from her two earlier marriages, and lavish entertainments were no longer required, she should have been financially secure. But, sadly, this was not the case. After years of keeping up with the Prince's lifestyle, and being forced to borrow when his extravagance had reduced their joint finances to almost nothing, she was deeply in debt. Her creditors were impatient, and she saw no way of paying them. She sold some jewels and closed Tilney Street. The Parson's Green house had already been sold, being replaced by Sherwood Lodge, on the river in Battersea, from there she wrote a sad letter to Thomas Coutts, on 11 September 1812: 'I have many thanks to return to you, my dear Mr Coutts, for your very kind letter and anxiety about me. I am ashamed to think how dilatory I have been in answering it, but at the time, and long after I got your letter I was so oppressed and miserable that I had not courage or resolution to take up my pen or indeed attend to anything.'[9]

Earlier in the year she had been shocked and saddened to hear that
her brother Jack had died without warning. He had married the widow
of a Captain Strickland, but the marriage seems to have been unhappy
and childless, the widow Strickland being described as 'barren'. They
appear to have been living apart when Jack died at Brambridge, William
Walmsley noting the funeral in his records, adding the words, 'subitanea
morte',[10] a sudden death. But although there were no children of the
marriage, there was a child, a girl, said to be Jack's, living at Red Rice.
She was apparently the fruit of an affair between Jack and a lady discreetly unnamed. She bore the Smythe family name, and the baptismal
names Mary Anne. She was usually known as Marianne, but Maria,
accepting responsibility for her after Jack's death,[11] nearly always
referred to her, and addressed her, as Mary. This second Mary, who was
about five or six at this time, eventually joined the household in Tilney
Street, addressing Maria as Mama, just as Minney did. For the first few
years after Jack Smythe's death, however, she seems to have remained in
Uncle Errington's house.[12]

Also in 1812, the whole country was shocked by the assassination of
Maria's old enemy, Spencer Perceval, in the lobby of the House of Commons. His assassin, John Bellingham, a man deranged by the failure of
his business, blamed the Prime Minister's policies for the troubles of
men like him. This was followed by a letter to the Prince Regent, signed
Vox Populi, and threatening him with the same fate if the price of bread
did not come down. Maria had no reason to like Perceval, but his murder appalled her. Though kind and considerate to her servants and, in
later years, when she had ample finances, more than generous to
Brighton charities,[13] she had little idea of the suffering of the urban
poor, and would not have understood why some people cheered when
they heard that Perceval was dead. Like many, she feared a revolution
akin to that in France, and possibly saw the murder of Perceval, and the
threat to the Regent, as the start of serious unrest.

In the years following 1812, Maria avoided the balls and assemblies
where she might meet the Regent, but though seen less in public she
never lost her place in the fashionable world. The dowager Lady Verulam wrote to Mary Frampton in July 1814, 'We met yesterday Mrs
Fitzherbert and her protégée. She was driving herself in one of the
fashionable carriages. They have four wheels and one horse and go at

a great rate'.[14] She entertained friends at Sherwood, guests sometimes arriving by river, and took up gardening, beginning a collection of rare plants. The *Brighton Gazette* commented on this on 24 September 1824, 'Mrs Fitzherbert is one of the most scientific botanists in the Kingdom and her protégée, Miss Seymour, is not deficient in that way'. Minney was still Mrs Fitzherbert's greatest joy, and they became good companions as she began to grow up. The Royal Dukes, especially York and Kent, remained frequent visitors and regular correspondents. Whatever had taken place between their brother and Mrs Fitzherbert, they saw no reason to be anything other than her 'affectionate and faithful' friends. The one thing they could not do was help with her money problems. In 1813 she was obliged to smother her pride and write to the Regent, asking him, once again, to increase her income to the promised amount. She approached him with deference, but with all the firmness of a wife who knew she deserved better treatment.[15] The letter went unanswered.

The early weeks of 1814 were the coldest anyone could remember. The Thames froze hard enough for a 'Frost Fair' to be held on the iced-over waters. On the Continent, in equally cold weather, the Russian, Prussian and Austrian armies were pressing the French back towards Paris, as Wellington marched towards Toulouse. In March the Emperor of Austria, Tsar of Russia, and King of Prussia rode into Paris as victors. In April Napoleon abdicated, and agreed to go into exile on Elba. Louis XVIII emerged from his exile in Buckinghamshire, and, escorted by the Regent, a troop of Life Guards, and cheering crowds, made a grand entry into Piccadilly. The capital was illuminated and Carlton House bedecked with flags. Lady Hertford hung a great banner across the front of Hertford House proclaiming, 'The Prince's Peace', and had her windows broken for her pains. Londoners were glad of the peace – but hated the Regent.

In June the state visit of the Tsar of Russia, King of Prussia and Metternich, representing the Emperor of Austria, threw London into a state of hysterical enthusiasm. Seen as saviours of Europe, they were cheered wherever they went. Not so their host the Regent; he was advised not to appear in the streets for fear of violent demonstrations in favour of the Princess of Wales. When he did venture out with his guests, he was booed and hissed. He was relieved when the visit was over.

Maria, though feeling herself to be greatly ill-used by the Regent, was pained by the way the crowds treated him. But she may have allowed herself to smile if she heard that, when the Regent presented Lady Hertford to the Tsar, the latter behaved as if he had not heard, and when the Regent repeated, loudly, 'My Lady Hertford', the Tsar gave her one glance and turned away.

1814 became known as 'the Year of Revelry', but to Maria it was a year of strict economies and increasing anxieties over the demands of her creditors. Having received no reply to her letter of the previous year, she wrote again in August 1814, stating her case bluntly:

> After the very ill success of my former application, it is with much painful reluctance and from the absolute necessity of my situation only that I am forced to address YRH upon the subject of my income, feeling as I do that all the pecuniary difficulties I endure originate from the very scanty allowance you made me for several years.

She had, she reminded him, shielded him from her financial difficulties at the time, knowing his own income was limited. 'To prevent you suffering uneasiness on that score, I was frequently driven by necessity to borrow money, and about six years ago, as you know, mortgaged my house to procure absolute necessities for yourself and me.' She acknowledged her increased income of four years ago, but added: 'This income I have not yet enjoyed, having been obliged to apply it, as far as I could, towards paying off of the old debts of former times – debts from which, with the most rigid economy, I have not been able to extricate myself.'

All these debts, she stressed, were incurred during the years when they were together, and added, 'I will not pain YRH by reminding you of how those debts arose or for whom they were contracted. Need I say more?' She then spoke of Minney :

> Under YRH's sanction, I have made myself responsible (and I have never for a moment regretted it) for the proper education and maintenance of my beloved child. She is everything I could wish her to be. Nothing is spared as far as I am able; and I should grieve, as her expenses increase with her age, if I had it not in my power to finish her education in the manner she deserves.

She told him she was going to live on the Continent, so this was the last time he would be troubled by a letter from her. If he would enable her to pay her debts then the

> many distressing discussions may be stayed which we ought both on every count to prevent becoming public ... Let me implore you, therefore, to answer this letter and to believe that, not withstanding all your prejudices against me and all the misery and wretchedness you have entailed upon me, I most sincerely wish you every degree of happiness, health and prosperity.[16]

It is hard to believe that the Prince failed to respond to such a letter, but no answer has survived. The creditors raised no cry when Maria went abroad, however, so perhaps he gave her some financial help or took responsibility for the debts himself. He did not raise her income to the promised amount and she seems to have made no further pleas for him to do so.

Maria and Minney left for the Continent in the autumn, and by February they were in Paris where Maria was received at the Tuilleries.[17] She planned to remain some time but, when the news of Napoleon's escape from Elba reached Paris, she hurried back to England, and awaited, with all the rest of the country, for news from the subsequent campaign. When Wellington's victory at Waterloo and Napoleon's second exile brought peace back to Europe, Maria did not return to France, and the following month she opened up Tilney Street again; a further indication that her financial affairs had been relieved. The Duke of Kent wrote to her on 22 September 1815, 'My ever dearest Mrs Fitzherbert, ... I write these few hasty lines before I set out for Windsor, to mention my intention of calling on you on Monday next the 25th towards one o'clock if that should suit you ...' The Duke was horribly embarrassed financially and struggling to sort out his affairs, the settlement of which was causing him 'worry and occupation ... beyond all description'. The only solution was to spend a few years abroad, where the living was cheaper. He wished to tell a sympathetic Maria all about his plans to settle in Brussels, and he ended his letter, 'All this however, we will talk over on Monday if you give me leave, when I shall be happy to learn your plans in return'.[18]

Maria's plans now centred entirely around Minney. She would be seventeen the following year, ready to be introduced into fashionable society as the Honourable Miss Mary Seymour. Graceful, charming, carefully educated and in every way enchanting, she was expected to win the admiration of all when she made her debut, and Mrs Fitzherbert, Sir George Seymour and the Regent himself were hoping to make her first Season as brilliant as she deserved.

12

The Queen's Trial

Sir George Seymour, Minney's eldest brother, had known 'Mrs Fitz' all his life. Away at sea during the Seymour Case, he heard only what his aunts reported, and agreed with them. Later he changed his mind and wrote:

> When on shore, I had always occasion to admire the maternal kindness with which she treated my sister ... As years drew on my former objection to her being with Mrs Fitzherbert weakened when I saw how consistently her care to my sister was administered; her house was always open to my brothers and myself, and she always consulted me about my sister's welfare.[1]

Minney accepted the protective presence of her brother without being on particularly intimate terms with him. But she had known and loved the Regent, her other 'protector', since early childhood, and her strong affection for him was unaffected by the estrangement between him and Mama. The £10,000 he had invested in her name at the time of the Seymour Case had almost doubled and would form her dowry, and the Regent would be watching her, with love and pride, as she danced her graceful way through her first Season.

On 7 January 1817, she attended a ball at the Pavilion to celebrate Princess Charlotte's twenty-first birthday. Maria did not attend, not having set foot in the Pavilion since parting from the Prince. The *Brighton Gazette* reported, 'The ball was opened by the Duke of Clarence and Lady Cholmondeley, Prince Esterhazy and the Hon. Miss Seymour'. The following week, the Grand Duke Nicholas of Russia was the guest of honour at the Pavilion, and another ball was held, the *Gazette* noting, 'The Grand Duke's partner during the ball was generally the Hon. Miss Seymour, ward of Mrs Fitzherbert'.[2] Dancing partners, admirers and suitors Minney soon had in plenty, but, though quickly learning the art of mild flirtation, she took none of them seriously.

When the Season ended, Maria and Minney went on to further entertainments in Paris. But Minney's first year in the *beau monde* had a sad ending. On 6 November Princess Charlotte, who had married Prince Leopold of Saxe-Coburg-Saalfeld in 1816, died, following the birth of a stillborn son. The whole country fell into profound and universal grief with unprecedented displays of public sorrow. When Mrs Trench wrote to Mrs Leadbetter, 'The nation would have resigned all the rest of the family to have saved her', she spoke for most of the ordinary people, weeping in the streets. The Regent felt too distressed to attend the funeral at Windsor, and Charlotte's mother, Princess Caroline, who had been travelling on the Continent since 1814, was not expected to return for her daughter's burial. Rumours of Caroline's immoral alliances with some of the servants travelling with her led to another enquiry (known as the Milan Commission) into her conduct in 1818. The evidence found was not conclusive.

The Regent was now without an heir. The unmarried Royal Dukes were obliged to leave their mistresses, marry German Princesses and do their best to produce a child. Adolphus, Duke of Cambridge, married Princess Augusta of Hesse Cassel in 1818 and produced a son who was the heir for a few months. The Duke of Clarence had already left Mrs Jordan, and, after a prolonged search, married Princess Adelaide of Saxe-Meiningen. The Duke of Kent, deeply grieving, parted from Madame de St-Laurent, after twenty-seven contented years, and wed the widowed daughter of the Duke of Saxe-Coberg-Saalfeld, sister of Prince Leopold, who gave birth to the future Queen Victoria on 24 May 1819. The Regent continued to press his ministers on the subject of a divorce from Caroline, possibly thinking of marrying again and producing another heir himself. 1818 was also a year for a royal marriage among his sisters. Charlotte, the Princess Royal, had finally been married at the age of thirty-one to the Hereditary Prince of Württemberg in 1797, leaving the way open for her sisters to escape from 'the nunnery' in their turn. Princess Mary married her cousin William, Duke of Gloucester, in 1816, and 1818 was, finally, Princess Elizabeth's year. Against her mother's opposition, but with the Regent's help, she married, on 17 April, aged thirty-seven, the unpreposessing Hereditary

Prince of Hesse-Homberg, with whom, to everyone's surprise, she was very happy.

Maria and Minney returned to Brighton for the New Year of 1818 but, mourning for Charlotte, had no heart for parties. There were no balls that winter at the Pavilion. The 1818 London Season brought Minney more admiration. The Duke of Clarence's eldest son, George Fitz-clarence, later Earl of Munster, was in love with her, but Maria could not regard him as a suitable husband, 'One of that family is enough', she is reputed to have said. Lord Arthur Hill, son of Lady Downshire, Maria's close friend, had also offered himself, without success, and Minney's Hertford second cousin, Lord Beauchamp, was only waiting for a smile of encouragement to declare his intentions. Maria might have looked favourably on him, but Minney withheld her smiles.

Universally admired as she was, Minney's love of flirtation and fail-ure to accept any of her train of suitors left her open to gossip. Her brother George heard unfortunate rumours that linked her name with a Mr Bruce, and wrote with disapproval to Maria, who replied:

> I ... can assure you with great truth that there is not the smallest reason for the reports that have been so industriously circulated concerning her. She is certainly an object of attraction ... and if a man happens to speak to her or is seen to join her walking it immediately sets people talking ... it is natural at her age to like being admired and I hope with her good sense as she grows older the love of flirtation will abate.

The cure for false rumours was an early marriage, as Maria admitted, 'I confess however miserable I shall be to part with her I am most anxious she should marry and I trust this spring may produce something deserv-ing of her'.[3] But hopes of the marriage Minney deserved were not fulfilled that year. She seemed in no hurry to settle down, and, child of the Romantic Age, was perhaps waiting for a great love to enter her life rather than a 'deserving' husband.

In the Autumn Queen Charlotte died, and the Regent wrote a birthday letter to Minney on 22 November 1818 expressing his grief:

> My beloved Minney, I take up my pen in the midst of the greatest grief and affliction possible (having so recently lost my best, most revered and most beloved of Mothers) to write you a few lines and to assure you that

notwithstanding I not only never can forget but that I do greet with emotions of pleasure the anniversary of the day that gave you birth.

He went on to wish her every kind of happiness, assuring her of 'Prayers that never could proceed with more sincerity and fervour from a real and natural parent, than are offered up to the throne of Mercies from the heart of him, who whilst he yet lives, never shall cease to be, my dearest child, your ever most affectionate Father by adoption. George PR'.[4]

If the Regent's prayers for Minney's future happiness included an early and splendid marriage, they went unheeded by the throne of Mercies. The following year she met the young Captain George Dawson and found herself suddenly and deeply attracted. At first Maria did not recognise the danger signs and found Captain Dawson perfectly charming, and quite suitable (he was a cavalry officer and the son of an Irish Earl) to be one of Minney's dancing partners, but nothing more. He was Lord Portarlington's third son, surviving on a very small income and, apparently, with no prospects. What she had not anticipated was that Minney would become completely infatuated. When she saw what was happening, she discouraged any further meetings between them, letting Captain Dawson know his attentions were not welcome. Captain Dawson had debts he could not possibly settle from his slender means and was, it was said, a heavy drinker and gambler. Minney was not the first young lady he had paid court to and later abandoned. Handsome, charming and a brave leader of cavalry he might be (he had had two horses shot from under him at Waterloo), but that was not enough for Maria, nor for Minney's brother, and certainly not for the Regent. When the Season ended Maria thought it wise to take Minney away to Paris, expecting this to put an end to the affair.

Minney, however, though aware of Mama's disapproval, had indicated to Captain Dawson that his attentions were not unwelcome to her. He followed them to Paris, and, to Maria's extreme annoyance, kept appearing in their company. Unbeknown to her, secret meetings between the two were arranged through messages carried by the teenaged Marianne Smythe. Though still at school in France, Marianne was staying with Maria in Paris, and had no compunction about deceiving her if it would aid Minney's romance.

Little notes, some of which survive, reached Captain Dawson almost daily via Marianne, giving hope of possible meetings, 'You will certainly see her tomorrow for we must go to Victorine's but today Mrs Fitzherbert went out or rather we three quite late', she scribbled on one occasion, and on another, 'If we go out at three (which is uncertain) I will go to a shop *en face de votre hôtel*. There is a possibility you must prepare for disappointment, as Mrs Fitzherbert may want the carriage'.[5]

Maria, suspecting that Minney and Dawson were secretly in touch, was furious with him and grieved to think that Minney might be deceiving her. Minney herself was torn in two directions. She could not bear to hurt Mama, would not in any circumstances marry a man Mama did not approve of, but could not resist Dawson's invitations to secret meetings, hoping that, given time, Maria's attitude might change. This inability to give Dawson up, but refusal to even think of marrying him without Mama's approval, was to be her dilemma, and Maria's anguish for years to come.

George Dawson was not content with brief assignations and smiles across Parisian salons, and had devised a scheme for gaining the support of the Duke of York in his effort to secure Minney's hand. He wrote a letter, setting out his case, to his friend Lord Alvanley, who agreed to show it to the Duke, who would then, it was hoped, persuade Mrs Fitzherbert to look more favourably on Captain Dawson. 'When I first met Miss Seymour', Dawson's letter began,

> she seemed as if she wished to avoid me: this and the repulsive manner of Mrs Fitzherbert gave me but little hope and I resolved to stifle every feeling of my heart ... one day I had the good fortune to meet her alone and it was on this occasion that I was made the happiest man in the world. I received the assurance that she was not indifferent to my attachment to her but at the same time she observed to me how insurmountable appeared the difficulties attending on eventual happiness! ... Miss Seymour from every circumstance connected with herself could look forward to making the most splendid marriage ... I know that I am nobody and have nothing.

The letter mentioned Dawson's aunt, Miss Caroline Damer, her provision for his elder brother, and the belief that she would do the same for him. It also claimed, 'The Duke of York was so kind as to promise he would do something for me! I feel that from the intimate terms upon which he is with Mrs Fitzherbert that nothing would do me so much good in her opinion as HRH being so good as to express to her his desire to serve me'.[6] The second part of Dawson's plan was to return to England hoping to meet the Duke and learn what help he might expect.

On 20 January 1820 Maria had heard, with grief and disbelief, of the sudden death by pneumonia of the Duke of Kent. As she mourned for him, news came on 29 January that George III had died, and the Regent was now King. Before she had time to wonder if this would in any way alter her position, word reached Paris that the new King was also dead. Stunned and silent, she and Minney spent a day in seclusion, no one knowing what sad thoughts and separate memories filled their minds. They saw no one until they heard that the rumour was false. The new King was still living, but gravely ill.

As often happened with him, George IV, as the Regent now was, recovered faster that his doctors dared to hope. Maria and Minney returned to Paris Society, and Tom Moore noted in his diary, 'George Dawson is gone off to England to try and make interest with the Duke of York to get the King's consent to his marrying Miss Seymour'.[7]

When Dawson arrived back in England he found his timing was wrong. The new King's illness had greatly alarmed the Duke of York, who had time for no one until his brother's return to health was assured. Nor was it the moment for the Duke to speak to Mrs Fitzherbert on Dawson's behalf, even if he had wanted to. She was still in Paris, and when she did make a brief visit to London, she had other things on her mind.

With health and strength returning, the King determined to rid himself of Caroline of Brunswick, who, whether he liked it or not, was now his Queen. Again he took advice on gaining a divorce. Her 'perfectly outrageous' behaviour in Italy with a certain Bartolomeo Pergami should, he said, provide sufficient grounds.

Caroline, calling herself the Queen of England, was preparing to return to London from Italy to claim her legal rights and be crowned. She had plenty of supporters in England, and Alderman Matthew Wood, a former Lord Mayor of London, was encouraging her to return at an early date. Her legal adviser, Lord Brougham, thought it more prudent to wait until the King's plans became clear, but the alderman had promised her rooms in his house in South Audley Street and she refused to wait.

Perhaps the thought of his second wife reminded the King of his first, because, to her surprise, Maria was informed that her income would be raised to the long-promised £10,000 a year from April. When Lady Anne Barnard heard of this she wrote, to a friend:

> I wish I had the leisure to make you laugh at a visit I had from the Fitz. in compliment by way to inform me of what I had asked her the truth of two months ago (which she then knew to be a fact but never told me) I mean the additional £4000 per annum now remitted her by the King. She affected not to care three straws about it – as he had not given it to her when she needed it. She said the Duke of Kent had asked if she would not find it convenient now. I told him the only way the money could give me any pleasure would be to have it in guineas and throw it at the King's head and knock him down with it – if you did – said he – he would pick up the gold and pocket the insult.[8]

Lady Anne, though supposedly a friend of Maria, often spread stories that were both unkind and only half true. Maria could not have had the reported conversation with the Duke of Kent: he had died early in January, well before her income was increased. Nor was she likely to have exchanged remarks of the kind Lady Anne quotes with any of the Royal Dukes, who invariably spoke of their brother with respect, as did Maria herself when talking to members of the family. Maria may have expressed some indignation that the long-promised allowance was given only when the time of her greatest need had passed, but she was disinclined to dwell on the wrongs of the past, being suddenly much concerned with the present.

On 5 June Caroline landed at Dover, and drove into London surrounded by a large crowd whose cheers could be heard in both Chambers as her coach crossed Westminster Bridge. The crowd escorted her to South Audley Street, amid shouts of 'No Queen, No King', and later gathered outside the windows of Carlton House shouting 'Nero, Nero'. The King left for Windsor. Lord Liverpool's government had advised that the best method of obtaining a divorce was to present a Bill of Pains and Penalties against the Queen in the House of Lords, the last clause of which would provide a divorce, should adultery be proved.[9] Before the Bill was presented, a fearful Maria sought assurance from Caroline's lawyer that she would not be called as a witness. She was afraid Lord Brougham might try to prove the King's 'Catholic Marriage' as a counter-attack against him if things looked bad for Caroline. Brougham assured her she would not be called, but she thought it wise to return to Paris, taking the papers pertaining to the marriage with her. Brougham did not tell her that, if need arose, he would call Henry Errington.

Maria spent an uneasy few months in Paris where news of the Queen's Trial, as it was popularly known, arrived daily. The 'trial' opened on 17 August. Thomas Creevey wrote to his stepdaughter Miss Ord, 'I cannot resist the curiosity of seeing a Queen tried. From the House of Lords or from Brooks' you shall have a daily account of what passes'.[10] Creevey may have enjoyed the 'curiosity' of it, but there was alarm in Parliament in case the massive crowd gathering in support of the Queen grew violent. Troops were poured into London on stand by, and barricades were set up around Westminster to ensure that the lords' carriages arrived safely. But there was no serious violence, the crowds confining themselves to shouting threats and breaking a few windows, including Lady Hertford's, though she had now been replaced in the King's affections by Lady Conyngham. Maria learned enough of all this to be glad she had left London.

The Queen, formally accused of committing adultery with Bartolomeo Pergami, her major-domo, was allowed to attend the proceedings in the Lords, but not to take part. She arrived on the first day wearing a huge black wig, her face heavily rouged. She shouted at the Italian witnesses if she did not like their answers, but much of the time she looked bored and sometimes fell asleep. When the main witness, her Italian servant Theodore Majocci, was called she looked shocked, and leapt to her feet shrieking 'Theodore' (or, some said, 'traditore', traitor), and left the chamber. This told against her, suggesting she was afraid of what he might say.

Majocci answered all the early questions about Caroline and Pergami's behaviour on board a boat sailing from Augusta to Tunis; yes, they had slept alone together under a tent constructed on the deck; and yes, they had taken baths together. But as the questions became more particular he became nervous, saying repeatedly 'Non me ricordo', I do not recall. By this time Caroline was spending most of the day in an antechamber playing backgammon with Alderman Wood.[11] The trial was the talk of the town, and the talk of Paris as well. From there Lady

Cooper complained to Frederick Lamb on 20 August, 'the Queen, the Queen and nothing but the Queen is heard of ...'.[12] The London and national papers reported the trial in full, the details shocking many. 'The newspapers accurately report the proceedings, horrible and disgusting as it all is', wrote Mrs Wellesley-Pole to Charles Bagot.[13] Princess Lieven, keeping Prince Metternich up to date, wrote 'What horrors in the newspapers! ... it is too disgusting. Is the Queen really a woman?'[14]

The Queen's supporters refused to believe the evidence, on the grounds that it was supplied by Italians and therefore not to be trusted. In the end, Lord Liverpool decided that, though hardly anyone present in the Upper Chamber believed the Queen to be innocent and though her behaviour had certainly been deplorable, if not downright disgraceful, it was virtually impossible to *prove* adultery. Although the Bill passed two readings in the Lords, the second one scraped through by only nine votes, and Lord Liverpool decided it unwise to let the Bill be debated in the Commons. Possibly he had heard that Brougham held proof of the 'Catholic Marriage', and thought it best to bring the whole unsavoury affair to an end rather than risk that matter being raised again. In addition, he knew that even the quietest crowd could become violent if angered, causing riots that could only be quelled by bloodshed. On 7 November he withdrew the Bill. Caroline was not found innocent; neither was she found guilty. Neither party had won, but both had been irreparably damaged.

Caroline lost much of her support once the trial ended and many thought it best if she left the country again, as a much-quoted little rhyme shows

> Oh gracious Queen we thee implore
> To go away and sin no more
> Or if that effort prove too great
> To go away at any rate.

The King was profoundly disappointed at the outcome; but even he could see that violent rioting in his capital city, with a possible return of the 'Catholic Marriage' question, was the worst way of beginning his reign. He may also have found his intense unpopularity among Londoners frightening as well as hurtful.

There was general relief when the affair ended, Creevey writing to

Miss Ord declared: 'The Bill is gone, thank God! to the devil'. Mrs Fitzherbert was possibly more relieved than anyone. She had not been panicking unnecessarily. Years later, Lord Brougham referred to the Queen's trial and Mrs Fitzherbert's marriage in his memoirs:

> We were not in possession of all the circumstances as I have since ascertained them, but we had enough to prove the fact. Mrs Fitzherbert's uncle Mr Errington, who was present at the marriage, was still alive and though he no doubt would have had a right to refuse answering a question to which an affirmative answer exposed him to pains and penalties of a praemunire ... it was almost certain that on Mrs Fitzherbert's behalf he would have waived the protection and given his testimony to prove the marriage, but even a refusal would have left the conviction in all men's minds that the marriage had taken place.[15]

When news of the Bill's withdrawal reached Paris, Maria, relieved of one anxiety, turned her mind to another, returning to London and the problem of George Dawson. The Duke of York had got round to thinking about Captain Dawson as well. He was too fond of Maria to think of speaking to her on a subject he knew to be painful, but he also knew Captain Dawson was a good soldier for whom he had promised to 'do something'. He offered to make him a lieutenant colonel, but warned that promotion would mean serving in the West Indies. This offer was welcomed by Dawson, who was not deterred by the thought of serving abroad. He deferred his departure for several months, hoping to marry Minney within that time and take her with him. Maria knew nothing of Dawson's hopes; she only knew that he was about to leave the country for faraway islands, and, as she and Minney prepared to pass the winter in Brighton, she devoutly prayed that his departure would mark the end of the affair, and that Minney would begin to forget.

13

George Dawson

Far from forgetting, on 1 December Minney sat writing to George Dawson, 'Our correspondence has never been interrupted notwithstanding Mama's strong wish that this should be the case ... the total silence I have pursued has hitherto left her in perfect ignorance as to what I have done about it, and will, I trust, remain so'.[1] Corresponding secretly was one thing, telling Mama she had decided to marry George Dawson was another, and she had promised Maria that she would never make such a decision without her agreement. Were she to do so, she told Dawson, Mama would say that as she could not answer for such a thing to my family, she 'would at once give me up to them'. This was not what Minney wanted. For the next eighteen months the three of them remained fixed in their positions: George Dawson never wavered in his desire to marry Minney; Maria's resolve to hand Minney over to the Seymours if she agreed to marry him was unshakable; and Minney, torn between the two, seemed fixed in permanent indecision.

George IV's coronation, on 19 July 1821, was the most splendid ever seen. He walked in procession from Westminster Hall preceded first by maids scattering nosegays, then by the Household Band and the Corporation of the City of London. Next came the peers in full robes and members of the Privy Council dressed in Elizabethan costumes designed by the King. Behind them, the crown, orb, sceptre and sword were carried by appropriate dignitaries. Then came the King himself, walking under a canopy of cloth of gold, his long crimson train stretching behind him, his hat decorated with ostrich feathers, and his curled wig hanging to his shoulders. The elaborate ceremony in Westminster Abbey lasted for a full five hours and was followed by a banquet in Westminster Hall. The King was finally driven back to Carlton House amid scenes of enthusiasm and, as darkness fell, there were fireworks in Hyde Park.

Support for Queen Caroline had fallen away after the end of the

'Trial', but the King had still feared she might disrupt the ceremony. Against the advice of her remaining supporters, she had arrived at the Abbey at six o'clock that morning, determined to enter; orders had been given, however, not to admit her, and she was turned away, humiliated, at every door. Eventually she walked back, defeated, to her carriage and drove off. The crowd, who had already gathered to watch the day's proceedings, shouted their derision as she left. In a few weeks she became ill with what was probably bowel cancer,[2] and died on 8 August, leaving a request to be buried in Brunswick as 'The Injured Queen of England'.

None of this distracted Maria from the problem of Minney and her Captain for long. Her distress was faithfully reported in Minney's letters to Dawson, who grew exasperated with 'Mama', claiming her rejection of him was based on 'vanity and ambition'. But, in spite of her agitation, Maria showed no anger towards Minney, who told Dawson, 'Mama's good humour towards me has not lessened'. Maria would not let their relationship deteriorate into bitter arguments over Captain Dawson. She was, however, quite willing to express disapproval when Minney showed extraordinary rudeness to Lord Beauchamp, turning her back on him at dinner and speaking only to her other neighbour. Greatly offended, he departed for Paris, leaving Maria to enquire the reason for Minney's conduct and remark that if she had intended to put an end to any friendship with Beauchamp she must have completely succeeded. Lord Beauchamp was very attached to Minney, but Minney had thoughts for no one but Dawson.

George Seymour also found a marriage between his sister and George Dawson unacceptable and, during 1822, wrote to Dawson and asked for a meeting. Whatever passed between the two men, Seymour's reaction was to propose a visit to Dresden for Minney and Dawson's was to fix his departure to the West Indies for October or November of that year. The elder Seymour sister, Horatia, was married to John Morier, who held a post at the Dresden Embassy, and it was hoped that a stay at a small German Court would divert Minney's thoughts.

Before plans for Dresden were finalised, Maria and Minney had a painful conversation in which, according to her account of it to Dawson, Minney used every argument she could think of, her devotion to him, her willingness to go to the West Indies with him, and her understanding of everyone's disappointed hopes concerning her future, but Maria simply repeated that if marrying Dawson was Minney's decision, then she would leave her to her family, and would herself retire from London, and indeed from the world. This sounds like the worst kind of emotional blackmail, but Maria knew that in the world she lived in a young woman's future was in the hands of her husband, and she was unable to believe that Captain Dawson could make Minney happy for long, or even provide for her adequately, and the thought of her darling child's ultimate unhappiness was more than she could bear.

Minney's solution was to escape from the situation, and she and George Seymour left for Dresden. In spite of the difference between them, Maria and Minney remained close, and long amiable letters passed between them as brother and sister travelled across Europe. From Sherwood on 29 July Maria wrote, 'Your letter, dearest Minney, gave me the greatest pleasure imaginable, for what I suffered all Wednesday it is impossible to describe. The wind was so high and the river so agitated that I did nothing but run from the house to watch the tide all day, and I worked myself up to a state of anxiety scarcely to be borne ...'[3] A week later she wrote, 'Your letter from Bruxelles, my dearest Minney, was a real satisfaction. Your journey having been so very pleasant delighted me very much. My thoughts have never been absent from you'.[4] Weekly letters followed giving whatever news she could find. Minney was told that her friend Harriet was to marry Lord Belfast, of whom Mrs Fitzherbert approved, 'Indeed I find him very deserving'. The suicide of the Marquess of Londonderry (formerly Lord Castlereagh) was mentioned, 'I am sure you must have been sadly shocked at the tragical end of poor Lord Londonderry', as was a gift of £5000 for Minney's brother Fred from the Marquess of Hertford and attributed to Lady Hertford's intervention, 'I must say she behaved most generously'. From Cheltenham she wrote, 'Here we have been a week ... we have got a very delightful house and everything comfortable. I hope I shall be benefited by the waters, for nothing on earth can be more dull and stupid. Millions of people here but such a group I never beheld ... not a human being I ever saw before ...' Her next letter gave a brief mention of Marianne, who was now living permanently with her: 'We all went to the Ball and Seymour danced with Marianne which pleased her very much. The first public Ball she ever was at.'[5] This reference to Marianne Smythe, at her first ball, in dull, stupid Cheltenham, confirms the impression that she was several years younger than Minney and not yet 'out' in London Society. She was also mentioned in a letter from Sherwood, 'Mary and I have never dined alone but twice since I came here ... I only want you of the party to make it perfection'.[6]

George Seymour wrote to Maria from Dresden commenting on Minney's present attitude towards Dawson:

> From conversations I have had with her it is impossible for me not to see that the infatuation towards him still continues and therefore to dread the effect that his meeting her again may have, but on the other hand I think she now feels that even if she does she stands pledged to you not to go on with the affair in any way and even with the weakness of decision which pervades her character there is a strong feeling of regard to a promise.[7]

Minney was still writing to Captain Dawson, light-hearted letters describing her journeys, the places she visited, and the entertainments she attended. One of particular interest was from Berlin, describing an event at a *soirée*:

> the lady of the house thought it proper to present every one person to me and I could not help remarking afterwards upon her carrying about a large picture which she was showing everybody and appearing to draw their attention upon me. I could not account for this until I was told someone had spread the unaccountably ridiculous report of my being the King of England's daughter and to improve the idea a print of Princess Charlotte had been carried about to prove the likeness that was said to exist between us. I could not help laughing when all this was told me ...'[8]

There are those who believe that Minney, though clearly Horatia Seymour's child, might have been fathered by the King when Prince of Wales, but clearly Minney herself thought it a ludicrous suggestion.

Maria's name crept into most of Minney's letters. She and Lady George Seymour and their young daughters were to meet Minney and her brother in Paris, and spend the winter there. Shortly before leaving, however, she heard that Dawson had been telling his friends that he would have given up all hopes of marrying Miss Seymour had he not received ample encouragement from her. No gentleman, at that time, bragged like that about a young lady when no marriage had been arranged. Maria, mortified on Minney's behalf, wrote to George

Seymour, 'It is so humiliating to her I cannot bear it'. To Minney she wrote, 'The purport of my writing to you is to implore you to come to a final resolution upon this business. You must decide and that decision must be done immediately'.[9] The years of anxiety over Minney's future, the lack of communication between them on the subject, and Minney's inability to make a decision, were becoming too much for Maria, who admitted that 'neither my health nor spirits can stand it any longer'.

Minney was upset in her turn, and wrote a long letter reporting Maria's distress, and ultimatum, to Captain Dawson, still waiting in England. Dawson's patience with Mama, if he ever had any, came to an end on 14 October when he wrote:

> I will content myself with observing that this was the most impolitic, weak and ridiculous act she could have been guilty of. It was tyrannical and foolish and the only result she could possibly have expected from it had she considered, would have been the giving you further proof of the return you meet with for sacrificing your feelings under the circumstances of the moment to selfish pique and the implacability of a mind entirely swayed by the feelings of revenge as well as the most petty, vulgar and illiberal sentiments.[10]

Bearing in mind that George Dawson had very little to offer Minney, that he could provide her with neither home nor adequate income, and that George Seymour and the King shared Maria's view, this seems an extreme outburst. Almost all the young men in Minney's circle were more acceptable than he was. Admittedly he loved her, but so did many others.

But Minney, deep in love herself, did not rebuke him. She had become adept at keeping everybody happy, especially Mama, and she assured her again that she never would consider marrying George Dawson while she knew the thought of it caused such distress. All was smoothed over, and Maria travelled to Paris as planned. 'Mrs Fitzherbert received me with great kindness', Minney wrote to Dawson, as he prepared to sail for St Vincent. Minney and Mama were more deeply involved with each other than George Dawson could understand. His last letter, just before sailing on 2 November 1822, was not so much full of sadness at parting from Minney as of bitterness against Maria:

> At this moment, when all my thoughts and ideas are of the most serious

nature I feel that if I am not doomed to return, the injuries I have received which I shall not be able to forgive or to lose sight of the bitterness of them, will be that Mrs Fitzherbert has been guilty of to me. For her sake I hope that God will be more merciful to her than I know she deserves and, if my life is sacrificed, may she not feel the pangs of conscience at her latter end, which she richly deserves for having caused and prolonged my misery.[11]

With that, Lieutenant-Colonel George Dawson sailed for the Indies.

Maria's eldest brother, Walter, died at Brambridge on 14 November, and Minney told George Dawson later in the month, 'I have thought her a good deal out of spirits'. Wat's widow and daughters had to move out of their home at Brambridge, the estate passing to the remaining brother, Charles. Maria felt both sympathy and concern for them, guessing perhaps at problems to come. In the same letter to Dawson Minney wrote, 'I hear very bad accounts of the King's health ... He is said to have gout, but I fear this is not really the case and that it is his mind that is affected. I have lately known of so many little instances that corroborate the idea ...'[12] Whatever news Minney heard about the King's ill health Mrs Fitzherbert would have heard too. Although they had not spoken for years, she still felt concern for him, and this news contributed to her low spirits.

They remained in Paris until the spring, and she and Minney went out a great deal during the London Season of 1823. In December she opened up her Brighton house for Christmas and New Year. On 14 December, she wrote to Minney, who was still in London:

Your letter this morning, my dearest Minney, gave me much pleasure, for I am so unused to be at Brighton without you that the sight of it quite revived me, particularly to hear that you are to come to me on Saturday. Pray do not disappoint me. You will be welcomed here by more than myself, for I have given out that I shall not receive company until your Ladyship makes your appearance. There are several strangers here who don't know what to do with themselves and they will be very glad to have a lounging place for dinner and for one evening. But I am determined not to kill the fatted calf until you arrive ... There is nothing gay going on, but I have promised to be very gay when you come. You will be delighted at the great improvements. The Chain Pier is beautiful and I have a delightful view of it from my windows.[13]

The Brighton press had welcomed Maria's return, 'The poor of Brighton', announced the *Brighton Gazette* on 18 December, 'to whom Mrs Fitzherbert is endeared by her benevolence will have reason to rejoice at her return, and we hope she may make a protracted stay with us.' 'In her the poor ever find a pitying and relieving friend', echoed the *Brighton Herald*. Since receiving her full allowance of £10,000 a year, Maria now had more than enough money for her own needs and gave generously to all the local organisations that relieved the poor.

The following spring George Dawson returned to England. His brother, Lord Portarlington, had added Damer to the family name, and Dawson was now known as Colonel Dawson Damer. He lost no time in writing to Maria.

> Madam, I feel the greatest diffidence in taking the liberty of writing to you. Although you once flattered me with your friendship, so many years have elapsed and so many unfortunate circumstances have taken place since that period that I own I have come to the determination of addressing myself to you with considerable embarrassment. My object in doing so is to request your permission to have an interview with Miss Seymour.

Surprisingly, in view of all the ill feeling that had existed between them, he added, 'I can't help flattering myself that you will peruse this letter with some indulgence'. He then told her that he had remained abroad until he had paid off all his debts, returning, 'free of encumbrances', and that, if she would listen to his side of the story of his long attachment to Miss Seymour, she would realise that all the 'disagreeable impressions' she had of him were due to them both being the 'victims of malicious persons who circulated calumny to keep up the annoyance which I unfortunately caused you'.[14]

Maria's reply was brief:

> Sir, I have received your letter requesting an interview with Miss Seymour. Her sister Mrs Morier being in Town it appears to me that her house and under the protection of her family would be the properest place for you to see her.
>
> I beg leave to observe that Miss Seymour is entirely her own mistress and must decide for herself.
>
> My feelings have been so harassed upon this sad subject and I have been made so completely miserable and unhappy that I must beg

your permission to decline entering into the details contained in your letter.[15]

If a meeting took place at Mrs Morier's London house, no decisions were made, and Minney continued to live with Maria.

In April Minney wrote sadly to Dawson Damer from Brighton:

> I am to be reduced to the alternative of making one of the two beings most interested about me wretched. This would sound a strong term and I am but too constantly reminded of how justly it would be applied to her I am living with, who during the last five months we have been here, though almost constantly so ill ... has repeatedly with tears in her eyes expressed how thankful she was for having passed the first tranquil period of time she had known for years since she had been here, which I cannot but know to be owing to the cessation of communications, true and false, about us that were constantly afforded her in the whirl of Paris and London Society.[16]

By the summer Maria's health and spirits had recovered, and Minney left her to spend some time in Paris with her brother Horace. In the New Year Maria gave a ball, something she had not done for years. On 28 January 1825 the *Brighton Gazette* reported:

> On Tuesday night Mrs Fitzherbert gave a splendid ball, with one of the most sumptuous suppers that had taken place this Season. The company was composed of all the Fashionables at present in Brighton. The rooms were elegantly decorated and the supper table was set forth with every kind of ornament ... There was the most superb table of gold plate and the most valuable china. The carriages began to set down at half past eight o'clock, and continued until near one o'clock.

She had not forgotten how to be a grand hostess.

On 1 May she returned to Tilney Street, and in July Minney finally agreed to marry George Dawson Damer, with her brother's consent. Colonel Dawson Damer was beginning to look more like a suitable husband. He had saved hard to pay off his debts, he had remained totally faithful to Minney for six difficult years, and it looked as if his inheritance of Came, the house in Dorset owned by his aunt, was almost certain. Maria, though not exactly giving them her blessing, accepted Minney's decision. There was no talk now of leaving the world in grief and misery, and she and Minney remained on the closest terms.

Minney's difficulties, however, were not over. The King still had to be approached.

Minney wrote him a respectful, humble, beseeching letter, revealing a determined but still very troubled state of mind. She begged for his indulgence towards a letter, 'written in the most trying moment of my life when I stand most in need of all my strength of mind and possess so little ...' She throws some light on the attitude of her brother and Mrs Fitzherbert, 'It would be disingenuous in me to attempt to conceal from Your Majesty that time has not reconciled Mama or my brothers to the step upon which my future happiness depends though it may have made them withdraw the opposition every consideration allied with their interest for me had made them so long continue'. She acknowledges that he too must condemn her plans, but begs nevertheless for his 'sanction and support', implores him not to withdraw his, 'countenance and protection', from her, and asks him to recollect, 'how much happiness and misery are in his hands'. She signs herself, 'Your Majesty's most devoted, attached and dutiful servant, Mary G. E. Seymour'.[17]

The King, though in bad health and great pain, for which he took large amounts of laudanum, often rendering himself almost senseless, kept a clear head on this occasion. He had forgotten much, denied and reinvented much, but he had never forgotten Minney, the beloved child, and he promptly sent for Mr Forster, his solicitor. The marriage was 'lamentable' and Minney's decision a, 'sad imprudence'; he later told the Duke of York that, while he did not refuse to agree to the match, he intended to see that every penny of the dowry was placed in Minney's name alone; half of it could be used at her discretion, and the other half of the capital she could, at a later date, divide among any children she might have. This would mean that she and her children would always be financially secure.

These details were read out to Maria and Minney in Tilney Street by the Duke of York, who reported back to the King that 'Both ladies appeared most affected by the extreme kindness of your letter, and after Miss Seymour, who was so nervous as to be hardly able to speak, had retired, Mrs Fitzherbert expressed herself in most feeling terms of acknowledgement of your goodness'. Maria had thought it right to mention Dawson Damer's likely inheritance, and the Duke ended his letter, 'She at the same time told ... that Lieutenant-Colonel Damer had in the course of last week applied to Lady Caroline Damer from whom he had received for answer ... that she thought it right to acquaint him, that she had in her will bequeathed to him the Came estate'.[18]

Maria had been reassured by the King's arrangements, but Dawson Damer felt himself insulted, telling George Seymour he thought it 'unusual, degrading and clearly betraying a want of confidence in me'.[19] In the end he had to swallow his pride, and he and Minney were married on 20 August at St George's Hanover Square. The King sent Minney a jewel, and a letter in which he asked her to 'be always good to my dear old friend Mrs Fitzherbert'.[20]

Maria was not at Minney's wedding. It had always been agreed that Minney should be married from her brother's house, with the Seymours as her witnesses. As Catholics, Maria and Marianne were not expected to attend the church, and Maria felt it more tactful, in all the circumstances, to give her blessings to Minney in private, leaving town before the wedding day. Her 'goodbyes' to her darling child were hard to say, but not because she hadn't accepted Minney's decision. Minney had told George Dawson Damer at the end of July, 'There never was anything equal to Mrs Fitzherbert's goodness for she appears to have put any feelings of her own away'.[21] But there was still sadness in the parting. From now on, Tilney Street and the house on the Steine would seem empty without her, and the presence of quiet Marianne Smythe, though welcome, could not make up for the loss of Minney.

Minney spent the time before her wedding at her brother's apartment at Hampton Court, and Maria wrote to her from Buxton, yet another watering place, where she and Marianne had gone for a few weeks. 'I will not revert to my parting with you, dearest', she began, 'the distress that occupied my mind at the idea of a separation from you affected me so much that I could not say half that I wanted to say to you, but ran out of the house, as fast as I could, so as not to annoy you by my sufferings. I am glad Hampton Court was made agreeable to you.'[22] Minney wrote several notes to Mama during these busy weeks before her wedding, and Maria replied affectionately. Marianne is mentioned in one of them, 'Mary desires her kind love. She would have written but this place affords no subject for letters, for we are living in the most perfect retirement quite *au bout du monde*'.[23] Unlike Minney, Marianne was never an ardent letter writer. Maria wrote again on 21 August:

It is quite impossible my dearest, dear Minney, to express to you half of what my feelings are at this moment. Your dear letters of Friday and Saturday I have received, and feel much gratified that at the moment you had so much to occupy you, you should think of me. Though I cannot help feeling that I do deserve it, from the very great and tender attachment I have ever felt for you since your birth. No mother I am certain ever loved her own child more dearly than I have loved you. I pray to God from morning to night that your happiness may be as complete as I wish and as you deserve.[24]

She longed to see Minney before the couple's departure for for France and Italy, but this proved difficult to arrange; instead she sent a bank note with the brief message, 'Pray accept the enclosed to buy Hats and Bonnets at Paris. I wish I was able to make it thousands instead of hundreds'.[25]

Still vigilant on her darling's behalf she wrote again on 7 September, Minney being now somewhere in France, 'I hope you are at this moment safely arrived. I watched the weather all day on Tuesday. The day here was beautiful and I trust you had a good passage. Pray direct all your letters for me to Tilney Street as Whale [her butler] will know where to find me, for if I am pretty well, I am going on a tour of visits'.[26]

The visits began a few days later when she and Marianne went to Hooton, the house of Sir Thomas Stanley and his wife Mary, Maria's niece. They were warmly welcomed. She wrote that 'Nothing can exceed the kind attentions of the inhabitants'. She also expressed great relief at leaving odious Buxton, 'I really think I should have died had I stayed longer'. She and Marianne were surrounded by family, 'Louisa [Wat's wife] and her children are all here and four of Sir Stanley's boys are now at home. I am quite charmed by them. You cannot think what well-behaved handsome creatures they are'.[27] She received 'very kind invitations' from the Cholmondeleys and the Seftons, but had to send her excuses because she had firmly promised to be at Chatsworth by 8 October. This was a quieter and, from her point of view, a more congenial Chatsworth than the one she had visited long ago with the Prince of Wales, when Georgiana was Duchess. The present Duke was Georgiana's only son. 'No one', she wrote to Minney, 'could be kinder than he has been to me.' He had been one of Minney's admirers, but from a discreet distance. He never married. He knew Minney well enough to recognise her handwriting when a letter arrived, dated from Nantes, and took it to Maria himself, knowing she would be overjoyed. 'We often talk of you', she wrote in her reply. 'The Duke seemed very much pleased at your having bought so many French hats etc. He is greatly occupied with ladies' dresses. He says you dress remarkably well.' Now in her sixties, Mrs Fitzherbert, was no longer 'greatly occupied' with fashion herself. 'He expects everybody to be dressed here as if going to a Ball, and looks rather shy if you have not a fresh gown for every day. This is rather a bore for me, for I hate the trouble of dressing up and in this particular I am afraid I don't stand very high in his estimation.'[28]

Though surrounded by the kindness of friends and enjoying her visits, Maria was sometimes 'out of spirits', slipping into a state of mind she called 'the dismals'. At these moments it was the thought of Minney's return that lifted the dark mood. 'I constantly pray to God to spare my life that I may be blessed by the sight of you again', she wrote from Chatsworth. While there she caught a 'violent cold' which kept her in bed, and delayed her next visit, which was to Swynnerton, her old home. She was welcomed there by her nephew, Thomas Fitzherbert. From Swynnerton she went on to Trentham, where Lady Stafford was 'constantly lamenting' that Minney was not her own daughter-in-law. Her son, Francis Leveson Gower, was one of the long list of those who had wanted to marry Minney.

By 7 November Maria was back in Tilney Street and from there 'Dearest Min' received her next letter. 'I arrived here the day before yesterday, rather glad to get to my fireside before the very bad weather sets in ... I ought to be, and indeed am, very much pleased with my tour. It is quite impossible to tell you all the kind attentions and courtesies I have received from everybody.'[29]

Throughout the winter letters passed regularly between Minney and Mama, and then, in mid January, came the letter that filled Maria with excitement, and anxiety. She replied almost at once, 'Your letter of the 31st I received the day before yesterday. The contents made me laugh at the ridiculous account you give of yourself not a syllable of what you say shall pass my lips ...' Minney had confided that she was pregnant.

Maria urged the travellers to come home, 'It is now quite necessary you should return to England instead of remaining abroad. I have been enquiring all over London to get a house for you, for I cannot bear the idea of your not having a Home somewhere and since I have had your last letter I am more anxious than ever'.[30] But at the end of February Minney and Dawson Damer were still in Italy. Maria was by now even more worried and wrote to Minney in Naples:

We are all looking forward with great anxiety to your safe arrival in this country ... I cannot tell you dearest the delight with which I look forward to once more embracing you, my dearest child ... only if, my dear Minney, taking so long a journey in your situation will not be detrimental to you, for God's sake don't hesitate but set out immediately ... You can have no idea of the anxiety which we all feel to have you amongst us.

She also assured her, 'You may depend upon finding on your arrival a comfortable House and everything you can want, therefore make your mind easy upon that score'.[31]

Arrangements for buying a house for the Dawson Damers fell through, however, at the last minute, and in the end it was to Tilney Street, large, comfortable and familiar, that Minney returned. The journey had been slow, and it was only a matter of weeks before her confinement.

Dawson Damer was about to change careers. Lady Glengall had suggested he stand for Parliament in the Irish constituency of Tipperary, and he was on the hustings in Clonmel when Minney's baby daughter was born. The joy and relief at the safe arrival of this child was felt not just by the father and Maria, but by Marianne, the Seymours, and all their wide circle of family and friends. They had shared the anxious weeks as the mother-to-be travelled back from Naples, and they had all known of too many deaths and still births to be easy until it was over.

Maria wrote joyfully to George Dawson Damer two days later: 'I have the best news possible to send you. Our dear Minney has had a very good night and Doctor Herbert says she is quite well ... She desires a thousand loves to you and bids me tell you the Baby is in a very flourishing state.'

Maria was not so absorbed by the baby as to forget about Dawson's election hopes. 'I have just had a very delightful note from Glengall [Lady Glengall's son] of the proceedings. We are very happy your address is so much approved. How surprised they will be to see you on Monday. We shall be all anxiety to hear how you are received.' Marianne gets another of her brief mentions in the same letter, 'You may

depend on hearing again either from me or Mary by Monday's post ...'
The letter ends, 'God Bless you, My Best wishes attend you'.[32]

Lady Glengall, eager for her man to win the election, wrote, 'impudently' in Maria's opinion, to Lady Caroline Damer asking for £2000 for election expenses. Dawson knew nothing of this, and Maria spoke immediately to his sisters. 'I have seen your sisters', she informed him. 'They are both very indignant at Lady Glengall's conduct. Lady Louisa writes today to Lady Caroline to tell her we are very much annoyed at the report of Lady Glengall writing her for money, and particularly on your account who are perfectly ignorant of such an application ... They both desire to be kindly remembered and are very anxious for your return, in which', Maria added firmly, 'all the inhabitants of this House most lovingly join.'[33] A baby, an Irish election and a lot of goodwill on both sides had brought them together, and from this time onwards Minney, George Dawson Damer and Maria Fitzherbert were a united trio.

14

Marianne

Towards the end of the year, while in Bath ('that detestable place') taking the waters, Maria heard that the Duke of York was seriously ill. Shortly after the New Year she learned, from Sir Henry Halford, that the Duke's condition was very grave indeed, she replied sadly: 'Your letter has grieved me to the heart ... I have long thought his case deplorable, but now I begin quite to despair, and to feel that there is no chance of his recovery. Alas! what a loss the country, his family, and his friends will sustain. I am sure none will feel or lament it more than I shall'.[1]

The Duke died on 5 January 1827. Mrs Fitzherbert was right in believing many would mourn and miss him. Charles Greville once wrote of him, 'He is the only one of the Princes who has the feelings of an English Gentleman. His amiable disposition and excellent temper have conciliated for him the esteem and regard of men of all parties and he has endeared himself to his friends by the warmth and steadiness of his attachments, and through the implicit confidence they have in in his truth, straightforwardness and sincerity'.[2] Maria regarded him as the best friend she had ever had. They had corresponded for years, their long letters covering a wide range of topics, but they had agreed that, when one of them died, all the letters should be destroyed. Lord Stourton commented 'when Sir Herbert Taylor gave her up her own correspondence, she was for two years employed in the perusal and burning of these most interesting letters ...'[3] He added, that, if she had 'entertained mercenary views', she could have obtained any price she had chosen to ask for the correspondence which she claimed provided the best private and public history from the end of the American wars to the Duke's death. She stayed in Brighton until May that year, but, out of respect for the Duke's memory, gave no large parties.

The publication of Thomas Moore's biography of Sheridan that year reminded everyone of the 'Catholic Marriage Question', and 'The Subject', as Maria called it, was being talked about again. Sir William Knighton, the King's Private Secretary, was claiming that such a marriage had never taken place, and John Croker recorded a conversation with the King in which his Majesty insisted there was no truth in 'that absurd story of my supposed marriage'.[4] The King was one of the few people who knew that a marriage certificate existed, and it would have suited him very well if it could be acquired and destroyed. After Maria's death, Charles Greville wrote, 'One remarkable attempt was made by Sir William Knighton ... Although a stranger to Mrs Fitzherbert, he called one day at her house where she was ill in bed, insisted upon seeing her and forced his way into her bedroom. She contrived to get rid of him without him getting anything out of her'.[5] The King knew Maria had always kept her documents in a locked box in her room, and no one knew better than him the layout of the rooms in both her houses. Knighton must have brushed past her servants and gone without hesitation to the right room. There is, of course, no proof that the King connived at this rash attempt, but he would certainly have benefited had it succeeded. One can only imagine Maria's outrage.

In spite of recurring ill health, grief over the death of the Duke, and annoyance over the resurgence of the old Marriage Question, Maria continued to play her part as a hostess in Brighton and London. On 24 February 1827 Prince Puckler-Muskau, a visitor from Germany, wrote, 'I spent this evening at Mrs F.'s, a very dignified and delightful woman, formerly, it is affirmed, married to the King. She is now without influence in that region, but still universally beloved and respected – *d'un excellent ton et sans prétention*. In this house one sees only the *beau monde*'.[6] John Croker claimed that she liked Brighton because everyone there treated her like royalty, 'They don't *Highness* her in her domestic circle but they *Madam* her prodigiously, stand up longer for her arrival than for ordinary folks ...'[7]

In the early summer of 1827, the Count de la Garde visited Brighton, and noted in his diary that he saw Maria at Mass in the Catholic Chapel in High Street:

> I found myself in a pew near Colonel Stonor, whom I already knew and at the end of Mass we went out together ... On our way I asked the Colonel who was the lady who heard Mass in a room adjacent to the

chapel whose regular and noble countenance retained traces of great beauty. It is Mrs Fitzherbert, he answered, the Madame de Maintenon of England; the regularity of her features, at an advanced age, her exemplary piety, the qualities which distinguish her, the marriage which she contracted with the King in her youth, although not valid or recognised like your celebrated Marquise, give her nevertheless a remarkable resemblance to Mlle d'Aubigne ...[8]

Most English Catholics believed that there had been a marriage, but few spoke of it as openly as Colonel Stonor seems to have done.

The Count also gave the only contemporary description of Marianne. He attended a ball at the Ship Hotel and was introduced to her by a Mrs Concannon, who told him who she was while they watched her dance the quadrille. The Count was charmed:

I had singled her out from her companions; all were beautiful, full of the bloom of youth, but, probably by a kind of national instinct, I found something French about her, which immediately attracted admiration. Pale, with an enchanting purity, her dark lashes surrounded eyes of a beautiful blue and gave her whole face a character at once tender and melancholy. In a word, the soft and delicate aspect of her features equalled the grace of her movements ... While refreshments were being offered Mrs Concannon took the opportunity of presenting me to Miss Smith, to whom I offered my arm while awaiting the commencement of the next dance. If I had been charmed by all the grace which was so admired in her, how much more was I when I conversed with her.[9]

Marianne was now of an age to enjoy the London Season, and, on leaving Brighton, she and Maria joined Mrs Wat Smythe and her daughters, Louisa and Charlotte (known to their aunt as Lou and Cou), to enjoy the balls and breakfasts of the London Season. On a glorious June day, they were preparing to go to a breakfast near Richmond, hosted by Lords Castlereagh and Chesterfield, when they received the news that Uncle Errington had died. Young Louisa wrote in her diary, for 30 June 1827, 'It certainly was not an unexpected event and it is only to be wondered at that he arrived to such an advanced age, but however expected the event I could not help wishing it had not happened today ... We did not get to Richmond Hill till after four, when we found Aunt Fitz very cross and the rest of the party rather in a fuss'.[10] The evening was warm, food was served in the garden, and dancing and fireworks went on late into the night, but Mrs Fitzherbert might have wished for somewhere more private to remember her uncle, and the part he played with unfailing kindness in her troubled past.

The Errington estates were left to the second son of Mary Stanley (Frances Smythe's daughter) and legacies to the great nieces, Louisa, Charlotte and Marianne. Louisa, preparing for the Almacks Ball, wrote in her diary for 4 July, 'We went to Tilney Street, and drove all over the Town to get black beads. Mama did not go to Almacks, therefore Mary and I went with Minney. We went *en noir*, but did not look so *triste* as our costumes bespoke us'.

Back in Brighton for the New Year of 1828, accompanied by the Smythes, Maria gave an elegant dinner for twelve on 1 January, and on the 25th she gave a ball of which Louisa wrote, 'The Ball was universally considered charming. Aunt F. looked *à merveille*, and everybody seemed in high force'.

In the spring a marriage began to be talked about between Marianne and Captain Edward Jerningham, second son of Lord Stafford. Maria hinted of this to Minney, in Paris, but later had to admit: 'I have little hopes of the event I announced taking place. Everything we could wish for or desire except that odious commodity money, which on the part of the young man is very deficient'. This must have sounded familiar to Minney:

> The person's name and connections are most desirable in every point of view and the father and mother ... have written such kind and affectionate letters upon the subject that we are both charmed and so would you be if you knew all ... The young man is Edward Jerningham, second son of Lord Stafford, very amiable, good-looking and gentlemanlike. His brother I believe is now in Paris. Therefore for Heaven's sake don't say anything about it to a human being. There are unfortunately ten younger children, their fortune five thousand each, which is so very trifling that though I shall give Mary at present twenty thousand added to this, they could not exist without a further addition. I have written to beg they will endeavour to do something more. If this is not acceded to, the marriage cannot take place.[11]

Marianne took a practical view. According to Mama, 'Mary has not seen enough of him to be much attached and feels the smallness of his fortune would be a great drawback to their mutual comfort, for it really would not enable them to have the common necessaries and comforts of life and if they should have children they would absolutely be paupers'.

More money was found by the Jerninghams, and the marriage went ahead on 16 June 1828. Maria gave a splendid breakfast at Tilney Street on the day, and the servants were allowed a ball of their own in the evening, in the bride's honour. Maria wrote to Marianne the following day, 17 June 1828:

> Though half dead with fatigue I will not let the post go without scribbling a few lines to you, dearest Mary. I long to hear you got safe to Tunbridge and that you found your new habitation comfortable. I never passed a more melancholy day than I did yesterday. After you left me I really felt quite alone in the world. Minney came to me about seven o'clock and we went to Lady Stanley's a little after ten. My servants were very anxious to get me out of the house that they might begin their amusements. They were all in high spirits and kept up the ball till near six this morning ... Say a thousand kind things from me to my son-in-law and believe me ever most affectionately.[12]

She wrote again on 21 July:

> Your welcome letter has given me the greatest pleasure and delight to hear that my little girl has been received in the manner you mention. It really affected me so much that I have shed abundance of tears. I should have behaved very ill had I been present, for kindness and joy such as you have received is very affecting ... you would laugh at me if at this moment you could witness the large drops that trickle down my cheeks.

She had become very fond of Marianne over the last few years and was obviously pleased with this marriage. She continued

> The Stanleys take their departure this morning. They and Minney quite well. I am going to her and shall show her your letter and I shall do the same at Cumberland Place [the Smythes' house]. I have great delight in doing so. I shall enjoy seeing their faces when they read all the grand and great doings and the delightful welcome you have received from all both high and low.

The Smythes had always been jealous of Marianne, and Lou had commented unkindly on Edward Jerningham. The letter ended, 'I trust, my dear Child, that I shall live to have the gratification of seeing you as happy and as much beloved as you deserve'.[13] She had written to Minney the previous November, 'It is a great consolation, at my advanced age, to have those I love the most (yourself and Mary, my two children) both well and happy, and to receive from them kindness and affection and to end my days in peace and quietness'.[14]

The year 1829 began happily for Maria, whose days were by no means ending yet. The newly-wed Jerninghams ('the Jams', as she sometimes called them) had joined her in Brighton for Christmas, and Minney and George Dawson Damer, who now had a second daughter, Blanche, arrived with Louisa and Charlotte Smythe for the New Year. Eager for the young to enjoy themselves, Maria a gave a fancy dress ball. The *Brighton Gazette* for 14 January gave it a rapturous write up:

> Mrs Fitzherbert's grand Fancy Dress Ball was not only the most splendid party given during the present Season but the most splendid ever seen in Brighton. There were more than two hundred present, including all the Fashionables now residing in the town. No magnificence can be conceived greater than that displayed in the various dresses which were exceedingly rich ... The fine rooms of the noble mansion ... lighted up, presented a most brilliant and dazzling appearance; and on the supper table every delicacy was seen in profusion. Kirchner's excellent quadrille band was in attendance.

Along with all the 'Fashionables', there were 'Army and Navy officers in number'.

Later in the year Maria finally managed to buy a London house as a present for Minney. The property was in Upper Grosvenor Street, and was purchased from a Mr Rigby for £13,000. Lady Caroline Damer died in 1829, and the house at Came was now the Dawson Damers' country home. From this time onwards Maria's letters to Minney are punctuated with thanks for fine pineapples, melons and peaches from the Came hot houses. Also in this year, Marianne gave birth to a son, Augustus.

In the early months of 1829 a Bill for Catholic Emancipation was introduced into the Commons. In March Maria wrote to George Dawson Damer, asking 'What is to happen next about the Catholic Question? News arrived very early here announcing the majority of Government'.[15] Getting the Bill through Parliament had never been the problem. The problem had always been George III, and his interpretation of his coronation oath. Now his son was following the example of his 'revered and sainted father'. He called the Cabinet to Windsor and, after six hours of quoting his father, of weeping and praying and of much drinking of brandy, he dismissed them all. Later he learned there were not enough opponents of Emancipation to replace the Cabinet he had sacked. He sent for Wellington, who told him him that royal consent was necessary to prevent violent uprisings in Ireland. The King gave in and signed the Bill the following month, tears rolling down his rouged cheeks. It was a very long time since he had said the Catholic religion was the only one fit for a gentleman.[16]

Catholic men could now stand for Parliament and take their seats if elected. They could hold any office, judicial or administrative, with the exception of Lord Chancellor or Lord Lieutenant of Ireland, and the nine Catholic peers could take their seats in the House of Lords. These changes, long in coming, were welcomed by English Catholics, but were absolutely crucial to the Irish, who had demanded for years the right to return Catholic Members to Parliament. Apart from one query to Dawson Damer about the procedure in the Commons, none of Mrs Fitzherbert's letters contain any reference to Emancipation. She had retained the habit of keeping very quiet on matters of religion.

The Catholic question had been brought into the Westminster limelight this time by Daniel O'Connell, an Irish barrister who had for a number of years been the leader of agitation in Ireland for Catholic rights. He brought matters to a head in 1828 when he was elected as MP for County Clare, but was not permitted to take his seat. After the Bill was passed, O'Connell stood again for Clare in 1830, was elected and duly took his seat. Known as the Liberator in Ireland, he was never liked by English Catholics. They had gained themselves relief from most of the penal laws by years of tactful representation, demonstrations of loyalty to the Hanoverians, and consistently quiet behaviour. They believed they would have gained Emancipation as well, without O'Connell, and regarded his method of political agitation as unacceptable if not dangerous. It must also be admitted that his personality jarred on them. When, later, he called Lord Alvanley a 'bloated buffoon' in the House of Commons he was immediately challenged to a duel, George Dawson Damer acting as Alvanley's second. O'Connell had taken a vow never to fight another duel and it was his soldier son Morgan who met Alvanley and Dawson Damer at dawn on Wimbledon Common, on

5 May 1835, while Minney and Mrs Fitzherbert waited nervously at home. Shots were fired and honour satisfied, but neither man was wounded.[17] In a letter to Lord Stourton, Maria referred to O'Connell, rightly or wrongly, as 'very mischievous'.[18]

The King's health was beginning to cause anxiety in early 1830. He had never really recovered from giving consent to Catholics entering Parliament: 'Let them get a Catholic King in Clarence', he had muttered at the time, referring to the brother who would become King on his death, and implying that this event was now not far away. London and Brighton were full of rumours of the King's ill health, and indeed of his approaching death. Croker recorded that his master was always announcing his imminent departure into the next world. 'I shall be dead by Saturday', he frequently foretold. His condition noticeably improved, however, and Maria told George Dawson Damer that she was in no way surprised, 'for I knew the man'.

But the improvement did not last. In June Minney passed on the news that the King was failing. She had already sent a concerned message to him through Sir Henry Halford, one of several doctors attending him, and received a message in return sending his, 'very affectionate love'. Maria, who had heard conflicting stories about the King's condition, decided to ask Sir Henry for accurate news of the man she had never ceased to regard as her husband. She enquired with the greatest possible discretion, as a letter to Minney shows:

> I have frequently intended writing to Sir Henry but have always delayed it for fear of being thought intruding and curious, but your letter has given me courage and I have by this night's mail dispatched a letter for him under cover to Whale [her butler] to leave at Sir Henry's door, for if it were known, in this gossiping place, that I had written or had received a letter a thousand falsehoods would have been afloat.[19]

Sir Henry replied on 3 June, from Windsor, where the King was, with only Lady Conyngham, Sir William Knighton and the Duke of Cumberland admitted to his room:

> My dear kind Madam, I have not written a letter, nay not a note, since I came to Windsor on Sunday night, excepting to such of the Royal Family as required information and as it was my duty to give it. But I yield most

willingly to our friendship what I should withhold on any other possible ground and motive.

Though with hardly any time to write, as the King's condition worsened, Halford thought Maria entitled to the same information as the royal family. 'The King', he told her, 'has been and continues excessively ill, with embarrassment and difficulty of breathing ... What will be the result I can hardly venture to say with confidence ...' [20]

Maria read no optimism in this letter, and decided the time had come for her to send the King a last message of respect and affection, ending the long silence between them. After much thought she wrote:

Sir, After many repeated struggles with myself, from the apprehension of appearing troublesome or intruding upon Your Majesty, after so many years of continual Silence, my Anxiety respecting Your Majesty has got the better of my Scruples, and I trust Your Majesty will believe me most sincere, when I assure you how truly I have grieved to hear of your Sufferings. From the late account, I trust Your Majesty's health is daily improving, and no one can feel more rejoiced to learn Your Majesty is restored to complete Convalescence, which I pray to God you may long enjoy, accompanied with every degree of happiness you can wish for or desire.

I have enclosed this letter to Sir Henry Halford, as Your Majesty must be aware that there is no person about him through whom I could make a Communication of so private a nature, attended with the perfect conviction of its never being divulged. [21]

Carefully composed, free of anything that could embarrass him if found by any 'person about him', it is yet so very touching when read now, by those who know her story, and all the suffering he had caused her.

Having sent the letter, she left Brighton for Tilney Street, where she waited in case the King sent some message, or called her to his bedside. Sir Henry reported that he had delivered the letter and that the King received it with every sign of pleasure and placed it beneath his pillow. She continued to wait. No word came from the King, and in the early hours of the morning on 26 June 1830, just as Henry Halford came into his room, and with only time to give the old doctor his hand, George IV died. [22] An hour or two later, the great bell of St Paul's began to toll telling Londoners that their King had passed into another world. It is said that a friend of Maria's heard it, and made his way to Tilney Street to tell her that she was once again a widow. [23]

After the King's death Maria went through a time of great sadness. She told Lord Stourton that nothing had 'cut her up' so much as getting no reply from her letter to the King. She had hoped for a sign, however small, to show that all they had shared in their time of happiness still had some meaning for them both, and that they had made their peace before he died. Sir Henry Halford could have told Maria that George was almost blind by the end, and could not have read her letter. Knowing it came from her, and guessing its contents were private, he was unlikely to have asked any of those around him, Lady Conyngham, Knighton or Cumberland, to read it to him. George did not wish his near-blindness to be generally known, which may be why Sir Henry made no mention of it.

George IV's obituary in *The Times*, savagely attacking him, did nothing to lift Maria's spirits.[24] Lady Conyngham's departure from Windsor, almost as soon as the King had breathed his last, taking with her several carriage loads of plate and jewels, confirmed Maria's opinion that she had never really cared for the King, and that he had died a lonely death. George Dawson Damer had insisted on going racing at Ascot during the King's last days, seeing no reason to stay at home with Minney, whose affection for 'Prinny' had never changed, and whose grief and anxiety over his suffering was overwhelming her. The people of London showed no signs of grief; later generations would appreciate his interest in the arts, his collection of paintings, the building of Regent Street, the transforming of Windsor Great Park, and the fantasy Pavilion at Brighton, but in the summer of 1830 his faults were uppermost in people's minds and his passing was met with indifference. His brother, the Duke of Clarence, now William IV, refused to wear mourning. Maria must have felt that only she, Minney and his surviving sisters wept for the dead King, remembering how he had once been.

The funeral took place at nine in the evening of 15 July at Windsor. The coffin was carried to St George's Chapel, by six dukes and four eldest sons of dukes, between lines of Grenadier guardsmen, every fifth one carrying a burning torch. The procession was led by the Guards' trumpeters, drummers and fifers, and behind the coffin were carried the crown of Hanover the crown of England and the sword of state. At the rear walked William IV enveloped in a splendid purple cloak. It was impressive pageantry, but there were few signs of grief in either the chapel or the town. William IV talked audibly during much of the service, and left before the end, leaving the rest of the congregation to witness the lowering of the coffin into the grave, while minute guns were fired in the Long Walk.

A month after the King's death, on 25 July, her seventy-fifth birthday, Maria wrote of her low spirits in a letter to Minney:

> I was so worried with all the *tracasseries* of yesterday that I could not sleep, and therefore I got up early and went to ten o'clock church. I am just returned when I found your dear little note and the beautiful fan you were so kind as to send me. It is too fine for me, but very beautiful, and I beg you to accept my best thanks for it ... Don't wish me happy returns of this day. I do not desire them for myself. I often regret (though I am told it is wrong) that I ever was born, but I won't touch upon this subject, as I don't wish to hurt your feelings ...[25]

In addition to her sadness, Maria was worried about money again. Most of her annual allowance came from a mortgage on the Pavilion, and she was full of anxiety in case the new King would not agree to its payment. Without it, she told Minney, 'I shall be penniless'. Marianne, writing to her husband during George IV's last illness when Maria first began to worry, showed how calm and sensible a young woman she had become. 'Mama's despatch to the Bank concerning *certain private papers* proved extremely satisfactory and it appears that in the event of the King's death that sum at least cannot be taken from her, not that I have the least apprehension on the subject myself, for what she now enjoys is surely her right and as such who would attempt to deprive her of it?'[26]

Marianne was right. In September the new King and Queen visited Brighton to take possession of the Pavilion, and the question of her income was settled. Creevey recorded a conversation between the Duke of Sussex and Mrs Herbert Taylor, on 23 September 1830: 'You'll be glad to hear, Ma'am, that the King has continued to Mrs Fitzherbert the same pension she had before – I am very glad of it, Sir, it does His Majesty great honour. Oh, Ma'am, the whole family made a point of it'.[27] Honouring her with a visit to her house on the Steine, the King was shown some of her papers, and was moved to tears to think that she had possessed all this clear evidence of her marriage to his brother and yet kept silent. His offer to make her a Duchess was refused. Lord Stourton explained her reasons:

> He asked what amend he could make her, and offered to make her a Duchess. She replied that she did not wish for any rank; that she had borne through life the name of Mrs Fitzherbert; that she had never disgraced it, and did not wish to change it; that therefore she hoped His Majesty would accept her unfeigned gratitude for his gracious proposal, but that he would permit her to retain her present name.[28]

The King insisted that she use the royal livery, authorised her to wear widow's weeds for his late brother, and to put her servants into mourning. She was to dine with him and his family at the Pavilion at the earliest possible date.

This she did, and wrote to Minney, 'My reception was most flattering. I was overwhelmed with kisses from males and females; the Princess [Augusta] was particularly gracious. I felt rather nervous never having been in the Pavilion since I was drove away by Lady Hertford. I cannot tell you my astonishment at the magnificence and the total change since my first acquaintance'.[29] She had watched the exterior change into Nash's delicate Indian façade, but nothing had prepared her for the changes within. The long corridor had lost the bamboo furniture and chinoiserie that she remembered, and now held chairs and settees of ivory-veneered sandalwood. Beyond was a glorious mixture of stylised palm tree columns, carpets woven with dragons and serpents, great painted glass chandeliers shaped like water-lilies, and silk draperies of crimson and gold, all combining to present George IV's conception of 'the Splendour of the Crown'.[30]

The visit was the first of many. King William and Queen Adelaide planned to spend part of each year in Brighton and to entertain in royal style. Mary Frampton wrote in her diary the following February, 'The magnificence of the parties given by the King and Queen at the Pavilion are spoken of as realising the ideas of the entertainments described in the Arabian Nights ... The King consults Mrs Fitzherbert much as an old friend in matters relating to the fêtes'.[31]

As was customary, any portraits of Maria found in the late King's possession were returned to her, but one small locket with a tiny portrait by Cosway, covered with half a diamond and set in gold, could not be found. There were rumours that such a jewel had been seen on

George IV's neck during the last days of his life. She tentatively approached the King on the subject and he sent her a message by Sir George Seymour:

> The King sent for me yesterday evening to desire I would tell you that he had caused inquiries to be made about the little picture of yourself in a gold case, and that he had every reason to to believe it was not removed from the late King's neck. Sir Frederick Watson confirms this circumstance, which must afford you some satisfaction however melancholy it will be, and I believe they are right as it was seen on his neck a twelve month back also.[32]

The question was finally settled by the Duke of Wellington, who passed the truth on to Minney. Once again, it was Mary Frampton who heard the story and recorded it:

> The Duke of Wellington when one evening sitting next to Mrs Damer said to her with some hesitation: 'I dare say you may like to know something of the lost jewel', but added, 'perhaps I had better not tell you.' She pressed him however to continue when the Duke proceeded to state with some confusion that in his office as First Lord of the Treasury it had been his duty to remain till the very last with the body of the King, who had given him strict injunctions not to leave it, and had desired to be buried with whatever ornaments might be upon his person at the time of his death. The Duke was quite alone with the body then lying in an open coffin and his curiosity being excited by seeing a small jewel hanging round the neck of the King he was tempted to look at it, when he found it was the identical portrait of Mrs Fitzherbert covered with a diamond, for which an unsuccessful search had been made. The Duke added: 'I leave it to you to communicate this or not to Mrs Fitzherbert as you may think best for her.' As Mrs Fitzherbert scarcely ever alluded to her former connection with George IV, Mrs Damer doubted as to the propriety of naming this to her; but one day when the conversation between them led that way she ventured to tell the discovery. Mrs Fitzherbert made no observation but soon large tears fell from her eyes.[33]

No one will ever know what went on in George IV's mind. Several people remembered him stipulating that he was to be buried with the locket round his neck, but what did his wearing of it signify? He had for years been rewriting his own life in his mind, changing events and inventing new ones. The story of his claim to have led a cavalry charge at Waterloo, and to have frequently asked Wellington to confirm this, is well known. Towards the end of his life he was fond of telling Lady Melbourne's daughter, Lady Cowper, how he had visited her mother, one of his early mistresses, every day during her last illness. Lady Cowper had hardly left her mother's side during the last weeks of her life and she knew that he had never called.[34] As, sick and lonely, he realised that Lady Conyngham was simply feathering her nest and cared little for him, he may have looked back on his other loves, and, among them all, Maria must have stood out. It would not have been difficult to persuade himself that he had always been true to the wife of his heart and soul, and now wore her image to prove it. This would have made him feel a better man than he really was, and have helped him to forget how badly he had treated her. By the end, he possibly believed that it was all other people's fault, and that he had been forced to abandon her. Holding on to the idea of himself as the faithful lover, and reliving the days when he was young and handsome and admired by everyone, may have consoled him. Knowing that he died with her portrait round his neck may well have consoled Maria.

15

Endings

In the years that followed, Maria recovered her spirits. In spite of bouts of illness and increasing fatigue, she remained a part of London Society, receiving invitations to both St James's Palace and the Pavilion. William IV wanted to make public her marriage to his brother, feeling that justice demanded it, but the Duke of Wellington had 'set his face like a flint' against that. She welcomed an increasing brood of 'grand-children' – Minney and Marianne's children – to her Brighton house, all of them addressing her as 'Granny'. She still gave her elegant dinners, and in the early summer of 1831 Minney's letters to George Damer, fighting an election in Tipperary, give a glimpse of her enjoying the London Season: 'She is so gay. Today she dines with the Fremantles to meet the Landgravine and she is bent on going to the Opera to see Taglioni and has engaged a box with Lady Guildford ...'[1]

She returned to Brighton for Christmas and the New Year, and was frequently present at the 'Splendid Pleasures' at the Pavilion when William IV and Queen Adelaide were in residence. The *Brighton Herald* for 29 January 1831 reported on one of them:

> Upwards of 800 of the inhabitants and gentry of the country had the honour of receiving cards of invitation ... It was a very late hour before the most brilliant entertainment ever witnessed in this town concluded ... His Majesty conversed with his guests, particularly with Mrs Fitzherbert, who looked exceedingly well and whose sweetness and dignity of expression are proof against the attacks of time.

Sir George Seymour, acting as secretary to the King, stayed with Maria during the early months of 1831, and his diary, though in note form, adds to the picture of life in Brighton that winter. On 2 January he wrote 'Mrs Fitzherbert unwell', but not, it seems, for long, as the next day's entry noted, 'The Belfasts and Lady Aldborough dined with Mrs Fitzherbert', and the same evening, 'Played whist late with Mrs Fitzherbert'. On 26 January he recorded that, 'Mrs Fitzherbert had a very nice children's Ball at which Blanche made her debut'.[2] Blanche was one of Minney's daughters, aged three.

Since showing her papers to the new King, and being accepted by him as one of the family, Maria felt free to talk openly of her marriage. On the same day as he recorded the 'very nice Children's Ball', George Seymour wrote, 'Mrs Fitzherbert showed me a certificate dated December 15 1785 and a will of twenty-four sides of letter paper with four codicils signed and sealed by the Prince and written in his own hand, but without any witnesses' signatures, dated January 10 1796'. Mary Frampton, recorded the following month, 'Mr Humphrey Weld [one of Thomas Weld's sons] told me that he had seen the certificate of Mrs Fitzherbert's marriage to the late King when Prince of Wales and that since his death she talked openly of it'.[3]

Part of Maria's respect for the Duke of Wellington may have been because he saw the parliamentary reform, about which the whole country was talking this year, as being 'dangerous'. The 'reform', causing so much talk was intended to redistribute the parliamentary seats on a fairer basis, get rid of the pocket boroughs, where the member was virtually appointed by the local landowner, and to widen the franchise. It was a far cry from the universal suffrage of today, but it seemed a gigantic change to people of the time. The year 1830 had been one of revolution on the Continent. In Paris, Charles X had been forced to abdicate (finding refuge with the Welds in Maria's former home at Lulworth), and her friend the young Duke of Orleans had received the crown instead, as King Louis-Philippe, the 'Citizen King'. Riots were breaking out all over England: there were those who supported reform, those who believed a measure of reform would quieten the rioters, and others who were afraid reform would lead to more and more demands, and eventually to full-scale revolution. Maria was among the latter. She had never forgotten the terror of the Gordon Riots. Nor could she forget how many people she knew had died in revolutionary France. She agreed with Wellington that the Reform Bill held dangers.

Minney's letter to her husband on 23 May confirmed this. 'Yesterday I dined in Tilney Street where I met the Jerninghams, Smythes, Mr Bruce and Mr Weld. His reforming ideas do not suit Mama, who though she has no opinion, is I see in her heart very anti-reformish ...'[4] Maria remained in London for the summer and in May wrote to Minney, now enjoying a long visit to Ireland with her husband: 'though many think we are on the eve of revolution, everything in the great world goes on as usual – balls, dinners and Ascot races'.[5] In August she expressed similar fears: 'The town is quiet but at the smallest signal from Lord Grey is ready to rise, we are in a sad state. God knows what will happen ... He [the King] does everything Lord Grey wishes and I am sorry to say is only occupied with dinners and balls'.[6]

Lord Grey had triumphed in the election and a Whig government, committed to reform, was established. New peers were created that summer to ensure that next time the Reform Bill was introduced it would be passed by the Lords. Maria's comments to Minney were unfavourable: 'You will see an extraordinary list of Peers. I understand there are to be fifteen more made to get the majority in the House of Lords. Several have refused accepting this dignity and several that ought not from birth or situation are very anxious to be appointed. This is lowering the Peerage sadly'.[7]

In spite of this sudden interest in politics, Maria found time to worry over Mrs Wat and her daughters. On 5 September she wrote hurriedly to Minney in Ireland:

I must send you a few lines as you will probably see in the paper an account that a robbery has taken place at the Smythes' whilst they were at home about nine o'clock. When the servants were at supper some thieves got in at the garret window and finding nobody in that part of the house they have carried off every earthly thing of bijouterie both of Mrs Wat's and of the poor girls. They literally have nothing left of any sort or kind ... Their house is full of Bow Street Officers who gave them very little hopes of recovering their losses.[8]

Though genuinely fond of Mrs Wat, Maria had never had any illusions about her, and added, 'Of all the things that could have happened to to Mrs Wat nothing could be more distressing to her than the loss of her finery'.

A pre-Coronation party was given by the Duke of Devonshire at his house in Chiswick, and Maria described it for Minney: 'The Duke was in higher force than ever I have seen him. A remarkably good dinner, the illuminations, fireworks, and the house and grounds beautifully lit up. By nine o'clock dancing began, and I felt rather tired and came away. There was dinner for a hundred guests and the scene was altogether very gay.' Unfortunately, though the weather was fine, Maria caught a chill, 'Since then I have been confined by another attack of influenza and have not been able to leave my house. I have had three dinner invitations from the Palace and have been obliged to send excuses'.[9]

She missed the Coronation held later that month, but told Minney, 'The Coronation by all accounts went off beautifully and everybody seemed pleased'. This included the Smythes who, 'all went to the Coronation in the Chamberlain's box and were quite delighted. It was a little amusement and diverted their minds for they have been sadly worried by their loss'.[10]

The pageantry of a coronation did not, however, divert those rioting for parliamentary reform, as Maria, her fears increasing, noted in a letter to Minney from Tilney Street on 18 October:

> I have been *so* much worried and alarmed by all the riots that have been going on here these days that I could settle to nothing. The alarm everybody is in of what may happen is sadly increased by the accounts from different parts of the country. It is so similar to what happened in France that it is really quite *frightful*. Your friend Lady Georgiana (Bathurst) is for setting off to China and I believe if it was not for the sea voyage I should like to go there too.[11]

Hardly serious about escaping to China, Maria decided to go to Brighton, inviting the Smythes to join her explaining, in the same letter: 'Poor little Lou is looking ill ... from the fright of their house being broken into. It has had such an effect upon her that she never dares go to sleep and is often obliged to have things given in the night to quieten her nerves.' The stay in Brighton with Aunt Fitz calmed Lou's nerves better than medicines, and in December her engagement to Sir Frederick Hervey Bathurst was announced. Maria approved, writing to Minney, 'Lou is completely happy and delighted and I am half in love with Fred Bathurst myself. I think him so good-looking and so amiable. I wish he were not quite so shy but I hope he will upon better acquaintance get the better of that. I think dear Lou has a great prospect of happiness of which she, you know, is so deserving'. The practicalities had to be dealt with, and she added, 'He is not what is called rich at the present but all Lady Fremantle's property will come to him at her death'.[12]

Fred Bathurst's shyness made it difficult for the subject of money to be broached. Mrs Wat and her daughters were in financial difficulties as Charles Smythe had persistently refused to give them 'one farthing' of the income due to Mrs Wat after her husband's death. He now owed them in the region of £2000 and was adamant that they would get nothing. Mrs Fitzherbert found his behaviour 'quite disgusting' and did everything she could to persuade him to make proper payments. The matter was in the hands of lawyers, but they were doing little to help Mrs Wat, who, in turn, was doing nothing to curb her expenses. Mrs Fitzherbert consulted her friend Colonel Gurwood, the Duke of Wellington's secretary, who seems to have been acting as an unofficial secretary to her as well at this time. He went to Brambridge on her behalf but Charles simply repeated that Mrs Wat and her daughters would get nothing.

An undated letter to Gurwood from Maria, which must have been written late in 1832, describes a visit from Charles Smythe's daughter, Caroline McNotty. McNotty was her married name, but whether Charles had been married to her mother, and what had happened to Mr McNotty, is not clear. 'To my great surprise' Maria wrote:

> On Saturday morning who should enter my room but Mrs McNotty telling me that she had left her Father at Worthing very unwell ... She says he is so altered I should scarcely know him ... the only thing she tells me now on his mind is a thorough determination of never paying Mrs Smythe a farthing ... he has quarrelled with everyone, not only his friends but his acquaintances and nobody goes near him.[13]

Maria sent him conciliatory messages, saying she too was in old age and ill health but did not wish to leave this world with enmity to anyone, particularly himself. Charles died soon afterwards, on 20 October 1832, Colonel Gurwood willingly representing Maria at the funeral in Brambridge and helping to sort out Charles's papers. £50,000 was to be left in trust until his granddaughter, Emma McNotty, reached the age of twenty-one, when it was to be divided between her and her mother. In the meantime, Mrs Fitzherbert and Marianne were to be joint executors. If Caroline and Emma both died before Emma reached her majority, or if she married without Mrs Fitzherbert's approval, the money was to go to Marianne.

It seems that Maria was always left with responsibility for her brothers' affairs, but she had not seen her sister Frances for nearly eighteen years. Charles had tried to arrange a meeting of reconciliation between the two sisters but Maria had refused. As she explained to Gurwood:

> I and Lady Haggerston have quarrelled more that twenty years ago about some trifling money concerns for she has always been, where money was concerned, a counterpart to himself [Charles Smythe] but now she is in possession of 8 or 9000 per annum she perhaps may alter her conduct. She has added so much to the miseries of my life that though I forgive I cannot forget and we have not seen each other for seventeen or eighteen years.[14]

Lady Haggerston is not mentioned again in any of Maria's surviving letters.

Invitations from the 'Royalties' never ceased to be showered on her, but she was beginning to find the King's family hard to bear. The King's sons by Mrs Jordan lived with him and the Queen, and the eldest, now Earl of Munster, had a depressed and difficult personality. Maria, though fond of him, thought he caused most of his problems himself, and wrote to Minney, '*Entre nous* I think he is not right in the upper-storey'. The Queen, unable to produce a healthy heir herself, found it difficult living with the quarrelling FitzClarences, and Maria's sympathies were probably with her. But invitations from royalty could only be refused on grounds of serious ill health. 'Much as I like Brighton' she confided to Minney:

> I feel uncomfortable with respect to the Royalties. That happy family last year at the Pavilion is very different now … I am engaged to dine there every Sunday during their stay in Brighton which they told me was not to prevent my dining there other days of the week. They are all very kind to me and I feel grateful, but you know how it generally is …[15]

The one member of the royal family Maria was always pleased to see was Princess Augusta, the King's unmarried sister. Several affectionate notes from the Princess have survived, all similar to one sent from St James's on 1 January 1832: 'I have been so unfortunate as to miss you when you called at my House. May I therefore hope that you will dine with me tomorrow Monday at a little after seven o'clock. I shall be most happy to welcome you to my pretty little den.'[16] The two women had known each other a long time, Augusta was intelligent and thoughtful, and they always had much to talk about.

In spite of her involvement with the royal family, her fears of revolution and her worries over the Smythes, the greater part of Maria's thoughts and concerns always remained with Minney and Marianne, 'my children'. Marianne's marriage had proved a happy one, but she and Edward Jerningham were 'very unfortunate with their children', as Maria once put it. Augustus, their first born, was a healthy child, doted on by Maria. After a visit with her she wrote to Marianne that their friends, the Brisbanes, 'could talk of nothing but their admiration of your little Augustus and laughed heartily at his telling them I had a *Roman Catholic nose*'. But their second child, a girl, died in infancy. A second son, William Edward, seemed healthy, but when he was a few weeks old the family went to stay with the Jerningham grandparents, from where Marianne wrote to say that the baby was ill and likely to die. Maria replied in great distress:

> I cannot tell you, my dearest Marianne, how miserable your letter of yesterday made me ... I trust in God you may be able to send me more favourable accounts tomorrow ... if it pleases God to take the dear baby to Himself, you, my dearest, must exert all you fortitude and submit to His will. If my poor prayers for his restoration should be of any avail he has them from the bottom of my heart for I really had taken such an affection for that dear baby that no one but yourself and Edward could feel more interested about him.[17]

The child died a few days later, leaving Marianne in 'sad tribulation'. (In later years Marianne had another daughter, Emma, and a son, Fitzherbert, both of whom survived into adult life.)

The Dawson Damers were luckier with their children but had problems over money, leading to endless indecisions about where to live. George Dawson Damer was sometimes in Parliament and sometimes out, but did not hold a paid post. He had income from the estate at Came, and had remained in the army on half pay, but now talked of selling his commission and trying to become one of the King's equerries. Maria wrote to the King on his behalf and received promises in return, but no action, which annoyed her.[18] The Dawson Damers found it more economical to live abroad for much of the time. To her credit, Maria never criticised George during these years of changing plans and shortage of money, though she may, privately, have wished for a more settled life for Minney.

In the spring of 1833 the Duke of Wellington, always very gentle in his approaches to Maria, tactfully mentioned to Minney that it was time to dispose of the late King's papers, which included many letters from Maria. Minney passed this on to Maria who was filled with alarm. Wellington, one of the late King's executors, agreed with Maria that the letters should be returned to her and then burnt, together with any she held from him. Any she particularly wanted to keep could be put aside. Maria wrote to Gurwood on 23 August, 'The Duke of Wellington and Lord Albemarle are to come at twelve o'clock tomorrow morning. I am frightened to death for fear of setting my house on fire, I shall be heartily glad when this business is finished'.[19]

The burning took place in the presence of the Duke, Lord Albemarle and Lord Stourton on 24 August, and Maria was able to report to Gurwood, 'I am sure you will be glad to hear that the Duke of Wellington and Lord Albemarle have just left me and thank God my mind is relieved by having all the papers except some particular ones, committed to the flames. Nothing can have been more kind in every respect than your friend the Duke'.[20]

The documents retained by Maria, and placed in a box sealed by the Duke, Lord Albemarle and Lord Stourton, were deposited in Coutts' Bank. They are listed by both Lord Stourton and George Seymour as the marriage certificate; the Prince's will of 1796; a letter from the clergyman who married them (with a note by Mrs Fitzherbert attached); a letter from George IV while still the Prince of Wales referring to the marriage; and the deed mortgaging the Pavilion at Brighton to Mrs Fitzherbert.[21] George Seymour noted in his diary for 28 August:

> Mrs Fitzherbert acquainted me she was very happy and had a load taken off her mind by having arranged the future disposition of her papers ... these five other documents had been sealed and deposited at her Banker's with a label saying they were only to be opened should the said three Trustees think it essential to produce them if her character was assailed in future'.[22]

Maria had, however, made no arrangements for the papers after the deaths of Lord Stourton, Lord Albemarle and the Duke of Wellington, whose agreement was needed before the seals could be broken. Various requests to open the box were made in order to refute articles in the *Edinburgh Review* in 1838, 1841 and 1842, which were felt to be derogatory. The Duke of Wellington vetoed any breaking of the seals. Lord Stourton died in 1846, leaving his Memoir with his nephew Charles Langdale. Lord Albemarle died in 1851 and the Duke of Wellington in 1852. It was uncertain who now had responsibility for the box of documents. In 1854 Lord Holland's *Memoirs of the Whig Party* were published posthumously. In them he claimed that Mrs Fitzherbert had told a friend of his, unnamed, that she cared nothing for the marriage ceremony, knew the marriage was illegal and was 'nonsense', and that she had told the Prince so. Again pleas were made to the Bank to have the box opened to defend Maria's good name, that being the reason she had deposited the documents. Permission was refused, and Langdale prepared to publish Lord Stourton's Memoir. A limited edition was published in 1856.[23] The contents of the box were named, including the marriage certificate. The box, still sealed, was removed to the Royal Archives at Windsor for discreet keeping by Edward VII.

This, however, was all in the future. At the time, Maria felt her business had been completed, and left for Aix-la-Chapelle to take the waters and enjoy her new peace of mind.

Maria wrote to Lord Stourton from Paris, on 7 December 1833:

> I went to Aix-la-Chapelle: the waters did wonders and I find my health is so improved by change of scene, that I determined to pass my winter on the Continent ... I have taken a very quiet apartment and live very retired, seeing occasionally some friends. The Duke of Orleans[24] came to see me the moment I arrived, with a thousand kind messages from the King and Queen desiring me to go to them, which I accordingly have done ... I really think I never saw a more amiable family: so happy and united.[25]

Lady Warrender wrote to Colonel Gurwood, 'I saw Mrs Fitzherbert at the Embassy and her manner to me was, as it has always been, most kind. I was surprised to see her so little changed in the ten years which have passed since you and I used to meet so often at her fireside'.[26]

Minney was staying in Paris with her Mama, and Countess Granville (wife of the British Ambassador), gave the Duke of Devonshire a less tranquil picture of Maria's Paris life: 'Mrs Damer is so flustered and hysterical with the universal hubbub that she invited a party to Fitz. two days ago. Granville amongst the number went and found Fitz. was gone to the Opera and nobody at home'.[27] Minney was finding Maria difficult and wrote to her husband: 'Mama has had a regular fit of gout which had she submitted to it patiently would have done her good ... she certainly does not suffer as much as she says ... I have been obliged to make her excuses for a dinner at the Tuileries tomorrow ... It is odd that she does not like people to know that she has gout and begs I will not publish it in England'.[28] Maria recovered her good humour, if not from her gout, and Minney continued in her next letter: 'I sat with her last Sunday in the darkened bedroom ... she was very amusing about her younger days and told me it was the forty-eighth anniversary of her marriage with the King December 15th 1785.'[29]

Princess Augusta wrote from Brighton on 1 January 1834:

> It was but yesterday, my dearest Mrs Fitzherbert, that I was talking of you and saying how truly sorry I was that you were not here; and this morning I had the great pleasure of receiving your most kind letter. It was *a pleasure indeed* and I thank God you have given me so good an account of your health. I shall be reconciled to your being far away if it is for your good; otherwise we all lament your absence from Brighton at this house ... Accept of my kindest wishes ... that you may return to England in the spring when none of your friends will be happier to see you than, my dearest Mrs Fitzherbert, your very sincere and attached friend.[30]

But when the spring came, Maria was in no hurry to return. In May she wrote to Marianne, 'I have left the Hôtel de Londres for the last month. There were so many disagreeable things there that finding my old apartment at the Hôtel Bristol empty I have taken possession of it and am very comfortable'.[31] In August she went to Aix and then on to Spa, from where one of her letters to Minney, dated 12 August, ended with a sad postcript: 'August 12. A melancholy and memorable recollection'. The date was George IV's birthday, celebrated so often in Brighton, years ago, when Maria and the Prince were still happy together. She was beginning to feel her age and wrote wistfully to Minney regarding plans for the winter: 'I wish I could make myself some years younger and my health better. I should then have much pleasure in joining you anywhere you and George might propose but alas! *mes beaux jours son passés,* and I must make up my mind to my armchair and my fireside. I am not fit for anything else'.[32]

A few days after her return to London she was surprised to be sent for by the King. He told her he had had a gift specially made for her, and presented her with a pair of diamond bracelets. She told George Damer, 'The value was nothing to me, but the kind manner that accompanied it was very flattering. I have shown them to everyone as the first and only present he ever gave me'.[33] In October she went on visits to her two Smythe nieces. Louisa was now Lady Hervey Bathurst, and Charlotte was married to Augustus Craven and living at Brambridge.

She returned to Brighton for Christmas and New Year and stayed until the following April, when she left threatening never to return. A letter from Miss Lucia Jeffreys to Minney, dated 23 June, gives a partial explanation:

> Our kind friend Munster wrote me word that they had been to Norwood and that Mrs Fitzherbert was going to reside there for some time, to visit the Gipsies I suppose? She went away from here so disgusted with Brighton that she told the Brisbanes she really thought of not coming here next winter. All the business of the ungrateful behaviour of Barratt and losing the election at the Alms House did for poor Brighton.[34]

The Norwood referred to was one of the Fitzherbert estates, where the family had told Mrs Fitzherbert she could live for as long as she liked. She seems to have stayed there for a few months, but by late October was back in Tilney Street. She did return to Brighton for the winter, apparently willing to forget Mr Barratt and the Alms House election.

She still entertained in some style, as Thomas Raikes later recalled:

> She kept a very handsome establishment in Tilney Street and Brighton, where the best society was always seen, everyone without formality evincing the nuance of respect which tacitly acknowledged her elevated position, while the service of plate and handsome dinners, and a numerous train of servants all grown old in her service, gave the house at least a seigneurial, if not a royal appearance.[35]

She was also seen at St James's. Lady Georgiana Grey told Minney, 'Mrs Fitzherbert was at St James's last night, looking beautiful, and young as ever'.[36]

When she returned to Brighton for Christmas 1835 she found a new, larger and grander Catholic chapel, dedicated to St John the Baptist, had been built further to the east.[37] There is no evidence that she contributed to its cost, though in 1827 she had endowed the Brighton mission with £1000 worth of French bonds, providing an income of about £50 a year. About this time she acquired a private chaplain, William Lopez, a Portuguese priest.[38] According to accounts settled by Minney after Mrs Fitzherbert's death, William Lopez lived in lodgings in Brighton, paid for by Maria, in addition to receiving fees for his services as a chaplain.[39] He said Mass regularly in her house, Dr Cullin, the priest in charge at St John the Baptist's, providing one of his altar boys as server. By now she was frequently confined to the house by rheumatism, and hearing Mass at home, something she remembered from her earlier years, was appreciated.

The Damers did not join her in Brighton or London that year, but long letters from Minney and George never ceased to arrive. From Paris Minney wrote saying the French King and Queen, 'asked most kindly after you and expressed a wish to see you in the spring'. From Baden she mentioned meeting Count Charles de Morny, the French Minister, 'He enquired very attentively after you, dearest Mama, and said no one he had met in England had made the impression of being *grande dame* half as much as yourself'.[40]

She did appear as a *grande dame* on some occasions, but her manners remained as unaffected and natural as before. William Saunders, a young upholsterer who had worked in her Brighton house between 1832 and 1836, remembered that he had, 'revered her as a lady who could talk to a young working man as well as to a Prince'. He had been called in to help her rehang her collection of silhouettes, hundreds in number, and recalled, 'For some time I worked at them, Mrs Fitzherbert telling me where to place them. Every now and then she interrupted the work to ask me some questions about myself ... She was very pale, in fact her face was as colourless as wax, which made her bright dark eyes seem all the brighter by contrast ...'[41]

On 4 August 1834 Maria wrote to Marianne in Baden: 'I am sure you will be glad to hear dear Minney is quite recovered from her confinement ... I sincerely hope it will be the last. Four little girls and one little boy is quite sufficient.'[42] Minney had given birth to a daughter, Constance; it was her last child.

One of Minney's daughters recalled later that 'Mrs Fitzherbert was very fond of us children and liked having us with her ... I well remember what a beautiful old lady she was, with brilliant dark eyes, and a bright charming manner.[43] Anita Leslie, descended from Minney's daughter Constance, remembered her great grandmother saying her mother had told her that kissing Mrs Fitzherbert's cheek was like touching the petals of a flower.[44]

One of the last letters she wrote was to Lady Cecilia Buggin, second wife of the Duke of Sussex,[45] asking after the Duke, who was recovering from influenza. Lady Cecilia replied on 15 February 1837:

> I told him of your kind enquiries. He desires me to thank you and give you his love, and say how sorry he is that you have been ill, and we both trust you will take care of yourself and escape this horrid complaint which seems to spare nobody. I believe the best way is to remain within doors, and I'm sure the advice given to you to do so is the best and the only sure way to avoid it.[46]

Maria stayed 'within doors', until a sunny day in March when she went for a carriage ride. The next day she was unwell with symptoms of influenza. Now in her eighty-first year and frail, her condition deteriorated rapidly, and the Damers, Jerninghams and Dr Halford were sent for. There was nothing Henry Halford could do. It was time for William Lopez to be called. The last sacrament was given and prayers for the dying begun. Marianne had not yet arrived, but Minney's older children were brought into the room, one of them remembered 'our parents took us into the room where she lay dying. The Priest was saying the last prayers over her the words of which ... made such an impression on my mind that I have never forgotten them – "Proficiscere, anima Christiana de hoc mundo", Go forth Christian soul from this world'.[47]

Prayers were said for her in every Brighton church that Sunday, and she died the next evening, 27 March 1837, at about seven o'clock, having been unconscious for several hours. It had been a wild and windy day with fitful sunshine, and she died when the tide was ebbing and daylight had gone.

Minney's grief was overwhelming. She wanted everything done to make the funeral both splendid and dignified. This was the last thing she could do for Maria, the only way she could show how much she had always loved her. George Seymour wanted a simple, private funeral, but Minney took no notice. Dr Cullin agreed it was appropriate for Maria to be buried in his new church, a vault being created in the centre aisle to receive the coffin. In the meantime her body was brought down to her dining parlour, the coffin covered with a crimson cloth. The room was transformed by William Lopez into a *chapelle ardente*, with an altar where he could say Mass, and where anyone who wished could come and pay their last respects. The windows were hung with black to exclude the daylight, tall candles burning round the coffin upon which Minney had placed white roses.

The King was informed of her death while walking on the terrace at Windsor, and, deeply affected, went to find the Queen to pass on the sad news himself. Marianne had not arrived in time to see Mama before she died, which added to her grief. Quiet and amenable as she had always been, she allowed Minney to make the arrangements, and agreed to whatever she decided. The funeral took place on 6 April. The *Gentlemen's Magazine* for May 1837 reported:

> Her mortal remains were removed on the 6 April from her mansion on the old Steyne to the Roman Catholic Chapel at the Eastern part of Brighton for interment. The funeral procession consisted of six mourning coaches and the private carriage of the deceased ... High Mass was performed by the officiating minister, Mr Cullin. The coffin was afterwards lowered into a grave eleven feet deep, constructed in the centre of the Chapel.

George Seymour's account noted that the hearse was drawn by six horses decorated with black plumes and velvets, accompanied by two mutes and four pages, and that the mourning coaches were also decorated with plumes and velvets, with a page to each coach. At the rear followed Maria's empty barouche.[48] The Earl of Munster, representing the King, George Damer, George Seymour and Edward Jerningham, were the chief mourners. Mr Saunders later recalled that, 'I saw the funeral cross the Steine. There was an enormous crowd, such as I never saw before in Brighton; to us it seemed like a State Funeral, but it was not'.[49]

Minney had been right to choose a funeral the people of Brighton could take part in, lining the streets to watch the final journey of the great lady they had always regarded as their Queen of Hearts. They

made their silent farewells as the cortège passed at walking pace across
the Steine, along the sea road and inland again to the Catholic chapel.
The Times noted that, 'The chapel was hung with black and was full of
well-dressed persons who were admitted by ticket to view the ceremonies'.[50] The *Brighton Patriot* reported:

> The whole of the chapel was darkened by black tapestry hung over the
> windows. The only light proceeded from the wax candles around the
> coffin, from around the altar and a few from the sides of the chapel ... The
> pillars by the side of the altar, and the pews and front of the gallery were
> hung with black and the whole of the floor of the chapel were covered with
> black cloth. The altar alone, and the masterpiece of modern art, the rep-
> resentation of the baptism of the Messiah, in the most pure white marble,
> remained unobscured by sable drapery ... The choir, though not power-
> ful, was effective and sung well in tune ... The music selected for the
> occasion was the ancient Gregorian chant which was sung in a solemn and
> most impressive style.[51]

Dr Cullin was assisted by William Lopez and by several other priests
from the area, all in gold and black vestments. When the Requiem was
over, the coffin was lowered into the vault, while the choir sang the
Benedictus. Dr Cullin then said the Our Father in English, perhaps for
the benefit of the many Protestants present. The chapel was kept open
until early evening so that those unable to attend the Requiem could pay
their respects by the open vault.

In her will Maria left legacies to her servants, to Mrs Wat and her two
nieces, Louisa and Charlotte, and to several of her friends.[52] Her jewels
were already divided into two for Minney and Marianne, and her two
paintings by Gainsborough went to George Damer. Her two houses,
Tilney Street and Brighton, were to be sold, and the money invested in
the form of a trust, the income to be paid to Mary Emma Georgina
Damer, the beloved Minney. With her final act Maria had made sure
that Minney would live comfortably.

The will had a moving codicil addressed to Marianne and Minney,
who could hardly have read it without tears:

Maryanne Jerningham and Minney Damer!
This paper is addressed to my two dear children who I am sure will strictly
comply with a few requests I wish to make: Life is uncertain and my health
and speech are often so much distressed that I am fit for nothing. Still my

anxiety is great respecting them. I pray to God they may both live long with sincere affection and attachment to each other. I am confident this will be the case, the thought reconciles my mind at taking a long farewell of them. I have loved them both with the tenderest affection any Mother could do and I have done to the utmost of my power for their interests and comfort. God bless them both as well as all those that belong to them.[53]

She was right about her 'two dear children' living in affectionate attachment; her will had favoured Minney, but Marianne accepted this gracefully. Minney wrote to Colonel Gurwood, 'I cannot find a term that is strong enough to express my admiration at Mary Anne's conduct. It is quite admirable, right minded, unselfish and straightforward ... I feel I would have been quite incapable of acting and thinking as they both do'.[54]

Minney commissioned John Carew to sculpt a memorial to Mrs Fitzherbert to go on the wall of St John the Baptist's chapel adjacent to the vault, and composed the words to go beneath it,

> In a vault near this spot are deposited
> the remains of
> MARIA FITZHERBERT She was born on the XXVI of July
> MDCCLVI
> And expired at Brighton on the XXVII of
> March MDCCCXXXVII
> One to whom she was more than a parent
> has placed this monument to her revered and
> beloved memory, as a humble though feeble
> tribute of her everlasting gratitude and affection
> R I P

Letters of condolence were received from all the royal family, even from the Duke of Cumberland in Hanover, where he was now King, who had never been a friend of Mrs Fitzherbert. The Duke of Sussex, who like his dead brothers, York and Kent, had been deeply fond of her, wrote thanking Minney for sending him 'a mourning ring enclosing some of the hair of my late invaluable friend, your adopted Mother, whose loss I most deeply deplore. No one ever respected and loved her more than I did'.[55] Lady Louisa Stuart, one of Mrs Fitzherbert's few remaining contemporaries, wrote on 30 March to her nephew, George Damer: 'I always believed poor Mrs Fitzherbert very amiable, and respected her character even in the old days, when party set in full tide against her ... No woman that ever enjoyed the confidence of a Prince kept so clear of abusing it, or meddled so little in matters of state'.[56] Dr Cullin wrote to Minney in June:

> I was fully authorised by her to contribute in her name to all our little charities. She usually headed the list in our collections and she regularly gave five pounds annually towards the support of the Charity School. Then came something for the clothing of the poor, for coals in winter. The sick, the aged, the widow, the orphan were all helped by her. Easter was commonly the pay time. The sums varied from fourteen to twenty pounds, sometimes more rarely less. I recollect I received from her at the Easter of last year twenty pounds with a few additional pounds for the clothing of the little boy who served her Mass ...[57]

Lord Greville, writing in his memoirs, summed up what so many had thought about her, 'She was not a clever woman, but of a very noble spirit, disinterested, greatly beloved by her friends and relations, popular in the world, and treated with uniform distinction and respect by the royal family'.[58]

But perhaps the Earl of Munster's hauntingly sad letter to Minney, describing how he revisited her Brighton house, gives the best idea of the deep sense of loss experienced by those who had known and loved Maria, and were left knowing that a portion of their own lives had gone with her, and could not be replaced:

> I have been over the old house on the Steine. I had no idea the whole house and furniture would be so exactly as she left it. What scenes did every object recall to my remembrance! The dressing room with most of the Indian ink profiles there ... The white bed in the corner of her bedroom. That sad room. On entering the drawing room I almost expected to see you on the sofa behind the screen – all as you saw it the last time. I went down to the dining room, where as a boy I used to dine sometimes five days out of seven, and you came down to desert. I recalled it as our theatre where we used to act. And then, as hung with black on the last sad occasion, when she left us for the last time.[59]

The Question of Children

Did Maria Fitzherbert and the Prince of Wales have children? The pregnancy rumours of 1786 died away, and were never repeated. The writings of men like Lord George Gordon and Nathaniel Jefferys, the embittered jeweller, accusing Mrs Fitzherbert of secretly marrying the Prince, never even hinted at offspring threatening the proper inheritance of the crown. Seeing no children from Mrs Fitzherbert's first two marriages, and no further signs of a pregnancy, her contemporaries seem to have concluded that she was unable to bear children and asked no further questions.

Only one person put the question during her lifetime. James Ord, a young man brought up by the Jesuits in Georgetown, his fees paid by the British Embassy, wrote to her from America asking if he was her son by the Prince, born in 1786.[1] He received no reply, which proves nothing either way. Shane Leslie, investigating Ord's claim, found nothing to connect him with Mrs Fitzherbert.[2]

After her death many other claims began to be made, causing anxiety in royal circles. The 'Fitzherbert marriage', though illegal, would, if put to the test, have been found canonically valid by the Church of England,[3] just as it had been by the Church of Rome, and the succession to the throne could have been challenged by any child of the marriage holding proof of parentage.

On 10 June 1839, *The Times* reported that a Mrs Sophia Elizabeth Guelph Sims had asked the Lord Mayor of London for help in 'proving that she was the daughter of Mrs Fitzherbert by George IV', and published part of their conversation:

> The Lord Mayor – What proof is there that there was any child at all resulting from what you call the union, but what everybody knew could be no union at all ...?

Mrs Guelph Sims said Mrs Fitzherbert knew nothing about it.

The Lord Mayor – What! were you born without her knowledge?

Mrs Guelph Sims – She supposed that her child was stillborn, and was never told to the contrary ... The Lord Mayor – If George IV knew it, I am sure he would have made provision for you ... I can only tell you that the Lord Mayor cannot do it.[4]

It is possible that Mrs Fitzherbert did give birth at some time, and was told the child was stillborn when in fact it was living, but there was no evidence that Mrs Sims was that child.

In 1841 Lord Stourton wrote to Lord Albemarle, 'I have been appealed to by a Court of Law, by a Judge of the land, in testimony of no child being born from this illegal contract [the 'Fitzherbert marriage'] ... I have moreover, in common with his Grace [the Duke of Wellington] been appealed to by an imposter, assuming to have been the issue of this connection'.[5] Lord Stourton never believed Mrs Fitzherbert had had a child by the Prince and more than once asked her to make this clear. His certainty, though not proof, nevertheless carries weight.

In January 1857, Charles Bodenham wrote from Paris to Lord Fielding:

There's a jolly French widow – fair, fat and forty, with whom Alick Fletcher has been closeted six hours today on affairs of state and she got three crowns tattooed on her! The Lady of the three crowns is a daughter of George IV by Mrs Fitzherbert ... Alick says the three crowns affair is a state secret: that on this account the Duke of Wellington and Lord John Russell refused Charles Langdale the inspection of Mrs Fitzherbert's papers.[6]

It is difficult to know what to make of this facetious letter, but it shows that talk of possible children persisted and was believed by some. When W. H. Wilkins began research for the first biography of Mrs Fitzherbert (published in 1905), he was given access to letters and other material by 'descendants of Mrs Fitzherbert's connections and legatees', only on condition that the question of possible children was considered closed.[7] He agreed, but the question did not go away.

In 1910 some Americans visited St John the Baptist's church, Brighton, claiming both to be Mrs Fitzherbert's descendants and that their family had erected her memorial monument. Canon Johnson, the priest in charge, thought it proper to notify Minney's surviving daughters, who had the following lines added below the monument's inscription:

> In loving remembrance of our dear Mother Mary Seymour (Honble. Mrs G. L. D. Damer) the adopted daughter of Mrs Fitzherbert who placed this pious memorial of affection and gratitude here in 1837. She died in 1848. Her only surviving children Blanche Haygarth and Constance Leslie placed this record in 1910.[8]

The American visitors, whoever they were, took their claim no further.

Also during Canon Johnson's time at St John's, the baptismal records for the year 1800 were found to have been carefully cut from the church register. A letter of Canon Johnson's, preserved in the parish archives, suggests that, if Mrs Fitzherbert and the Prince had come together again in 1799, then a child might have been born in Brighton in 1800, and that the missing pages possibly contained a record of his or her baptism. No record would have contained the names Maria Fitzherbert and George, Prince of Wales, but something about the wording, or the child's names, may have suggested that they were the parents, and caused the removal of the pages. Against this, Mrs Fitzherbert and the Prince were not reunited in 1799, as Canon Johnson thought possible; their reunion took place on 16 June 1800, as Lord Stourton's account makes clear. Their meetings during 1799, had, on Mrs Fitzherbert's insistence, always taken place in company. Leaving aside Lady Anne Barnard's assertion that Mrs Fitzherbert and the Prince lived 'as brother and sister' after their reunion, no child could have been born to them before the spring of 1801. Mrs Fitzherbert, though visiting Brighton in the summer of 1801, had no connection with the town in 1800, not having been there since 1794.

Shane and Anita Leslie, both Mrs Fitzherbert's biographers, favour the idea that Marianne Smythe was Mrs Fitzherbert's daughter by the Prince, not her niece. As evidence, they quote Mrs Fitzherbert's letter to Marianne following her wedding to Edward Jerningham, 'Say a thousand kind things from me to my son-in-law',[9] and Fred Seymour's reference to Mrs Fitzherbert in a letter to Minney, 'The most gracious lady who has always been so active in promoting your interests with the Sovereign, even to the prejudice of her own daughter',[10] meaning Marianne. Mrs Fitzherbert had had sole responsibility for Marianne since her childhood and for that reason Marianne could be accurately be described as an 'adopted daughter'. It was Mrs Fitzherbert who had arranged the match with the Stafford Jerninghams, provided the dowry, and played the role of the bride's mother at the wedding. It may therefore have seemed quite natural to her, the day after the wedding, to speak of the bridegroom as a 'son-in-law'. Fred Seymour possibly used the word 'daughter', knowing Marianne to fill the role of an 'adopted daughter' as well as a niece. Minney, a Seymour, who originally had had the Hertfords as official guardians and had older brothers, and even the King, to share responsibility for her future, was usually described as Mrs Fitzherbert's *protégée*. But whatever lay behind the words used in these letters, they are not enough, on their own, to prove Marianne's parentage, and it would be unwise to exaggerate their significance. The Leslies were not, however, the only ones to believe Marianne Smythe was Mrs Fitzherbert's daughter; she died in 1859 and, because her daughter Emma married Basil Fitzherbert of Swynnerton, a document was added to the Swynnerton papers, recording that:

> Edward Stafford Jerningham born at Haughley, August 4, 1801. Married June 16, 1828 Marianne Smythe said to be the daughter of John Smythe, the great grandson of Sir John Smythe, the third Bart of Eshe Co. Durham. If she was a daughter of John Smythe, she cannot have been legitimate, for John Smythe had no children by his wife, widow of Captain Strickland. She is also generally described as niece of Mrs Fitzherbert and treated ostensibly as her niece, but many indications point with considerable probability to the conclusion that she was a daughter of Mrs Fitzherbert by George IV.[11]

The 'many indications' are not given, and even when this document is placed with the two references used by the Leslies, there is still not sufficient evidence to prove Marianne was Maria's daughter. But there is enough to make anyone interested in Maria look closely at what is known of Marianne Smythe to see if the Leslies and the Swynnerton document could be right.

The exact year of Marianne's birth is not known, but it is known that her birthday was 12 May,[12] and all the references in Maria's letters and elsewhere indicate that she was several years younger than Minney. She returned from school in France to live with Maria in 1822, and is mentioned for the first time in a letter to Minney from Cheltenham, in

September of that year, when Minney was nearly twenty-four, and Marianne about fifteen or sixteen, the age at which English girls usually returned from French convents. She was probably in her very early twenties when she married in 1828, this being the first marriage to be talked of, with Maria, confident that Marianne was young enough to receive other offers, determined to cancel the arrangement if the Jerninghams could not provide more money. The existing evidence suggests that Marianne Smythe was born in 1806 or 1807. Mrs Fitzherbert's movements for those two years are known. In May 1806 she was in London, in the public gaze, awaiting the outcome of the Seymour Case, which ended in early June. In May of the following year, she was taking an active part in the London Season, again very publicly. On 6 June, Mrs Calvert went to an assembly at Tilney Street, noting in her diary that it was a grand affair,[13] with hundreds of guests, and all the Royal Dukes present. Had Mrs Fitzherbert been pregnant that Season she would hardly have planned that ambitious entertainment so close to her expected confinement. Moreover, she was fifty-one that summer, almost certainly beyond child-bearing age. But the most convincing argument against the claim is that Mrs Fitzherbert, who always felt she owed George IV consideration and respect, and was careful to avoid causing him embarrassment, even after they parted, would never have presented a child of their marriage into gossiping London Society, where the truth might be guessed at. In addition there is no reason to suppose that the child referred to by Mrs Fitzherbert in her letter to Lady Anne Lindsay, just after her brother Jack's death in 1812: 'I have got an addition to my family, a dear lovely little Girl about six years old, a Legacy of my poor brother',[14] was some other child, and not the Marianne Smythe who appeared in her household and began to be metioned in her letters in 1822. It seems, therefore, almost certain that, when Mrs Fitzherbert presented Miss Smythe as her niece, she simply spoke the truth and Society believed her, there never being the faintest rumour to the contrary during their lifetimes.

Claims continued to be made, but none successfully, and claims are still made by those who believe they are descended from George IV and Mrs Fitzherbert, but, like the earlier claimants, none have produced clear documentary evidence, most basing their claim on 'family tradition'.

Lord Stourton told Lord Albemarle that when he urged Mrs Fitzherbert to add a note to her marriage certificate declaring there had been no issue, she had 'smilingly refused on the score of delicacy'. Among her papers, passed down to Lady Constance Leslie, was found one in Lord Stourton's hand declaring, 'I Mary Fitzherbert moreover testify that my union with George Prince of Wales was without issue'.[15] A space was allocated below for the signature, but she had not signed it. If the marriage was childless, why had she left it unsigned? The answer could be that she did have a child or children who were either still-born or died in early infancy, a common occurrence at the time, or who were taken away and brought up in secret. Or possibly she still believed she should refuse to answer the question on the 'score of delicacy', a phrase no one would use today, but which had a clear meaning for her generation and class, preventing any public comments on matters connected with marital intimacy.

In spite of many claims, there is no evidence that proves Mrs Fitzherbert did have children, but it is impossible to prove that she did not. The question will go on being asked, Mrs Fitzherbert, who could have answered it, having refused to do so, and the discovery of fresh evidence to settle the matter now being unlikely.

Notes

Notes to Chapter 1: Mary Anne

1. *Jerningham Letters, 1780–1843*, ed. Egerton Castle (London, 1896), i, p. 182, letter from Lady Frances Jerningham to her daughter, 27 May 1799.
2. Shane Leslie, *Mrs Fitzherbert* (London, 1939), i, p. 7.
3. Denis Gwynn, *Bishop Challoner* (London, 1946), p. 130; John Milner, *Life of Richard Challoner* (London, 1949), p. 12.
4. *Brambridge Catholic Registers, 1766–1869*, ed. R. C. Baigent, Catholic Records Society, 27 (1927), p. 5.
5. W. H. Wilkins, *Mrs Fitzherbert and George IV* (London, 1905), i, illustration facing p. 4.
6. *Boys at the Liège Academy, 1773–1788*, Catholic Records Society, 13 (1910). The Harry Smythe referred to in some of Mrs Fitzherbert's letters was of the next generation but may have been Henry's son.
7. James Munson, *Maria Fitzherbert: Secret Wife of George IV* (London, 2001), p. 18.
8. *Brambridge Catholic Registers, 1766–1869*, ed. R. C. Baigent, Catholic Records Society, 27, pp. 6–8.
9. Priests training on the Continent for work in England dropped their family names and assumed new ones to make discovery, later, less likely. William Walmsley's real name was William Caldwell. Like all priests of that time he would have been addressed as 'Mr' not 'Father'.
10. Brambridge Hall was destroyed by fire on 15 February 1782, after it had passed out of Smythe hands, so it is impossible to know where the chapel was when they lived there. A Victorian mansion was built in the park on a different site. This has now been made into flats.
11. *Brambridge Catholic Registers, 1766–1869*, ed. R. C. Baigent, Baptismal Register, Catholic Records Society, 27, p. 15. The godfather was Thomas Fitzherbert; this may have been Thomas Fitzherbert of Swynnerton, who later became Mary Anne's father-in-law, but the Brambridge Registers also

show that a Thomas Fitzherbert was living in the area at this time, who could have been the godfather.

12. *Jerningham Letters*, ii, appendix, pp. 399–408.

13. Munson, *Maria Fitzherbert: Secret Wife of George IV*, pp. 19 and 93.

14. Basil Whelan OSB, *Historic English Convents of Today: The Story of English Cloisters in France and Flanders in Penal Times* (London, 1905), appendix 1, pp. 253–61; *Jerningham Letters*, i, pp. 19, 29, 33, 34–35.

15. Charles Langdale, ed. *A Memoir of Mrs Fitzherbert with an Account of Her Marriage to George IV* (London, 1856), pp. 113–14.

16. Wilkins, *Mrs Fitzherbert and George IV*, ii, an illustration facing p. 122, shows a satchel embroidered by Mrs Fitzherbert. William Saunders told William Wilkins 'I remember especially an ottoman covered with needle-work (done by Mrs Fitzherbert herself, the maid said) some two feet long, a bunch of roses on a maroon-coloured ground', ibid., p. 282.

17. *Jerningham Letters*, ii, p. 321.

18. A reference to Marianne Smythe, thought to be Jack Smythe's illegitimate daughter.

19. Wilkins, *Mrs Fitzherbert and George IV*, i, p. 13.

20. Joan Berkeley, *Lulworth and the Welds* (Gillingham, Dorset, 1971), pp. 132–34, 137, and 141, covers Edward Weld's education, Grand Tour, the death of his first wife, his accomplishments and lifestyle.

21. *Brambridge Catholic Registers, 1766–1869* ed. R. C. Baigent, Marriage Register, 13 July 1775, Catholic Records Society, 27.

22. Gwynn, *Bishop Challoner*, pp. 142–43, friends of the Duke of Norfolk had put the Catholic view to the government and it was agreed that when Catholics attended Church of England churches in order to marry it would be regarded not as an act of religious conformity, but as a 'ceremony prescribed by law of the Land for the civil legality of the marriage'.

23. Frampton, *The Journal of Mary Frampton, 1779–1846*, ed. H. G. Mundy (London, 1885), quoted in Shane Leslie, *Mrs Fitzherbert*, i, p. 9.

24. Wilkins, *Mrs Fitzherbert and George IV*, i, p. 14, has accounts of the young Mrs Weld given to William Wilkins by Charles Weld Blundell, who heard them from his great uncle, Joseph Weld, who died in 1863.

25. Berkeley, *Lulworth and the Welds*, p. 154.

26. Frampton, *The Journal of Mary Frampton, 1779–1846*, quoted in Shane Leslie, *Mrs Fitzherbert*, i, p. 9.

27. Berkeley, *Lulworth and the Welds*, p. 156.

28. Swynnerton Papers, quoted in Shane Leslie, ed., *The Letters of Mrs Fitzherbert* (London, 1940), p. 332.

29. *Britwell Catholic Registers, 1765–1788*, Baptismal Register, 18 December 1775, Catholic Records Society, 13 (1910).

Notes to Chapter 2: Thomas Fitzherbert

1. Anita Leslie, *Mrs Fitzherbert* (London, 1960), p. 24.
2. *Boys at the Liège Academy, 1773–1791*, Catholic Records Society, 13 (1910).
3. *Jerningham Letters*, ed. Egerton Castle (London, 1896), i, p. 158.
4. Ibid., p. 34.
5. Dennis Gwynn, *Bishop Challoner* (London, 1946), p. 216.
6. Bernard Ward, *The Dawn of the Catholic Revival, 1781–1803* (London, 1909), preface to volume 1, quoting an article by Charles Butler published in the *Catholic Spectator*, 7 (1824).
7. Gwynn, *Bishop Challoner*, pp. 225–26.
8. Lady Forrester's Autograph Book, quoted in Shane Leslie, *Mrs Fitzherbert* (London, 1939), i, p. 11.
9. Ibid., p. 12, Swynnerton MS Book of Deeds.
10. Johanna Harting, *Catholic London Missions from the Reformation to 1850* (London, 1903), pp. 101–10.
11. John Mawhood, *The Mawhood Diary, 1774–1790*, ed. E. E. Reynolds, Catholic Records Society, 50 (London, 1956). John Mawhood was a London cloth merchant and friend of Bishop Challoner. There are references to Mass, Vespers and Compline at the embassy chapels on almost every page of his diary.
12. Shane Leslie, *Salutation to Five* (London, 1958), pp. 40–41; George Damer heard this story from Mrs Fitzherbert and left a record of it, found, years later, by Shane Leslie at his family home at Glaslough. The Leslies were descended from Constance Leslie, youngest daughter of Minney Dawson Damer, Mrs Fitzherbert's adopted daughter.
13. John Kirk, *Biographies of English Catholics in the Eighteenth Century* (London, 1909), ed. J. H. Pollen and Edwin Burton, p. 84, Kirk claims that Mrs Fitzherbert had 'an only son who lived but a few months'. He gives no date for the birth and there is no record of it in the Swynnerton MS Book of Deeds, nor is there a record of a baptism or burial. He may have got the story from Sir Thomas Clifford's *History of Tixall* (1817), who used exactly the same words to describe the event, Munsen, *Maria Fitzherbert: Secret Wife of George IV* (London, 2001), p. 44. Lady Anne Lindsay claimed that there was a child who 'died as soon as born', ibid., pp. 44–45, which might have meant a still birth. If this was the case it would account for the lack of a baptismal record. None of Mrs Fitzherbert's surviving letters mention this birth.

14. Shane Leslie, ed. *Letters of Mrs Fitzherbert* (London, 1940), p. 164, 29 July 1822.

15. Kirk, *Biographies of English Catholics in the Eighteenth Century*, pp. 85–86.

16. Ian Gilmour, *Riot, Risings and Revolution* (London, 1993), pp. 342–70, gives a detailed account of the Gordon Riots.

17. Mawhood, *The Mawhood Diary, 1774–1790*, ed. E. E. Reynolds, Catholic Records Society, 50, pp. 158, 159, and 160.

18. Kirk, *Biographies of English Catholics in the Eighteenth Century*, p. 86.

19. *Brambridge Catholic Registers, 1766–1869*, ed. R. C. Baigent, Catholic Records Society, 27, (1927), p. 15, the record of her death was inserted beside that of her baptism.

20. Stanley Ayling, *Fox: The Life of Charles James Fox* (London, 1991), letter from Charles James Fox to Richard Fitzpatrick, p. 25.

21. Shane Leslie, *The Letters of Mrs Fitzherbert*, p. 183, Mrs Fitzherbert to Minney Dawson Damer, 15 November 1825.

22. Kirk, *Biographies of English Catholics in the Eighteenth Century*, p. 87.

23. Wilkins, *Mrs Fitzherbert and George IV* (London, 1905), i, pp. 21–22. 'Mr Fitzherbert's will was proved July 4, 1781, by Henry Errington (Mrs Fitzherbert's uncle), from it these particulars are taken'. Ibid., p. 22 n. 1. Other accounts say the income was £1000 a year.

24. Ibid., p. 22.

25. Ibid., p. 22 n. 2.

26. *Brambridge Catholic Registers, 1766–1869*, ed. R. C. Baigent, Catholic Records Society, 27, p. 11, the Highbridge house was one mile from Brambridge. The house still stands, though much changed.

27. Chatsworth Papers, quoted in Shane Leslie, *Mrs Fitzherbert*, i, p. 16.

Notes to Chapter 3: 'Who the Devil is that Pretty Girl?'

1. Shane Leslie, *Salutation to Five* (London, 1958), p. 41. Mrs Fitzherbert's own version of the meeting after the opera was told to George Dawson Damer, and was recorded by him immediately after hearing it. His note was found by Shane Leslie among the Leslie's family papers.

2. Christopher Hibbert, *George III: A Personal History* (London, 1998), p. 100.

3. Alan Palmer, *Life and Times of George IV* (London, 1972), p. 20.

4. The Duke of Gloucester's son, William Frederick, and his daughter, Sophia Matilda, were given incomes by George III. William later married George III's daughter Princess Mary.

5. Chatsworth Papers, quoted in Shane Leslie, *Mrs Fitzherbert* (London, 1939), i, p. 22.

6. Chatsworth Papers 628, a note by Georgiana Devonshire, July 1784, quoted in Brian Masters, *Georgiana, Duchess of Devonshire* (London, 1980), p. 132.

7. Langdale, ed. *A Memoir of Mrs Fitzherbert with an Account of her Marriage to George IV* (London, 1856), p. 141

8. Chatsworth Papers, quoted in Shane Leslie, *Mrs Fitzherbert*, i, p. 21, 9 July 1784.

9. Henry, Lord Holland, *Posthumous Memoirs of the Whig Party*, ed. Henry Richard, Lord Holland (1854), quoted in Shane Leslie, *Mrs Fitzherbert*, i, p. 32.

10. Crawford Muniments (Balcarres), quoted in James Munson, *Maria Fitzherbert: Secret Wife of George IV* (London, 2001), p. 137. In 1785 Mrs Fitzherbert told Lady Anne Lindsay she was sorry for 'our poor little friend at The Hague', and that she regretted that her own marriage to the Prince was the 'cause of a thing [a marriage to the Dutch Princess] so much to his advantage not taking place'.

11. Munson, *Maria Fitzherbert: Secret Wife of George IV*, p. 128.

12. Wilkins, *Mrs Fitzherbert and George IV* (London, 1905), i, pp. 65–66.

13. Langdale, *A Memoir of Mrs Fitzherbert*, pp. 117–18.

14. Fitzherbert Papers, ii, quoted in Shane Leslie, *Mrs Fitzherbert*, i, pp. 33–34.

15. Ibid. Fitzherbert Papers, i, appendix 1, pp. 353–70.

16. Crawford Muniments (Balcarres), quoted in Munson, *Maria Fitzherbert: Secret Wife of George IV*, p. 136.

17. Munson, *Maria Fitzherbert: Secret Wife of George IV*, p. 142.

18. *Lord Colchester's Diary*, ed. Charles, Lord Colchester (1861), i, p. 68, 'I learned that the Rev. Burt, of Twickenham, actually married the Prince of Wales to Mrs Fitzherbert and received £500 for doing it', quoted in Leslie, *Mrs Fitzherbert*, i, p. 49; a letter from Burt to the Prince of Wales, 25 February 1791, was kept by Mrs Fitzherbert, with a note saying he was the clergyman who officiated at her marriage to the Prince. It was placed in the sealed box at Coutts' Bank along with other papers pertaining to the marriage, now in the Royal Archives at Windsor, Wilkins, *Mrs Fitzherbert and George IV*, i, pp. 102–4.

Notes to Chapter 4: Marriage

1. Orlando Bridgeman later became the first Earl of Bradford.

2. Wilkins, *Mrs Fitzherbert and George IV* (London, 1905), i, p. 99 and n. 'We the under-signed do witness that George Augustus Frederick, Prince of Wales, was married unto Maria Fitzherbert, this 15th day of December, 1785', signed by John Smythe, Henry Errington, the Prince and

Mrs Fitzherbert, published for the first time by William Wilkins in his biography of Mrs Fitzherbert, with the permission of Edward VII, in 1905, now in the Royal Archives at Windsor.

3. Rutland Papers, quoted in Wilkins, *Mrs Fitzherbert and George IV*, i, p. 132.

4. *The Life and Letters of Sir Gilbert Elliot*, ed. Countess Minto (1874), quoted in Wilkins, *Mrs Fitzherbert and George IV*, i, p. 133.

5. Denbigh Papers (Pailton House), quoted in Hibbert, *George IV, Prince of Wales* (London, 1972), p. 55.

6. Rutland Papers, quoted in Shane Leslie, *Mrs Fitzherbert* (London, 1939), i, pp. 52–53, 14 March 1786.

7. Ibid., p. 65, 16 May 1786.

8. *Walpole Correspondence*, ed. W. S. Lewis (Oxford, 1937–1956), quoted in Shane Leslie, *Mrs Fitzherbert*, i, p. 63, 13 February 1786.

9. Shane Leslie, *Mrs Fitzherbert*, i, p. 64, 17 March 1786.

10. Chatsworth papers, quoted in Shane Leslie, *Mrs Fitzherbert*, i, pp. 61–62, 6 February 1786.

11. Ibid., p. 62, 7 February 1786.

12. Fox's letter to the Prince, and the Prince's reply, quoted in Wilkins *Mrs Fitzherbert and George IV*, i, pp. 74–79, 10 December 1785, and pp. 81–82, 11 December 1785.

13. *Jerningham Letters*, ed. Egerton Castle (London, 1896), i, p. 33.

14. Jervis Papers, note by Lady Forrester (formerly Miss Jervis), quoted in Shane Leslie, *Mrs Fitzherbert*, i, pp. 48n., 49n.

15. Clifford Musgrave, *Life in Brighton* (Chatham, 1981), p. 90.

16. Ibid., p. 92.

17. Rutland Papers, quoted in Wilkins, *Mrs Fitzherbert and George IV*, i, p. 171, 18 July 1786.

18. *Hansard*, xxvi, quoted in Hibbert, *George IV, Prince of Wales*, pp. 65–66.

19. John Rolle (1750 –1842), Tory MP for Devonshire, he became Lord Rolle in 1796.

20. Langdale, *Memoir of Mrs Fitzherbert with an Account of her Marriage to George IV* (London, 1856), p. 163.

21. *Hansard*, xxvi, quoted in Stanley Ayling, *Fox: The Life of Charles James Fox* (London, 1991), pp. 158–59; Wilkins, *Mrs Fitzherbert and George IV*, i, pp. 191–94.

22. Langdale, *A Memoir of Mrs Fitzherbert*, p. 170.

23. *Hansard*, xxvi, quoted in Shane Leslie, *Mrs Fitzherbert*, i, p. 81.

24. Rutland Papers, quoted in Shane Leslie, *Mrs Fitzherbert*, i, p. 82, 4 May 1787.

25. Rutland Papers, quoted in Wilkins, *Mrs Fitzherbert and George IV*, i, p. 211, 28 May 1787.

26. Frampton, *Journal of Mary Frampton, 1779–1846*, ed. H. G. Mundy (London, 1885), quoted in Shane Leslie, *Mrs Fitzherbert*, i, p. 70.

27. Shane Leslie, *Mrs Fitzherbert*, i, p. 89, 1 August, 1787, the visitor was Dr Thomas Campbell.

28. The Princesse de Lamballe was Marie-Thérèse Louise de Savoie Carignan, an intimate friend of Marie-Antoinette and Mistress of the Household.

Notes to Chapter 5: Battle for the Regency

1. Wilkins, *Mrs Fitzherbert and George IV* (London, 1905), i, pp. 220–21. The unnamed 'habitué' was one of the very old Brightonians who remembered seeing Mrs Fitzherbert in their youth, and whose reminiscences Wilkins collected when preparing his biography.

2. Ibid., p. 222.

3. Jervis Papers, Lady Forester's Notebook, quoted in Shane Leslie, *Mrs Fitzherbert* (London, 1939), i, p. 100

4. Ibid., Fitzherbert Papers, ii, p. 101.

5. Wilkins, *Mrs Fitzherbert and George IV*, i, p. 228, 4 May 1788.

6. Munson, *Maria Fitzherbert: Secret Wife of George IV* (London, 2001), p. 227.

7. J. Galt, *George III: His Court and Family* (1820), 3, 22 July 1788, quoted in Ida Macalpine and Richard Hunter, *George III and the Mad Business* (London, 1991), p. 11.

8. *Diary and Letters of Madame D'Arblay*, ed. C. F. Barrett (1842), 4, quoted in Macalpine and Hunter, *George III and the Mad Business*, p. 31.

9. J. Campbell, *The Lives of Lord Chancellors* (1847), 6, Jack Payne's letter to Lord Loughborough, 1789, quoted in Wilkins, *Mrs Fitzherbert and George IV*, i, pp. 234–35.

10. *The Manuscripts of the Earl of Spencer, Historical Manuscripts Commission and Report*, quoted by Macalpine and Hunter, *George III and the Mad Business*, p. 36, letter from Dr R. Warren to Lady Spencer, 12 November 1788.

11. *The Life and Letters of Sir Gilbert Elliot*, ed. Countess Minto (1874), quoted in Stanley Ayling, *Fox: The Life of Charles James Fox*, (London, 1991), p. 161.

12. *Hansard*, xxvii, quoted in Hibbert, *George IV, Prince of Wales* (London, 1972), p. 95.

13. Shane Leslie, *Mrs Fitzherbert*, i, p. 91 n. 2, 5 February 1789.

14. Ibid., p. 94.

15. Macalpine and Hunter, *George III and the Mad Business*, p. 65.

16. *Correspondence of Charles, First Earl Cornwallis*, ed. C. Ross (1859), i, p. 406, 21 February 1789.

17. *Life and Letters of Sir Gilbert Elliot,* ed. Countess of Minto, quoted in Wilkins, *Mrs Fitzherbert and George IV,* i, p. 240.

18. W. E. H. Lecky, *History of England in the Eighteenth Century* (1878–90), quoted in Shane Leslie, *Mrs Fitzherbert,* i, p 92.

19. Harcourt Papers, quoted in Wilkins, *Mrs Fitzherbert and George IV,* i, pp. 249–50, undated letter from Lord Harcourt to his wife.

20. *London Gazette,* 27 February 1789, 'By His Majesty's command, the Physicians' report is to be discontinued from this day', Macalpine and Hunter, *George III and the Mad Business,* p. 86.

21. Mrs Harcourt's Diary of the Court of George III, in *Miscellanies of the Philobiblon Society,* 13 (1871–72), quoted in Macalpine and Hunter, *George III and the Mad Business,* p. 92. George III, speaking of the Regency Bill to his brother the Duke of Gloucester, declared 'Had it passed, no power on earth should have prevailed on him to resume Government'.

Notes to Chapter 6: Lady Jersey

1. Madeleine Bingham, *The Track of a Comet: The Life of R. B. Sheridan* (London, 1980), p. 216.

2. Thomas Raikes, *A Portion of a Journal Kept by Thomas Raikes* (London, 1857), quoted in Leslie, *Mrs Fitzherbert* (London, 1939), i, p. 98.

3. W. H. Wilkins, *Mrs Fitzherbert and George IV* (London, 1905), i, p. 276; James Munson, *Maria Fitzherbert: Secret Wife of George IV* (London, 2001), pp. 224–27.

4. Shane Leslie, *Mrs Fitzherbert,* i, p. 103.

5. Elisabeth Vigée-Le Brun, *Memoirs of Elisabeth Vigée-Le Brun* (London, 1989), p. 71.

6. *Despatches from Paris,* ed. Oscar Browning, letter from Robert Fitzgerald to Lord Leeds, 29 October 1789, quoted in Lucy Ellis and Joseph Turquan, *La Belle Pamela: Lady Pamela Fitzgerald* (New York, 1920), p. 189.

7. *The Life and Letters of Sir Gilbert Elliot,* ed. Countess of Minto (1784), quoted in Wilkins, *Mrs Fitzherbert and George IV,* i, p. 283.

8. Harcourt Papers, letter from Miss Dee to Lady Harcourt, quoted in Wilkins, *Mrs Fitzherbert and George IV,* i, p. 284.

9. *Claughton Catholic Registers,* Baptismal Register, Catholic Records Society, 20 (1916), 28 May 1791, pp. 310–11, 'William John, son of William and Mary Fitzherbert Brocholes, godparents: John Dalton, Maria Fitzherbert and George, Prince of Wales'.

10. Sister Frideswide Stapleton, *History of St Mary's Priory Princethorpe*

(Hinchley, 1930), p. 82. The sisters agreed to stay in England, living first in London then at Bodney in Norfolk and finally settling, in 1835, at Princethorpe near Rugby.

11. *Sussex Weekly Advertiser*, 3 September and 10 September 1792.

12. Musgrave, *Life in Brighton* (Chatham, 1981), p. 108; Munson, *Maria Fitzherbert: Secret Wife of George IV*, p. 243.

13. Arthur Aspinall, *Prince of Wales' Correspondence*, ii, quoted in Hibbert *George IV, Prince of Wales* (London, 1972), p. 126.

14. Gerald Campbell, *Edward and Pamela Fitzgerald* (London, 1904), p. 35. The Charles referred to was Lady Lucy's brother.

15. *Jerningham Letters*, ed. Egerton Castle (London, 1886), i, p. 49.

16. Mrs Harcourt's Diary of the Court of George III, *Miscellanies of the Philobiblon Society* (1871–72), 13, quoted in Wilkins, *Mrs Fitzherbert and George IV*, i, pp. 297–98.

17. Nathaniel Wraxall, *Memoir of Sir Nathaniel Wraxall, 1772–1784*, ed. Wheatley Wraxall (1884), quoted in M. J. Levy, *The Mistresses of King George IV* (London, 1996), p. 78.

18. Robert Huish *Memoirs of George IV* (London, 1884), i, p. 263.

19. Aspinall, *Prince of Wales' Correspondence*, ii, quoted in Hibbert, *George IV, Prince of Wales*, p. 131.

20. Wilkins, *Mrs Fitzherbert and George IV*, i, p. 310. This letter was found among Mrs Fitzherbert's papers after her death and was lent to William Wilkins 'by one who cherishes the memory of Mrs Fitzherbert'. Ibid., p. 310n.

21. Ibid., p. 310n.

22. Shane Leslie, *Mrs Fitzherbert*, i, pp. 110–13, Jack Payne's letters to the Prince from Hambledon and Brighton.

23. Ibid., p. 116. Brighton, 15 July 1794.

24. Ibid., p. 113–14, 21 August 1794.

Notes to Chapter 7: Caroline of Brunswick

1. P. H. Stanhope *Life of the Rt Hon William Pitt* (1867) ii, appendix 20, 24 August 1794.

2. Aspinall, *Prince of Wales' Correspondence*, iii (London, 1963–71), quoted in Hibbert, *George IV, Prince of Wales* (London, 1972), p. 134, letter from Queen Charlotte to her brother, the Duke of Mecklenburg-Strelitz, August 1974: 'She is not allowed to go from one room to another without her Governess … all her amusements have been forbidden her because of her indecent conduct.'

3. *Walpole Correspondence*, ed. W. S. Lewis (Oxford, 1937–65), quoted in Leslie, *Mrs Fitzherbert* (London, 1939), i, p. 121.

4. *Sussex Weekly Advertiser*, 13 April 1795.

5. Royal Archives, a letter to the Prince from Lord Chancellor Loughborough, 19 December 1794, quoted in Wilkins, *Mrs Fitzherbert and George IV* (London, 1905), i, p. 319, a copy was sent to Mrs Fitzherbert, via Miss Pigot, and was later placed in the sealed box at Coutts' Bank, though not listed by Lord Stourton, ibid., p. 319n.

6. *Malmesbury Diaries*, ed. 3rd Earl of Malmesbury (London, 1844), iii, quoted in Hibbert, *George IV, Prince of Wales* p. 144.

7. Swynnerton Papers, quoted in Shane Leslie, *Letters of Mrs Fitzherbert* pp. 331–32, letter from Charles Bodenham to Miss Dormer, 12 February 1854: 'I have heard my Father-in-law [Thomas Weld] say more than once that the Queen Charlotte … told her son before his marriage to the Princess Caroline: It is for you, George, to say whether you can marry the Princess or not'.

8. James Munson, *Maria Fitzherbert: Secret Wife of George IV* (London, 2001), p. 277, a letter from Mrs Fitzherbert to Lady Anne Lindsay tells of an earlier appearance of the Prince of Wales on horseback near Marble Hill House; however, the one on the eve of his wedding to Princess Caroline is the one Mrs Fitzherbert remembered in old age and recounted to Lord Stourton.

9. Royal Archives, Queen Victoria's Journal, 13 November 1838.

10. Lady Charlotte Bury, *Diary: Illustrative of the Times of George IV*, ed. John Galt (1839), 'When Orlando Bridgeman, now Lord Bradford, went to inform Mrs Fitzherbert of the Prince's marriage, she would not believe it until he swore that he himself had been present at the ceremony, and when he did so she fainted away', quoted in Wilkins, *Mrs Fitzherbert and George IV* i, p. 330

11. Alison Plowden, *Caroline and Charlotte: The Regent's Wife and Daughter* (London, 1989), p. 24.

12. Ibid., p. 22.

13. *Walpole Correspondence*, ed. W. S. Lewis (Oxford, 1937–65), Miss Berry to Horace Walpole, 28 September 1794, quoted in Shane Leslie, *Mrs Fitzherbert*, i, p. 121.

14. Aspinall, ed. *Correspondence of George, Prince of Wales, 1770–1812* (London, 1963–71), both letters dated Carlton House, 9.45 a.m. 7 January 1796, quoted in Plowden, *Caroline and Charlotte*, pp. 29–30.

15. Fitzherbert Papers, quoted in Shane Leslie *Mrs Fitzherbert*, i, appendix 2, pp. 372–386, the Prince's will was written in his own hand, signed and sealed, but without witnesses.

16. Macalpine and Hunter, *George III and the Mad Business* (London, 1991), pp. 229–40, gives the Prince's detailed medical history and makes an informed case for the Prince's strange behaviour, on this and other occasions, being due to inherited porphyria.

17. Shane Leslie, *The Letters of Mrs Fitzherbert* (London, 1940), p. 122, dated only 1796.

18. Wilkins, *Mrs Fitzherbert and George IV*, ii, pp. 61–62.

19. Ibid., p. 63.

20. Ragley Papers, quoted in Shane Leslie, *Letters of Mrs Fitzherbert*, p. 125, 16 December 1802.

21. Glenbervie, *Diaries of Sylvester Douglas, Lord Glenbervie*, ed. Francis Bickley, (London, 1928), quoted in Shane Leslie, *Mrs Fitzherbert*, i, p. 125.

22. Fitzherbert Papers, i, quoted in Shane Leslie, *Mrs Fitzherbert*, i, pp. 123–25, 11–12, June 1799.

23. Glenbervie, *Diaries of Sylvester Douglas, Lord Glenbervie*, ed. Francis Bickley, 31 March 1799, quoted in Shane Leslie, *Mrs Fitzherbert*, i, p. 123n.

Notes to Chapter 8: Reconciliation

1. *Jerningham Letters*, ed. Egerton Castle (London, 1896), i, p. 168.

2. Ibid., p. 161, 17 March 1800.

3. Crawford Muniments (Balcarres), quoted in Hibbert, *George IV, Prince of Wales* (London, 1972), p. 173.

4. MS Diary of Bishop Douglass, Archives of the Archdiocese of Westminster, 8 November 1800, quoted in Shane Leslie, *Mrs Fitzherbert* (London 1939), i, pp. 127–28. Bishop Douglas had known and approved of the appeal to Rome and recorded the audience with Pius VII as John Nassau reported it to him. Charles Bodenham wrote to Miss Dormer, in 1854, 'I had ascertained beyond a doubt when I was in Rome that she had sent a very confidential friend to the Pope to ask whether in these circumstances she was to consider the Prince her husband: and that the answer was in the affirmative'. Shane Leslie, *Letters of Mrs Fitzherbert* (London, 1940), p. 330.

5. Crawford Muniments (Balcarres), quoted in Hibbert, *George IV, Prince of Wales*, p. 173.

6. Royal Archives, George IV, box 7, wardrobe accounts, quoted in Hibbert, *George IV, Prince of Wales*, pp. 175–76.

7. *Jerningham Letters*, i, p. 188.

8. Ibid., p. 192.

9. British Library, Adair MSS, correspondence of Robert Adair, quoted in Amanda Foreman, *Georgiana, Duchess of Devonshire* (London, 1998),

p. 335, a note from the Duchess of Devonshire to Lady Melbourne circa 1800–1.

10. Langdale, *A Memoir of Mrs Fitzherbert with an Account of her Marriage to George IV* (London, 1856), pp. 129–30.

11. Chatsworth Papers, September 1782, quoted in Hibbert, *George IV, Prince of Wales* p. 25n.

12. P. H. Stanhope, Earl, *Life of the Rt Hon. William Pitt* (London, 1861–62), iii, pp. 294–97.

13. Chatswortth Papers, Duchess of Devonshire's Diary, 17 March 1801, quoted in Foreman, *Georgiana, Duchess of Devonshire*, p. 345.

14. The Memorandum of the Prince of Wales 15 April 1802, Papers of the Earl of Carlisle, *Historical Manuscripts Commission* (1897), quoted in Ida Macalpine and Richard Hunter, *George IV and the Mad Business* (London, 1991), p. 125.

Notes to Chapter 9: Minney

1. Lady Euston's affidavit at the Seymour Trial, quoted in W. H. Wilkins, *Mrs Fitzherbert and George IV* (London, 1905), ii, p. 78. The Seymour Trial affidavits were recorded in a Parliamentary Paper entitled 'The House of Lords, between Mary Georgina Emma Seymour, an infant, by William Bentinck Esq. her next friend, Appellant. The Earl of Euston and Lord Henry Seymour, Respondants'. Ibid., p. 68n.

2. Ragley Papers, Mrs Fitzherbert's letter to Lord Robert Seymour, 16 December 1802, quoted in Shane Leslie, ed., *Letters of Mrs Fitzherbert* (London, 1940), pp. 124–27.

3. Ibid., p. 125.

4. Shane Leslie, *Mrs Fitzherbert* (London, 1939), i, p. 163.

5. Ibid., pp. 151–58, Ragley Papers, letters exchanged during the year 1802 by the Prince of Wales and Lord Euston and Lord Henry Seymour.

6. Wilkins, *Mrs Fitzherbert and George IV*, ii, pp. 66–67.

7. Ragley Papers, 16 December 1802, quoted in Shane Leslie, *Letters of Mrs Fitzherbert*, p. 127.

8. Ibid., p. 126.

9. Ragley Papers, quoted in Shane Leslie, *Mrs Fitzherbert*, i, p. 149, 23 November 1801.

10. Ibid., pp. 168–69, Mrs Loch's Papers, 19 January 1805.

11. Ibid., p. 161, Calvert, Mrs, *An Irish Beauty of the Regency* (1911).

12. Lady Euston's affidavit, quoted in Wilkins, *Mrs Fitzherbert and George IV*, ii, pp. 77–78.

13. The Prince's affidavitl, sworn 24 November 1804, quoted in Wilkins, *Mrs Fitzherbert and George IV*, ii, pp. 71–74.

14. Ibid., p. 67.

15. Shane Leslie, *Mrs Fitzherbert*, i, p. 171, 1 July 1806.

16. *The Guardian Angel*, a cartoon by James Gilray, published by H. Humphrey 22 April 1805, based on a popular painting by Rev. Matthew Peters, *An Angel Carrying the Spirit of a Child to Paradise* (exhibited in the Royal Academy in 1782), implying that Mrs Fitzherbert was capturing Minney for Catholicism.

17. *Jerningham Letters*, ed. Egerton Castle (London, 1896), i, p. 274.

18. Fitzherbert Papers, iii, quoted in Shane Leslie, *Mrs Fitzherbert*, i, pp. 165–66, 16 June 1806.

19. Wilkins, *Mrs Fitzherbert and George IV*, ii, pp. 82–83, 17 June 1806. Caroline Browne was an illegitimate daughter of Lord Thurlow.

20. Calvert, *An Irish Beauty of the Regency*, quoted in Shane Leslie, *Mrs Fitzherbert*, i, pp. 160–61.

21. Madame Vigée-Le Brun's self-portrait in London's National Gallery confirms this.

22. Vigée-Le Brun, *The Memoirs of Elisabeth Vigée-le Brun* (London, 1989), pp. 253–54.

23. The house still stands, but is greatly changed inside and out. It is now used to house some of Brighton's homeless men.

24. Glenbervie, *Diaries of Sylvester Douglas, Lord Glenbervie*, ed. F. Bickley, (1928), ii, quoted in Ida Macalpine and Richard Hunter, *George III and the Mad Business* (London, 1969), pp. 233–34.

25. *Letters of R. B. Sheridan*, ed. C. Price (1966), ii, p. 216, 27 February 1804.

26. Fitzherbert Papers, iii, quoted in Shane Leslie, *Letters of Mrs Fitzherbert*, p. 128, 4 February 1804.

Notes to Chapter 10: Lady Hertford

1. *The Creevey Papers*, ed. H. Maxwell, (1905), quoted in Shane Leslie, *Mrs Fitzherbert* (London, 1939), i, p. 140, 5 November 1805.

2. *Sussex Weekly Advertiser*, 12 August 1805.

3. *The Creevey Papers*, ed. Herbert Maxwell, quoted in Shane Leslie, *Mrs Fitzherbert*, i, p. 138, 6 November 1805.

4. Ibid., p. 140, 8 November 1805.

5. Ibid., pp. 140–41.

6. Ibid., p. 141.

7. Ibid., title page.

8. Lady Charlotte Bury, *Diary: Being Illustrative of the Times of George IV*, ed. A. F. Steuart, (1908), quoted in Shane Leslie, *Mrs Fitzherbert*, i, p. 180.

9. *Jerningham Letters*, ed. Egerton Castle (London, 1896), i, p. 281.

10. *Sussex Weekly Advertiser*, 12 August 1806.

11. Shane Leslie, *Mrs Fitzherbert*, i, p. 179.

12. *Jerningham Letters*, i, p. 275.

13. Nathanial Jefferys, *Review of the Conduct of the Prince of Wales to Which is Added a Letter to Mrs Fitzherbert* (1806), ii, pp. 13–15.

14. Holland House Papers, quoted in Hibbert, *George IV, Prince of Wales* (London, 1972), p. 251.

15. Papers of the Earl of Carlisle, *Historical Manuscripts Commision*, quoted in Shane Leslie, *Mrs Fitzherbert*, i, pp. 182–83.

16. Calvert, *An Irish Beauty of the Regency* (1911), 25 July and 5 August 1807, quoted in Shane Leslie, *Mrs Fitzherbert*, i, p. 181.

17. *Sussex Weekly Advertiser*, 22 November 1807.

18. Ragley Papers, quoted in Anita Leslie, *Mrs Fitzherbert* (London, 1960), pp. 145–46.

19. Langdale, *A Memoir of Mrs Fitzherbert with an Account of her Marriage to George IV* (London 1856), p. 132.

20. Barbara Charlton, *Recollections of a Northumbrian Lady* (Stockfield, 1989), pp. 24–25.

21. *The Creevey Papers*, ed. Herbert Maxwell (1905), quoted in Wilkins, *Mrs Fitzherbert and George IV*, ii, p. 105.

22. Holland, *Memoirs of the Whig Party During My Time*, ed. Henry Richard, Lord Holland (1852–54), ii, quoted in Hibbert, *George IV, Prince of Wales*, p. 254.

23. *Private Correspondence of Lord Granville Leveson Gower*, ed. Castalia, Countess Granville (London, 1916), ii, quoted in Hibbert, *George IV, Prince of Wales*, pp. 254–55.

24. Langdale, *A Memoir of Mrs Fitzherbert*, p. 133.

25. Fitzherbert Papers, iii, quoted in Shane Leslie, *Letters of Mrs Fitzherbert*, pp. 129–31, dated only 1808.

26. Ibid., pp. 133–34, 18 December 1809.

27. Ibid., p. 135, 19 December 1809.

28. Holland, *Journal of Elizabeth, Lady Holland*, ed. the Earl of Ilchester (1908), ii, quoted in Hibbert, *George IV, Prince of Wales*, p. 268.

Notes to Chapter 11: The Prince Regent

1. Charles Langdale, *A Memoir of Mrs Fitzherbert and an Account of her Marriage to George IV* (London, 1856), pp. 143 and 144.

2. Glenbervie, *Diaries of Sylvester Douglas, Lord Glenbervie*, ed. Francis Bickley (London, 1928), quoted in Shane Leslie, *Mrs Fitzherbert* (London, 1939), i, pp. 192–93.

3. *The Creevey Papers*, ed. Herbert Maxwell (1905), 2 February 1811, quoted in Shane Leslie, *Mrs Fitzherbert*, i, p. 193–94.

4. Langdale, *A Memoir of Mrs Fitzherbert*, p. 144.

5. There was gossip about Mrs Fitzherbert's friendship with the young Count de Noailles which made the Prince of Wales furiously jealous, but it was unlikely to have been more than a mild flirtaion on her part, and unjustified boastfulness on his, James Munson, *Maria Fitzherbert: Secret Wife of George IV* (London, 2001), pp. 261–62.

6. Fitzherbert Papers, iii, quoted in Shane Leslie, *Letters of Mrs Fitzherbert* (London, 1940), pp. 138–39.

7. Langdale, *A Memoir of Mrs Fitzherbert*, p. 146.

8. The document giving her this mortgage was eventually deposited in Coutts' Bank, and later removed to the Royal Archives at Windsor.

9. Fitzherbert Papers, iii, quoted in Shane Leslie, *Letters of Mrs Fitzherbert*, p. 140.

10. *Brambridge Catholic Registers, 1766–1869*, ed. R. C. Baigent, Catholic Records Society, 27 (1927), p. 37.

11. Munson, *Maria Fitzherbert: The Secret Wife of George IV*, p. 338, quotes letter from Mrs Fitzherbert to Lady Anne Lindsay in 1813 referring to 'a dear lovely girl about six years old' received as a 'legacy' from her late brother Jack.

12. Portarlington Papers, quoted in Shane Leslie, *Letters of Mrs Fitzherbert*, p. 215, a letter from Mrs Fitzherbert to George Dawson Damer, 4 December 1829, refers to Marianne having had chicken pox 'while at Red Rice'.

13. *Brighton Gazette*, 18 December 1826, and 1 May 1825, and Dr Cullin's letter to Minney, 14 March 1844, quoted in Shane Leslie, *Letters of Mrs Fitzherbert*, Introduction, p. xxviii confirm this.

14. Letter from Lady Verulam to Mary Frampton, 2 July 1814, quoted in Shane Leslie, *Mrs Fitzherbert*, i, p. 198.

15. Fitzherbert Papers iii, Shane Leslie, *Letters of Mrs Fitzherbert*, pp. 141–42, undated.

16. Ibid., pp. 143–45, 16 August 1814

17. Shane Leslie, *Mrs Fitzherbert*, i, pp. 202–3.

18. Windsor Archives, quoted in Shane Leslie, *Letters of Mrs Fitzherbert*, pp. 146–47, 22 September 1815.

Notes to Chapter 12: The Queen's Trial

1. Memorandum of Admiral Sir George Seymour written for Lady Georgina Bathurst, quoted in Wilkins, *Mrs Fitzherbert and George IV* (London, 1905), ii, p. 134, by permission of members of the Bathurst family.
2. *Brighton Gazette*, 7 and 14 January, 1817.
3. Ragley Papers, quoted in Shane Leslie, *Letters of Mrs Fitzherbert* (London, 1940), pp. 161–62.
4. Fitzherbert Papers, iii, quoted in Shane Leslie, *Letters of Mrs Fitzherbert* (London, 1940), p. 158, 22 November, 1818.
5. Shane Leslie, *Mrs Fitzherbert*, i, p. 218, notes from Marianne Smythe to Captain George Dawson.
6. Ibid., Portarlington Papers, quoted in pp. 220–21.
7. *Diary of Thomas Moore*, ed. Lord John Russell (1853), 24 March 1820, quoted in Shane Leslie, *Mrs Fitzherbert*, i, p. 220n.
8. Barnard Papers, quoted in Shane Leslie, *Mrs Fitzherbert*, i, p. 212. Louisa, Lady Waterford told Augustus Hare that her great aunt, Lady Anne Barnard, had written a book like his *Family Memoirs*, but that hers was 'too imaginative', *The Story of My Life*, ibid., p. 42. It has been suggested that Lady Anne's letters and diaries may also be 'too imaginative'.
9. Hibbert, *George IV: Regent and King* (London, 1973), p. 154, 'Since Pergami was Italian, and not subject to English Law, and since the alleged offences had not taken place in England, it was impossible to institute a trial for High Treason which would otherwise have been the appropriate procedure'.
10. *The Creevey Papers*, ed. Herbert Maxwell (1905), 12 August 1820, quoted in E. A. Smith, *A Queen on Trial* (London, 1993), p. 69.
11. *The Private Letters of Princess Lieven to Prince Metternich, 1820–1826*, ed. P. Quennell (1937), quoted in E. A. Smith, *A Queen on Trial*, p. 91, Princess Lieven to Metternich, 2 September 1820, 'Do you know, *mon Prince*, what the Queen does in Parliament? – she plays backgamon ... with Alderman Wood'.
12. Smith, *A Queen on Trial*, p. 78, letter from Lady Cowper to Frederick Lamb, 20 August 1820.
13. Ibid, p. 81. Mrs Wellesley Pole, wife of William Wellesley Pole, later 3rd Earl of Mornington.

14. *The Private Letters of Princess Lieven to Metternich*, ed. P. Quennell, 23 August 1820, quoted in Smith, *A Queen on Trial*, p. 80, 23 August 1820.

15. *The Life and Times of Henry Lord Brougham Written by Himself* (London, 1871), quoted in Shane Leslie, *Mrs Fitzherbert*, i, p. 210.

Notes to Chapter 13: George Dawson

1. Shane Leslie, *Mrs Fitzherbert* (London, 1939), i, pp. 221–22, 1 December 1820.

2. *Annual Register*, 63 (1821), states that she had 'an obstruction of the bowel attended with inflamation', quoted in Christopher Hibbert, *George IV: Regent and King* (London, 1973), p. 204.

3. Fitzherbert Papers, iii, quoted in Shane Leslie, *Letters of Mrs Fitzherbert* (London, 1940), p. 164, 29 July 1822.

4. Ibid., p. 165, 6 August 1822.

5. Ibid., p. 169, 25 August 1822, and p. 170, 8 September 1822.

6. Ibid., p. 167, 6 August 1822.

7. Ibid., p. 168.

8. Fitzherbert Papers, iii, Shane Leslie, *Mrs Fitzherbert*, i, p. 237, October 1822.

9. Ibid., p. 240, part of this undated letter was mistakenly published, in facsimile, by W. H. Wilkins, as one addressed to the Prince, Wilkins, *Mrs Fitzherbert and George IV* (London, 1905), ii, between pp. 110–11; the error is noted in Shane Leslie, *Mrs Fitzherbert*, i, p. 240n.

10. Shane Leslie, Mrs Fitzherbert, i, pp. 240–41, 14 October 1822.

11. Ibid., p. 242–43, 2 November 1822.

12. Ibid., p. 245, Paris, 16 November 1822.

13. Fitzherbert Papers, iii, quoted in Shane Leslie, *Letters of Mrs Fitzherbert*, p. 171, 14 December 1823.

14. Portarlington Papers, quoted in Shane Leslie, *Mrs Fitzherbert*, i, pp. 249–51.

15. Ibid., p. 251.

16. Ibid., pp. 251–52, 9 April 1824.

17. Windsor Archives, quoted in Shane Leslie, *Letters of Fitzherbert*, pp. 174–75.

18. Windsor Archives, quoted in Shane Leslie, *Mrs Fitzherbert*, i, pp. 254–55, 19 July 1825.

19. Ibid., Ragley Papers, p. 256, 13 August 1825.

20. Ibid., p. 258.

21. Ibid., p. 257, 23 July 1825.

22. Shane Leslie, *Letters of Mrs Fitzherbert*, p. 176, 7 August 1825.

23. Ibid., Fitzherbert Papers, iii, pp. 176–77, 11 August 1825.

24. Ibid., pp. 177–78, 21 August 1825.
25. Shane Leslie, *Mrs Fitzherbert*, i, p. 258.
26. Fitzherbert Papers, iii, quoted in Shane Leslie, *Letters of Mrs Fitzherbert*, pp. 178–79, 7 September 1825.
27. Shane Leslie, *Letters of Mrs Fitzherbert*, p. 180, 18 September 1825.
28. Ibid., p. 181, 17 October 1825.
29. Ibid., pp. 182–83, 7 November 1825.
30. Ibid., pp. 184–86, 18 January 1826.
31. Ibid., p. 187, 27 February 1826.
32. Ibid., pp. 187–88, 16 June 1826.
33. Ibid., pp. 188–89, 20 June 1826.

Notes to Chapter 14: Marianne

1. Shane Leslie, *Mrs Fitzherbert* (London, 1939), i, pp. 263–64.
2. *The Greville Memoirs*, ed. Lytton Strachey and Roger Fulford (London, 1938), quoted in W. H. Wilkins, *Mrs Fitzherbert and George IV* (London, 1905), ii, p. 193.
3. Charles Langdale, *A Memoir of Mrs Fitzherbert with an Account of her Marriage to George IV* (London, 1856), pp. 142–43.
4. *The Croker Papers*, ed. Louis J. Jennings (1884), note of a conversation with George IV, 25 November 1825, quoted in Shane Leslie, *Mrs Fitzherbert*, i, p. 266–67.
5. *The Greville Memoirs* ed. Lytton Strachey and Roger Fulford, quoted in Leslie, *Letters of Mrs Fitzherbert* (London, 1940), p. 54–55.
6. Prince Puckler-Muskau, *Tours in England, Ireland and France, 1826–1832*, written in the form of letters to his ex-wife, quoted in Anita Leslie, *Mrs Fitzherbert* (London, 1960), p. 201, 14 February, 1827.
7. *The Croker Papers*, ed. Louis J. Jennings, quoted in Shane Leslie, *Mrs Fitzherbert*, i, pp. 203–4.
8. Count de la Garde *Brighton: Diary of a Visit* (Paris, 1934), extracts translated by Maurice Irvine, pp. 121–22.
9. Ibid., p. 123.
10. Diary of Louisa Smythe, *The Prettiest Girl in England*, ed. Richard Buckle (1958), quoted in Anita Leslie, *Mrs Fitzherbert*, p. 202, 30 June 1827.
11. Fitzherbert Papers, iii, Leslie, *Letters of Mrs Fitzherbert*, pp. 205–6, 1 April 1828.
12. Ibid., pp. 206–7, Swynnerton Papers, 17 June 1828.
13. Ibid, pp. 207–8, 21 July 1828.
14. Ibid., pp. 198–99, Portarlington Papers, 20 November 1827.

15. Ibid., p. 214.

16. Glenbervie, *Diaries of Sylvester Douglas, Lord Glenbervie*, ed. F. Bickley (1928), quoted in James Munson, *Maria Fitzherber: Secret Wife of George IV*, p. 238, Mrs St John told Sylvester Douglas that while talking to the Prince in 1790 or 1791, at Lady Salisbury's the latter had declared the Roman Catholic Church to be the 'only one fit for a gentleman', adding 'My God, that is my opinion and I do not care who knows it'.

17. Portarlington Papers, correspondence regarding the duel, Shane Leslie, *Mrs Fitzherbert*, i, p. 319. O'Connell's vow never to fight another duel was taken after a man he wounded in the leg died of blood loss. O'Connell never forgave himself and wore a black glove over the hand that had fired the shot whenever he attended Mass.

18. Shane Leslie, *Letters of Mrs Fitzherbert*, p. 303.

19. Fitzherbert Papers, iii, quoted in Shane Leslie, *Mrs Fitzherbert*, i, p. 273.

20. Ibid., pp. 273–74.

21. Ibid., Fitzherbert Papers, i, p. 276.

22. Waller of Woodcote Papers (Warwick), quoted in Hibbert, *George IV, Regent and King* (London, 1973), p. 335.

23. Shane Leslie, *Mrs Fitzherbert*, i, p. 277.

24. *The Times* obituary, 28 June 1830, attacked the late King's 'most reckless, increasing and unbounded prodigality', and, among other things, mocked the 'tawdry childishness of Carlton House and the mountebank Pavilion', and claimed his treatment of Queen Caroline was a 'stain on manhood'.

25. Shane Leslie, *Letters of Mrs Fitzherbert*, pp. 229–30, 26 July 1830.

26. Swynnerton Papers, quoted in Shane Leslie, *Mrs Fitzherbert*, i, p. 274.

27. *The Creevey Papers*, ed. Herbert Maxwell (1905), quoted in Anita Leslie, *Mrs Fitzherbert*, p. 215.

28. Langdale, *A Memoir of Mrs Fitzherbert*, p. 145.

29. Shane Leslie, *Mrs Fitzherbert*, i, p. 291, 10 September 1830.

30. Clifford Musgrave, *Life in Brighton* (Chatham, 1981), pp. 160–62, gives a detailed description of the Pavilion as it was at this period.

31. Frampton, *Journal of Mary Frampton, 1779–1846*, ed. H. G. Mundy (London, 1885), 8 February 1830, quoted in Shane Leslie, *Mrs Fitzherbert*, i, p. 296.

32. Ragley Papers, quoted in Shane Leslie *Mrs Fitzherbert*, i, p. 281.

33. Frampton, *Journal of Mary Frampton, 1779–1846*, ed. H. G. Mundy, quoted in Shane Leslie, *Mrs Fitzherbert*, i, pp. 281–82.

34. *The Journal of Mrs Arbuthnot*, ed. the Duke of Wellington and Francis Bamford (1950), quoted in Hibbert, *George IV, Regent and King* (London, 1973), p. 78.

Notes to Chapter 15: Endings

1. Portarlington Papers, quoted in Shane Leslie, *Mrs Fitzherbert* (London, 1939), i, pp. 298–99, 17 May 1831.

2. Ibid., Ragley Papers, pp. 296–97.

3. Frampton, *Journal of Mary Frampton*, ed. H. G. Mundy (London, 1885), 8 February 1831, quoted in Shane Leslie, *Mrs Fitzherbert*, i, p. 296.

4. Ibid., Portarlington Papers, p. 299, 23 May 1831.

5. Shane Leslie, *Letters of Mrs Fitzherbert* (London, 1940), p. 237, 4 May 1831.

6. Ibid., p. 238, 21 August 1831.

7. Ibid., p. 244, 9 September 1831.

8. Ibid., p. 242, 5 September 1831.

9. Ibid., p. 244, 9 September 1831.

10. Ibid., p. 243, 9 September 1831.

11. Ibid., pp. 254–55, 18 October 1831.

12. Ibid., Fitzherbert Papers, iii, pp. 261–62, December 1831.

13. Ibid., Fitzherbert Papers, ii, pp. 281–82, Paris, undated.

14. Ibid., p. 262, dated only 1831.

15. Ibid., p. 257, 26 October 1831.

16. Ibid., Fitzherbert Papers, iii, p. 264, St James's Palace, 1 January 1832.

17. Ibid., Swynnerton Papers, pp. 264–65, dated only August 1832.

18. Ibid., Portarlington Papers, p. 265, letter from Mrs Fitzherbert to George Damer, dated only 1832, and, ibid., p. 271, letter from George Seymour to Mrs Fitzherbert, 24 April 1833, show Mrs Fitzherbert's efforts on Damer's behalf.

19. Ibid., Fitzherbert Papers, ii, p. 277, 23 August 1833.

20. Ibid., p. 277, 24 August 1833.

21. Ragley Papers, quoted in Shane Leslie, *Mrs Fitzherbert*, i, pp. 306–7; Langdale, *A Memoir of Mrs Fitzherbert with an Account of Her Marriage to George IV* (London, 1905), p. 84. Wilkins, who saw the contents of the box when it was opened in 1905, claims that it also contained the letter from Lord Chancellor Loughborough to the Prince, 19 December 1794, regarding the continued payment to Mrs Fitzherbert of £3000 a year should the Prince die, and a copy of Mrs Fitzherbert's last letter to George IV, Wilkins, *Mrs Fitzherbert and George IV* (London, 1905), i, p. 319n. and ii, p. 216n.

22. Shane Leslie, *Mrs Fitzherbert*, i, p. 306.

23. Ibid., prelude, p. xii, only five hundred copies were printed and it was never reprinted.

24. Duke of Orleans (1810–1842), eldest son of King Louis-Philippe, grandson

of the Duke of Orleans who was once a friend of George IV when Prince of Wales.

25. Charles Langdale, *A Memoir of Mrs Fitzherbert*, pp. 109–11.

26. Shane Leslie, *Mrs Fitzherbert*, i, p. 312.

27. Ibid., pp. 315–16, 3 December 1833.

28. Ibid., p. 313, 2 December 1833.

29. Ibid., p. 314, 16 December 1833.

30. Fitzherbert Papers, iii, Shane Leslie, *Letters of Mrs Fitzherbert*, pp. 288–89, 1 January 1834.

31. Ibid., Swynnerton Papers, p. 289, 26 May 1834.

32. Ibid., Fitzherbert Papers, iii, p. 294, 22 August 1834.

33. W. H. Wilkins, *Mrs Fitzherbert and George IV* (London, 1905), ii, pp. 276–77, 30 September 1834.

34. Shane Leslie, *Mrs Fitzherbert*, i, p. 327, 23 June 1835.

35. Thomas Raikes *A Portion of a Journal, Kept by Thomas Raikes, Esq., 1831–1847* (London, 1857), iii, quoted in Wilkins, *Mrs Fitzherbert and George IV*, ii, p. 279.

36. Wilkins, *Mrs Fitzherbert and George IV*, ii, p. 280.

37. This church was built in the classical style with a severely simple interior, almost without decoration except for Edward Carew's two white marble Corinthian pillars each side of the altar, and his sculpture of the Baptism of Christ above it. The interior has since been greatly altered and extended, and is now highly decorated.

38. William Lopez may originally have been a priest at the Portuguese Embassy.

39. Ragley Papers, quoted in Shane Leslie, *Letters of Mrs Fitzherbert*, p. 40, a letter from Minney to her brother shows that William Lopez was paid six pounds a month for lodgings, in addition to £20 for his services as chaplain.

40. Fitzherbert Papers, iii, quoted in Shane Leslie, *Letters of Mrs Fitzherbert*, pp. 283–84, Count Charles de Morny had once wanted to marry Mrs Fitzherbert's niece, Louisa Smythe, but had not been accepted, and had not been regarded as suitable by Mrs Fitzherbert.

41. Wilkins, *Mrs Fitzherbert and George IV*, ii, pp. 281–82, William Saunders was still alive in 1905 and was interviewed by William Wilkins before the latter completed his biography of Mrs Fitzherbert.

42. Swynnerton Papers, quoted in Shane Leslie, *Letters of Mrs Fitzherbert*, pp. 301–2, 4 August 1836.

43. Wilkins, *Mrs Fitzherbert and George IV*, ii, pp. 283–84, Wilkins received the recollections of Minney's surviving daughters in 1905.

44. Anita Leslie, *Mrs Fitzherbert* (London, 1960), p 17, Constance Leslie

(Minney's daughter, and Annita Leslie's great grandmother), told her great grandchildren 'even when she [Mrs Fitzherbert] was old, my mother said that her cheeks felt as smooth as petals when you kissed her'.

45. Lady Cecilia Buggin was the Duke of Sussex's morganatic wife, and, as such, did not take his title. Later, after the Duke's death, she was created Duchess of Inverness by Queen Victoria, Wilkins, *Mrs Fitzherbert and George IV*, ii, p. 285n.

46. Ibid., p. 285, letter from Lady Cecilia Buggin to Mrs Fitzherbert, 15 February 1837.

47. Ibid., p. 286, Wilkins collected Minney's daughters' memories of Mrs Fitzherbert's death.

48. Sir George Seymour's papers, quoted in Shane Leslie, *Mrs Fitzherbert*, i, p. 345.

49. Wilkins, *Mrs Fitzherbert and George IV*, ii, p. 289n. 2.

50. *The Times*, 8 April 1837.

51. *Brighton Patriot*, 10 April 1837.

52. Fitzherbert Papers, iii, quoted in Shane Leslie, *Mrs Fitzherbert*, i, appendix 2, pp. 382–85. Mrs Fitzherbert's will, dated 26 April 1836.

53. Ibid., codicil of Mrs Fitzherbert's will, pp. 385–86.

54. Ibid., Fitzherbert Papers, i, p. 343.

55. Mrs Dawson Damer's Autograph Book, quoted in Shane Leslie, *Letters of Mrs Fitzherbert*, p. 51.

56. Ibid., Fitzherbert Papers, iii, pp. 45–46.

57. Portarlington Papers, quoted in Shane Leslie, *Mrs Fitzherbert*, i, pp. 325–26, 27 June 1837.

58. *The Greville Memoirs*, ed. Lytton Strachey and Roger Fulford (London, 1938), quoted in Wilkins, *Mrs Fitzherbert and George IV*, ii, p. 294.

59. Wilkins, *Mrs Fitzherbert and George IV*, ii, p. 294, 28 August 1837.

Notes to Appendix: The Question of Children

1. Anita Leslie, *Mrs Fitzherbert* (London 1960), p. 207.

2. Christopher Hibbert, *George IV, Prince of Wales* (London, 1972), p. 63n.

3. While accepting that Parliament could change the laws concerning legal marriages (as it had done in the Royal Marriages Act), the Church of England did not accept that Parliament could change the requirements for a canonically valid marriage.

4. *The Times*, 10 June 1839.

5. Letter from Lord Stourton to Lord Albemarle dated January, 1841, quoted in Shane Leslie, *Letters of Mrs Fitzherbert* (London, 1940), pp. 74–75.

6. Fielding Papers, quoted in Shane Leslie, *Letters of Mrs Fitzherbert*, pp. 332–33, Paris, 24 January 1857.

7. Shane Leslie, *Mrs Fitzherbert* (London, 1939), i, prelude, p. xv.

8. Ibid., p. 351, note by Constance Leslie, 'Owing to Monsignor Johnson's advice my sister and I added a few lines to the Epitaph with our mother's name owing to her effacing herself. Monsignor Johnson was told by some American tourists that they were Mrs Fitzherbert's heirs and had placed this monument to her memory'.

9. Swynnerton Papers, Shane Leslie, *Letters of Mrs Fitzherbert*, pp. 206–7, 17 June 1828.

10. Portarlington Papers, Shane Leslie, *Mrs Fitzherbert*, i, p. 390, 1 February 1824.

11. Ibid., Swynnerton Papers, appendix 3, p. 393–94.

12. Fitzherbert Papers, iii, quoted in Leslie, *Letters of Mrs Fitzherbert*, p. 298, Mrs Fitzherbert to Marianne Jerningham, 12 May 1835, 'May you have many, many happy returns, dearest Mary of this day ...'

13. Calvert, *An Irish Beauty of the Regency* (1911), 5 June 1807, quoted in Shane Leslie, *Mrs Fitzherbert*, i, p. 181, 'My sister and I went late to an Assembly at Mrs Fitzherbert's where were all the fine world. The Prince of Wales, the Duke of York the Dukes of Clarence, Cambridge and Kent were all there, dressed in full uniform'.

14. James Munson, *Maria Fitzherbert: Secret Wife of George IV* (London, 2001), p. 338.

15. Fitzherbert Papers, iii, quoted in Shane Leslie, *Letters of Mrs Fitzherbert*, pp. 68–69.

Bibliography

Stanley Ayling *Fox: The Life and Times of Charles James Fox* (London, 1991).

Mark Bence Jones, *The Catholic Families* (London, 1992).

Joan Berkeley, *Lulworth and the Welds* (Gillingham, Dorset, 1971).

Madeleine Bingham, *The Track of the Comet: The Life of R. B. Sheridan* (London, 1980).

Gerald Campbell *Edward and Pamela Fitzgerald* (London, 1904).

Barbara Charlton, *Recollections of a Northumberland Lady* (Stockfield, 1989).

Count A. de la Garde, *Brighton, Diary of a Visit, 1827* (Paris 1934).

Michael de-la-Noy, *George IV* (Stroud, 1989).

Lucy Ellis and Joseph Turquan, *La Belle Pamela: Lady Pamela Fitzgerald* (New York, 1920).

Boris Ford, ed., *Eighteenth-Century Britain*, Cambridge Cultural History (Cambridge, 1992).

Boris Ford, ed., *The Romantic Age in Britain*, Cambridge Cultural History (Cambridge, 1992).

Amanda Foreman, *Georgiana, Duchess of Devonshire*, London 1998).

Brian Fothergill, *The Cardinal King* (London, 1970).

Roger Fulford, *The Royal Dukes* (London, 1933).

Ian Gilmour, *Riots, Risings and Revolution* (London, 1993).

Dennis Gwynn, *Bishop Challoner* (London, 1946).

Johanna Harting, *Catholic London Missions from the Reformation to 1850* (London, 1903).

Christopher Hibbert, *George IV* (London, 1976).

Christopher Hibbert, *George III: A Personal History* (London 1998).

Jerningham, Lady Frances, *Jerningham Letters*, 2 volumes (London, 1896).

Carol Kennedy, *Mayfair: A Social History* (London, 1986).

John Kirk, *Biographies of English Catholics in the Eighteenth Century* (London, 1909).

Charles Langdale, *Memoirs of Mrs Fitzherbert: With an Account of her Marriage to HRH the Prince of Wales, Including Lord Stourton's Memoir* (London, 1856).

Shane Leslie, *Mrs Fitzherbert: A Life Chiefly from Unpublished Sources* (London, 1939).

Shane Leslie, *Letters of Mrs Fitzherbert and Connected Papers* (London, 1940).

Shane Leslie, *Salutation to Five* (London, 1951).

Anita Leslie, *Mrs Fitzherbert* (London, 1960).

M. J. Levy, *The Mistresses of George IV* (London, 1996).

Ida Macalpine, and Richard Hunter, *George III and the Mad Business* (London, 1995).

Stella Margetson, *Regency London* (London, 1970).

Brian Masters, *Georgiana, Duchess of Devonshire* (London, 1980).

David Matthew, *Catholicism in England, 1535–1829: A Social History* (London, 1936).

John Mawhood, *The Mawhood Diaries*, Catholic Records Society, volume 50 (London, 1956).

John Morris, *Catholic England in Modern Times* (London, 1892).

James Munson, *Maria Fitzherbert: Secret Wife of George IV* (London, 2001).

Clifford Musgrave, *Life in Brighton* (Chatham, Kent, 1981).

Venetia Murray, *High Society* (London, 1998).

Douglas Newton, *Catholic London* (London, 1950).

M. D. R. Leys, *Catholics in England, 1559–1829: A Social History* (London, 1961).

Alan Palmer, *The Life and Times of George IV* (London, 1972).

Alison Plowden, *Caroline and Charlotte: The Regent's Wife and Daughter* (London, 1989).

Trevor Pugh, *The Church of St John the Baptist, 1835–1985* (Brighton, 1985).

George Rudé, *Hanoverian London* (London, 1971).

E. A. Smith, *A Queen on Trial: The Affair of Queen Caroline* (Stroud, 1993).

Stapleton, Frideswide, *The History of Princethorpe Priory* (Princethorpe Priory, 1930).

Claire Tomalin, *Mrs Jordan's Profession* (London, 1994).

Michael Trappe-Lomax, *Bishop Challoner* (London, 1947).

Elisabeth Vigée-Le Brun, *The Memoirs of Elizabeth Vigée-Le Brun* (London, 1989).

Bernard Ward, *The Dawn of the Catholic Revival, 1781–1803* (London, 1909).

Basil Whelan, *Historic English Convents of Today: The Story of English Cloisters in France and Flanders in Penal Times* (1905).

Wilkins, W. H., *Mrs Fitzherbert and George IV*, 2 volumes (London, 1905).

Index